EXPERIMENTAL ECONOMICS

HOW WE CAN BUILD
BETTER FINANCIAL MARKETS

ROSS M. MILLER

Foreword by Vernon L. Smith

WILE

John Wiley & ~~Sons, Inc.~~

To My Wife

Contents

Foreword

Ross Miller was a double first for me: He was my first coauthor of an experimental paper, and my first student coauthor. Ever since our 1977 paper (with Charles Plott) I have been addicted to team research, the quality way to do experimental research because you have to cover design, theory, optimization (in complex "designer" markets), execution, and analysis in an integrated manner that exploits team economies of scope.

In this book, Ross writes engagingly and skillfully, blending salient issues in experimental methodology, and its astonishingly in-depth development since its inception a half century ago, with an intimate knowledge of financial markets and their history. In particular, he has an excellent grasp of the demonstration/testing power of the laboratory in showing how financially motivated participants interacting through institutions—exchange rule property right systems—solve the Hayek problem in the context of static, or even shifting, equilibrium environments: How can order create itself out of complexity? But in asset markets, chaos may reign where willingness-to-pay (or accept) depends critically on *expectations*, and there exist traders whose expectations may be driven by momentum factors (recent price changes), rather than fundamentals—whatever that might mean in an uncertain financial world committed to forward induction, but unambiguously defined in the laboratory according to standard theory. The laboratory that confirms equilibrium theory under far weaker conditions than modeled by any theorists, now fails to corroborate rational expectations theory under

conditions that any theorist would say are transparently simple for rational agents. What is going on here?

You, the reader, will learn much, not only about economics, but also
about economists, about the technology of experiment in economics and
what it has done for—or to—professional economics, and about the ac-
complishments and foibles of financial markets.

Enjoy yourself. It's an entertaining ride on the road to a better understanding of a financial world created we do not know how, whose upside
we love and whose downside we loath and fear; a world no one could
have invented, and that we may not learn to manage any better in the future than in the past. Experiments have taught us, however, the futility of
trying to attenuate price bubbles with circuit beakers and caps on price
increases and decreases; if anything, such interventions make them extend
longer and crash harder by creating an illusion of reduced downside risk.
On the positive side, experiments suggest that changing the mechanism
by which market prices transmit information to traders and investors can
reduce bubbles.

With all its alleged unreliability the market has fueled an economy
whose long-run performance is without peer. If we could completely
manage it, it might become more predictable, but also mask the true uncertainty in capital markets that caused it to emerge, and shaped its character, in the first place.

Vernon L. Smith
Professor of Economics and Law
George Mason University

Preface

On Wall Street, appearances are deceiving. Behind a façade constructed of the highest technology that money can buy lurks a market that is little more than an updated version of the bazaars of antiquity. Today's New York Stock Exchange (NYSE) dates back to a 1792 buttonwood tree on Wall Street when Spanish pieces of eight were the coin of the realm. The tradition of prices denominated in eighths (and then sixteenths) continued on the New York exchanges until 2001 when decimalization, the modern system long used by the rest of the world, was finally instituted after much resistance and several missed deadlines. Many other traditions, like the use of floor specialists to "maintain an orderly market," remain.

People are inclined to look back with nostalgia on the good old days, but in the financial markets, the old days were not always good. While Wall Street can do an admirable job of helping to fuel economic growth, the path of progress has been bumpy, punctuated by episodes of bone-rattling volatility that sometimes end with a crash. While the pillars of the financial community may be quick to point to the investing public's "irrational exuberance" as the source of this volatility, it is curious that most markets outside the financial arena conduct their business with considerably less drama. In other markets, faith rarely enters the picture, but financial markets would crumble without their daily dose of it.

While the Vatican has yet to assign a patron saint to Wall Street (although it could certainly use one), for economists, Adam Smith has assumed that role. This eighteenth-century Scottish philosopher expounded on the virtues of a market system freed from government interference and monopoly exploitation. Although Adam Smith is renowned as the father of economics, his ideas did not arise in a vacuum, but emerged out of the same environment that would spawn the industrial revolution. The physical world that surrounded Smith had been shaped by a former head of the British mint known for his success at keeping England's money safe from counterfeiters. But preserving the British currency was among the least of his achievements, for that public servant was Sir Isaac Newton.

Newton revolutionized the physical sciences by taking the perfect mechanical world thought into existence by René Descartes and then employing Galileo's experimental method to derive the laws that must logically rule that world. These laws could then be applied to real-world situations if one carefully took into account reality's imperfections. Newton's laws would function as the operating system for the industrial age. It was only natural that philosophers would take Newton's lead and begin to look for the laws that governed the operation of politics and the economy, creating what they called *social physics*.

Newton may have explained the physical world but he did not create it. His laws could be seen as interpreting divine intent even if the prevailing theology, which had intimidated Descartes and persecuted Galileo, did not concur. The logical holes in those laws—such as those eventually plugged by Albert Einstein's theories of relativity—were not problematic because God could mind the details. Indeed, physicists sometimes see themselves engaged in a game where God makes up the rules and physicists then try to discover them.

Adam Smith faced a similar problem when he advocated the virtues of free markets: Markets were good, especially when one considered the alternatives, but how did they work their magic? Following the lead of Newton, Smith dispensed with an explanation and observed that participants in a market acted as if they were collectively "led by an invisible hand" to the "natural price" for every good.

Physicists may have been able to set into motion an industrial revolution without knowing specifically how nature performs its miracles, but economists did not have this luxury. Smith's invisible hand does not operate with the clockwork precision and consistency that let inventors rely on Newton's laws. The manic-depressive financial markets, with their endless cycles of boom and bust, have repeatedly rocked the global economy. By the twentieth century, it dawned on economists that markets were too important to entrust to an appendage of dubious pedigree; if markets were to work properly, then, like any other mechanism, they needed to be consciously engineered to serve their function.

A satisfactory model of free markets only first appeared over a hundred years after Adam Smith made his original case for them. Building on the insights and mistakes of four generations of economic philosophers, Alfred Marshall published the first modern economics textbook in 1890. His magnum opus was not only an instant success, it was the dominant economics textbook for a generation and it continues to influence contemporary economics texts.

Like Adam Smith, Alfred Marshall also had difficulty coming to grips with the invisible hand. Marshall did, however, devise a workaround that would allow markets to operate perfectly without any form of intervention. He noted that if everyone in the market had perfect knowledge of everything that might affect it, each would have enough information to compute the natural price. In such an enlightened marketplace, everyone could agree upon the natural price for a good before its market opened. Marshall clearly stated that perfect knowledge was not required for markets to find their natural prices, but he was unwilling to provide the mechanism for how markets could work without it. The twentieth-century economists who followed Marshall assumed that markets worked perfectly for their theories' sake while acknowledging the imperfections of the real world that surrounded them.

It was not until the information age that economists would see the importance of fleshing out the invisible hand. As John von Neumann was drawing up the blueprints for the programmable electronic computer in 1945, Vienna-born economist F. A. (Friedrich August von) Hayek was publishing an article in the *American Economic Review* that praised the market for its computational abilities. Hayek's article was a defensive move taken against a rising tide of *market socialism* which advocated that under Marshall's assumption of perfect knowledge the government itself could not only directly compute market prices, it could rig the market to remedy a variety of social ills—most notably, the inequality of income—at the same time. Adam Smith's market was perfect on only one dimension—efficiency; market socialists believed that with the government's assistance, it could be perfect on every dimension.

Professor Hayek, who shared the 1974 Nobel Prize for his work in economics, pointed out that the government could not come close to performing the computations required of a perfect socialist economy. Although Adam Smith's invisible hand could do its job without knowledge of every economic detail, for government bureaucrats this information was essential to their task. In effect, the *market mechanism*—the rules and institutions that govern exchange—aggregated the information required to allocate goods without the need for any specific knowledge from buyers and sellers. As long as rules were established to guide and enforce the freely determined exchanges of the marketplace, *spontaneous order* would arise. (Hayek was well ahead of everyone on this point—it would be decades before physicists, biologists, mathematicians, and computer scientists appreciated the importance of spontaneous order in modeling the behavior of complex systems.) Hayek saw that if the government ever attempted the gargantuan task of compiling perfect knowledge about the economy, it would inevitably fail because people would be reluctant to tell their secrets to the government only to risk having that information used against them.

While F. A. Hayek was working to rehabilitate the free market, Edward Chamberlin at Harvard was among the majority of economists lined up against it. In the process of building his case for government intervention, Chamberlin invented the core methodology of *experimental economics*, the study of economic phenomena in a controlled environment. Armed only with a stack of index cards, he used his students as subjects in the first economic experiments. Before Professor Chamberlin developed these techniques, economists unquestioningly thought that economics, like astronomy, was a purely observational discipline. (Until only recently, many economics books continued to boldly maintain that economic experimentation is impossible.) Although physics could not develop a working theory without first embracing a scientific method based on experimentation, economics had managed nearly two hundred years without it.

The experimental findings that Chamberlin published, in which the market appeared to perform erratically, were at odds with the free-market theories of Adam Smith, Alfred Marshall, and F. A. Hayek. To emphasize the flaws he discovered, Chamberlin entitled the 1948 article reporting his results "An Experimental Imperfect Market."

Professor Chamberlin's scientific proof that markets were incapable of textbook perfection did little to discredit free markets; instead, it was the beginning of a new and exciting chapter in economic history. Could it be that the invisible hand did not care for the way that Chamberlin arranged his classroom market? Perhaps a different set of market rules might provide a more hospitable environment in which the invisible hand could work its magic? While Chamberlin was satisfied to continue running his imperfect markets for his classes, one of the graduate students who participated in the experiment, Vernon Smith, had to know more about how markets worked.

I had the privilege and exceptional good fortune to meet Vernon Smith when his work in experimental economics was beginning to attract the attention of the economics profession and as the practical application of experimental results to financial and other markets was becoming apparent. Vernon had been a Caltech (California Institute of Technology) undergraduate in electrical engineering before he went off to Harvard to study economics. Several members of the Caltech faculty, spurred on by Charles Plott, a young Caltech professor who had been Vernon's fishing buddy when they taught together a few years earlier at Purdue, had taken an interest in running experiments, not only in economics but also in the neighboring discipline of political science. (Caltech had erected no barriers between economics and political science; they were lumped together as "social science.") Vernon was invited to Caltech for a year (and ended up staying two) as one of a handful of Sherman Fairchild Distinguished Scholars on campus.

In the spring of 1974, Charles Plott and Vernon Smith jointly led a seminar course called "Laboratory Methods in Social Science." While the rising stars of Caltech's social science faculty dominated the seminar, I was one of the few "paying customers," as Vernon referred to the undergraduates brave enough to take the course.

Outside the calm of the Caltech campus, financial markets were in turmoil with skyrocketing oil prices bringing the stock market to its knees. (At the time I was living across a parking lot from Pasadena's largest brokerage office, where I would spend most early mornings before going to classes.) The other economics courses offered little that could explain what I saw in financial markets, but in Vernon and Charlie's class I was able with the class's assistance to build the world's first experimental market in which speculators played an active role.

In Caltech's crucible, the dominant theme for research in experimental economics was forged: Given that the market mechanism can be viewed as a computer, what is the best "program" for that computer to run? In particular, can we design markets that capture the Newtonian perfection of their theoretical counterparts even when the assumptions of theory are violated? Can markets be structured to promote rational choice rather than amplify and encourage irrationality that may lead to market bubbles? Finally, can we go the next step and program markets to be smart enough that they can achieve more than any theorist could have imagined?

While experimental economics is in hot pursuit of the perfect market, financial markets continue their volatile ways, as if they were stuck in the 1940s of Professor Chamberlin's Harvard classroom. While the physical Wall Street that runs from Trinity Church to the East River was paved long ago, the figurative Wall Street, which serves as the center of the global financial marketplace, is missing many cobblestones. But change is coming rapidly. In a world of supercomputers and high-bandwidth networks, Wall Street can only evolve or die.

Despite a surge in interest, experimental economics and its perspective on markets has remained largely confined to the academic world and a coterie of corporations and government agencies. The field encompasses so much that even an extended article cannot begin to explain what it is and what it can do. This book is designed to provide that explanation in the context of the financial markets. To liven things up, this book focuses on the occasional periods of market turbulence that can help us better understand where markets can go astray rather than those times when the markets operate smoothly. Whenever possible, I have drawn on my own experiences in investment management and risk management, which have often involved either preventing or remedying problems. Because Vernon, Charlie, and their Caltech colleagues got to me first, everything that I have seen in the academic and corporate worlds has been filtered through the lens of experimental economics. In this book, I share that view with you.

As I began to write this book, I set a number of guidelines for myself. First, I wanted the book to be as readable as possible, so that no prior exposure to economics or finance is necessary to appreciate most of its content. Moreover, this book is designed to be read straight from beginning to end, uninterrupted by notes or references (it is up to you whether you switch off your cell phone while you read it). For the reader who wants background information or pointers to further reading on a topic, I have collected notes by topic for each chapter at the end of the book. Included among the notes are references to several surveys and books of collected readings that provide gateways to topics for which I can provide only passing mention. Many of the references are freely available on the Internet, so links to them are provided. These notes also document the sources that I have drawn upon in writing this book, giving credit where credit is due.

Second, I wanted to avoid the "gee whiz" approach to my subject. Yes, experimental economics and the light it sheds on the financial markets are a true revelation, but I do not want you to just take my word for it—this book is designed so that you can experience that revelation for yourself. Furthermore, this book is as much concerned with solving the problems of the market mechanism as it is with demonstrating them. Sometimes we can make markets more perfect by changing their rules; other times we need to change them in more fundamental ways to make their behavior more intelligent.

Finally, I looked to balance my presentation along many dimensions. It is impossible for any serious discussion of markets to avoid politics. Indeed, political considerations are an important focus of the last part of the book. Nonetheless, the results of experimental economics can inform all but the most dogmatic political views. While the evidence compiled to date points to markets as possessing the virtues ascribed to them by Adam Smith and his descendants, the market mechanism is so powerful that its abuse can have dire consequences. Indeed, a long string of financial panics that culminated in the 1929 Crash led to a mistrust of markets that has never fully disappeared.

In this book, I attempt to take as scientific and open-minded an approach as possible, incorporating the ideas of economists from across the ideological spectrum that have contributed to our understanding of the market mechanism. For example, although F. A. Hayek and his better-known contemporary, John Maynard Keynes, were both frequently vilified as dangerous radicals, they were friends who disagreed about the way that government might save the capitalist system from the horrific threats posed by totalitarianism. Over time, events have come to cast Hayek and Keynes in a less extreme light, the great wisdom of their teachings overshadowing the politics of the moment.

Acknowledgments

Any special insights that I have brought to this book have come from my hands-on experience in experimental economics and finance. Over the years, several people helped me to gain that experience. Most notably, Charles Plott and Vernon Smith not only got me (and a whole generation of economists) started in experimental economics; we have continued to discuss developments in the field for the past 27 years. My first industry job, as head of GE's quantitative finance group at its Research and Development Center, provided me with the rare opportunity to work on the front lines of many key financial issues of the 1990s. The considerable time I spent in GE's far-flung trading rooms—John Sun's global trading room at Kidder Peabody, Charles Kaminski's fixed-income operation at GNA, and Mark Barber's commercial paper facility at GE Capital—enabled me to gain a broad understanding of the institutional details of finance. I would also like to thank Jack Welch, Dennis Dammermann, James Bunt, and James Colica for giving me carte blanche to peer into the nooks and crannies of GE Capital as leader of the quantitative risk management task force. Finally, I thank John Lewis for helping to launch me on my career as an institutional portfolio manager.

This book has particularly benefited from the extensive comments of Evan Schulman and Jan Nicholson, who have served as the book's godparents. Their enthusiastic support and constructive criticism has helped me to accomplish more than I ever thought possible.

This book is built on everything I could possibly absorb from the financial and academic worlds. I would like to thank Kenneth Arrow, Robert Baseman, Horace Wood Brock, Gunduz Caginalp, Colin Camerer, Jack Caouette, Samuel Dinkin, Martin Feldstein, David Greene, Bill Grey, Alex Kane, Stephen Kealhofer, Alexander Kelso, John Ledyard, Jonathan Leland, John McQuown, Haim Mendelson, Victor Neiderhoffer, Jack Praschnik, Stephen Rassenti, Mary Caslin Ross, Abraham Seidmann, Richard Spady, Michael Spence, Hal Varian, Ruth Whaley, Thomas Williams, Kenneth Winston, Steven Wunsch, and Richard Zeckhauser for all that I have learned from them.

In my background research for this book, I benefited greatly from my interviews with Seabron Adamson, Robert Bulfin, Jack Gribbin, Jerry Grochow, Evan Kwerel, Roger Noll, and Charles Polk.

Claudio Campuzano provided the support and encouragement during this book's development that is only possible from an editor with a deep understanding of what it is about. Pamela van Giessen has helped this book along its way with her skillful guidance. The diligence of Sujin Hong and the folks at Cape Cod Compositors was instrumental in the production of this book.

My closest relatives have all contributed in their own ways to my work on this book. My wife, Mary O'Keeffe, not only read the numerous drafts and helped guide the book on its way; she tolerated me and the book through its long journey into print. My children, Alison and Catherine, greatly contributed to the enjoyment of writing this book through our frequent discussions of the mechanics of writing and the use of language. My mother, Sara Miller, gave me the individual investor's perspective on finance, and my sister and fellow author, Dinah Miller, was a source of both concrete information and moral support.

Chronology of Major Events

Year	Actor(s)	Event
1604	Galileo	Experimental derivation of physical law
1610	Galileo	Sunspots and telescope
1628	William Harvey	Blood circulation
1644	René Descartes	Deterministic vision of the physical world
1687	Isaac Newton	Laws of classical physics
1705	John Law	Diamond/water paradox and paper money
1758	François Quesnay	*Tableau Économique*
1776	Adam Smith	*The Wealth of Nations*
1789	Jeremy Bentham	Utilitarianism
1803	Jean-Baptiste Say	Say's Law
1844	Jules Dupuit	Demand curve and consumer's surplus
1848	John Stuart Mill	Synthesis of supply and demand
1848	Karl Marx and Frederich Engels	*Communist Manifesto*
1862	William Jevons	Demand analysis
1874	Leon Walras	Early general equilibrium theory
1881	F. Y. Edgeworth	Economics of exchange
1883	Brooklyn Bridge	Steel-cable suspension bridge
1890	Alfred Marshall	Complete neoclassical synthesis
1899	Thorstein Veblen	Conspicuous consumption
1915	Albert Einstein	General relativity

Year	Actor(s)	Event
1929	U.S. stock market	October Crash
1933	Edward Chamberlin	Monopolistic competition
1936	John Maynard Keynes	Macroeconomics
1940	Tacoma Narrows Bridge	Modern suspension bridge collapse
1941	Wassily Leontief	Input–output model of the U.S. economy
1942	Joseph Schumpeter	Creative destruction and economic evolution
1944	John von Neumann and Oscar Morgenstern	Game theory
1945	F. A. Hayek	Markets as information aggregators
1945	John von Neumann	Architecture for the programmable computer
1945	Paul Samuelson	Modern mathematical economic analysis
1948	Edward Chamberlin	Classroom market experiments
1950	John Nash	Equilibrium concept for games
1951	Kenneth Arrow	Social choice theory and impossibility result
1952	Harry Markowitz	Modern portfolio theory
1953	Kenneth Arrow	Formal model of risk and uncertainty
1954	Kenneth Arrow and Gerard Debreu	Modern general equilibrium theory
1954	IBM	Mass-produced electronic digital computer
1960	Sidney Siegel and Lawrence Fouraker	Bargaining experiments
1961	William Vickery	Auction theory
1962	Vernon Smith	Double auction experiments
1962	Edward Thorp	Blackjack card counting
1964	William Sharpe (and others)	Capital Asset Pricing Model
1965	Paul Samuelson	Efficient markets and random walks
1965	Digital Equipment Corporation	Mass-market minicomputer (PDP-8)
1965	Eugene Fama	Efficient-market hypothesis
1970	George Akerlof	Lemons
1970	Amartya Sen	New impossibility results in social choice
1971	James Mirrlees	Optimal income taxation
1972	Robert Lucas	Rational expectations and monetary policy

Year	Actor(s)	Event
1973	Fischer Black, Myron Scholes, and Robert Merton	Option valuation
1973	Chicago Board Options Exchange	Exchange-traded stock options
1973	Hewlett-Packard	Programmable handheld calculator (HP 65)
1973	A. Michael Spence	Market signaling
1974	Amos Tversky and Daniel Kahneman	Individual irrationality experiments
1977	Ross Miller, Charles Plott, and Vernon Smith	Speculation experiments
1977	Michael Levine and Charles Plott	Agenda manipulation experiments
1978	F. A. Hayek	Private money
1978	Charles Plott and Vernon Smith	Market institution experiments
1979	Franco Modigliani and Richard Cohn	Money illusion and the stock market
1979	David Grether and Charles Plott	Preference reversal experiments
1980	Arlington Williams	Computerized experimental laboratory
1980	Sanford Grossman and Joseph Stiglitz	Information acquisition and efficient markets
1981	IBM	Mainstream personal computer
1981	Robert Axelrod	Evolution of cooperation
1982	Robert Bulfin, Stephen Rassenti, and Vernon Smith	Smart market for airport slots
1982	Robert Forsythe, Thomas Palfrey, and Charles Plott	Asset market experiments
1982	Chicago Mercantile Exchange	S&P 500 Index futures begin trading
1985	Ross Miller and Charles Plott	Market signaling experiments
1987	U.S. stock market	Black Monday

Year	Actor(s)	Event
1988	Vernon Smith, Gerald Suchanek, and Arlington Williams	Bubble experiments
1988	Charles Plott and Shyam Sunder	Information aggregation in asset markets experiments
1989	Sun Microsystems	"Pizza box" workstation (SPARCstation 1)
1989	Jeffrey Banks, John Ledyard, and David Porter	AUSM market for space station resources
1991	Colin Camerer and Keith Weigelt	Information mirage experiments
1994	FCC	First auction of electromagnetic spectrum
1994	Mordecai Kurz	Rational belief equilibrium
1995	David Porter and Vernon Smith	Bubble experiments with futures
1995	eBay	Internet consumer auctions
1996	Alan Greenspan	Irrational Exuberance speech
1997	U.S. stock market	Blue Monday
1997	Andre Shleifer and Robert Vishny	Limits of arbitrage
1997	IBM	Deep Blue defeats Garry Kasparov
1998	Global markets	LTCM crisis
1999	priceline.com	Initial public offering
2000	U.S. stock market	Internet bubble bursts
2001	State of California	Market-induced rolling blackouts
2001	U.S. stock market	Decimalization completed

PART I

BUBBLES AND EXPERIMENTS

1

Wind Tunnel Markets

On a typical Monday, the floor of the New York Stock Exchange is a beehive of activity from the opening bell at 9:30 in the morning until the closing gavel at four in the afternoon. October 27, 1997, however, was not a typical Monday. For exactly 30 minutes and 5 seconds—from 2:35:55 P.M. until 3:06:00 P.M.—all trading stopped. Traders who would normally be milling from post to post, gesturing madly to get the attention of one of the specialists who maintain the order books for each stock, prepared for trading to resume. On a few previous occasions, the entire exchange had shut down for a computer or power outage or to help members deal with a snowstorm; trading halts in individual stocks pending important news are an everyday occurrence. Now, for the first time in history, the government had brought the New York Stock Exchange to a complete standstill.

The day had started out as just another in a string of bad days when news of financial woes in Asia weighed on the U.S. markets. The problems had begun in July with the devaluation of Thailand's currency—the baht—and, with each passing day, it seemed like the crisis had spread so far through Asia's other emerging economies that its impact would eventually be felt in the United States. On Friday, the Dow Jones Industrial Average had closed a tad above 7700, down from 8200 a month earlier, but still up 200 percent from the beginning of its latest climb in 1990. This had been a most impressive run for the market. The Dow continued lower on Monday, declining steadily throughout the morning to fall below 7550 shortly before noon. The market then attempted to stage a rally, making it feebly

3

back to 7600 at the stroke of noon. As this rally faltered, panic began to spread through the market.

By one o'clock, the Dow had fallen to 7500 and the minds of traders on the floor, as well as those around the globe, undoubtedly focused on a market regulation that had never come into play before—the circuit breakers. This regulation required that all trading in U.S. stocks be automatically suspended for 30 minutes as soon as the Dow Jones Industrial Average declined 350 points from its previous close. Designed as a *time out* mechanism for the market, the circuit breakers forced traders to go back to their corners—providing them with the chance to reflect on their actions. This time could also provide the opportunity for a savior to step in and bail out the market. But, most important of all, the inventors of the circuit breakers hoped that their mere existence—even if they were never triggered—would reassure the market that a safety net was in place to catch a falling market, thereby nipping panic in the bud.

As two o'clock approached, it was clear that the circuit breakers overhanging the market had not allayed the panic; instead they had helped to fuel it. Disconcerted by the prospect of being locked into their positions when the market was shut down, many traders dumped stock while they still could. The very presence of the 350-point circuit breaker contributed to its being tripped soon after the half hour with the Dow just above 7360. Indeed, many traders believed that the circuit breakers had acted like a magnet. Instead of breaking the market's fall, each circuit breaker pulled the market down to it.

During their maiden voyage into market limbo, traders had time to contemplate something even more ominous—the next circuit breaker. If the Dow fell another 200 points, placing it down 550 points for the day, a second circuit breaker would be triggered—this one suspending trade for a full hour. Given that the first circuit breaker would not be lifted until after three o'clock and the market was scheduled to shut down at four o'clock, the tripping of the second circuit breaker would shut down the market for the day. This second circuit breaker proved to be an even stronger magnet than the first.

After mulling over the second circuit breaker, traders continued to sell like there was no tomorrow when the market reopened. For those traders whose capital would be wiped out by margin calls, forcing the liquidation of their positions at tremendous losses, there would indeed be no tomorrow. The anticipated plunge in the market tripped the second circuit breaker in just 24 minutes. The circuit breaker would have been tripped immediately except that the loss in each of the 30 stocks that made up the Dow would not register on the Average until buyers and sellers could agree upon a price at which to trade. With the market verging on mayhem, it took several minutes for most stocks to resume trading. As each Dow stock opened, the Average fell several more points to reflect its new, lower price. Because the market was now moving downward by leaps, the Dow overshot the second circuit breaker; trading halted for the day after the Dow had fallen 554 points to close at 7161.

Monday, October 27, 1997, quickly made a name for itself; indeed, it made several names for itself, the most popular of which was *Blue Monday*, which is how this book will refer to it. One name that was not available was *Black Monday*—it had already been taken by the record-breaking crash 10 years earlier on October 19, 1987. That plunge was so terrifying that the circuit breakers that were triggered on Blue Monday were instituted in an effort to prevent a replay of Black Monday's events.

After the market's early close at 3:30 P.M., the president of the New York Stock Exchange met with the press and proclaimed that the circuit breakers had worked as intended. Nonetheless, they were soon modified so that a 10 percent decline in the market rather than any specific point move would trigger them. In the future, changes in the settings for the circuit breakers would be largely automatic and would require only token administrative action. (The circuit breaker limits had only been minimally adjusted prior to Blue Monday.) Had the upgraded circuit breakers been in place on Blue Monday, it is doubtful that they would have been triggered at all. The only good thing that came out of the early close of the market was that it reset the circuit breakers. On the next day, another 350-point decline in the Dow would be needed to trip the first circuit breaker.

The market opened for trading on Tuesday the 28th with considerable fear. U.S. stocks had traded sharply lower overnight on the Tokyo, London, and world's other stock exchanges, but not low enough to make the tripping of the first circuit breaker a *fait accompli*. After an immediate decline of nearly 200 more points to clear out the so-called *weak hands* in the market—mostly traders receiving margin calls—the market abruptly reversed course. By the end of the day, it had rocketed up 334 points, recouping much of Monday's loss. Figure 1.1 shows the swiftness of both the decline and the subsequent recovery. Although few people felt the need to tag Tuesday with a name, *Happy Tuesday* was a common choice.

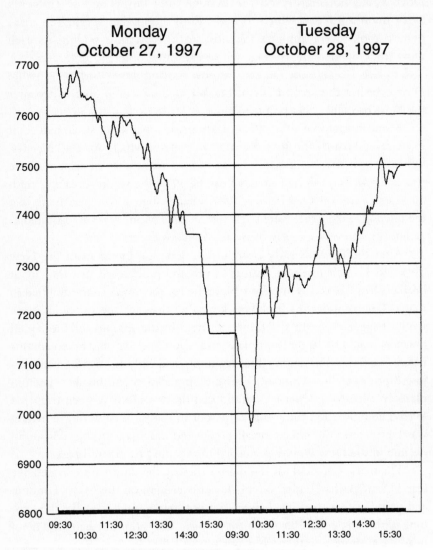

Figure 1.1 **Dow Jones Industrial Average on Blue Monday and Happy Tuesday**

Courtesy of the U.S. Securities and Exchange Commission.

Despite making banner headlines in newspapers and magazines around the world, Blue Monday has become little more than a footnote to financial history. The great bull market of the 1990s stampeded back to life, with the Dow topping 10,000 in less than two years. Monday did set a record for the largest daily point decline in the Dow; however, viewed in relative terms, the 7.2 percent decline was only the twelfth-worst percentage decline at the time. In addition, the rise in the Dow and the trading volume for the next day's rebound both set records. But all these records were quickly and repeatedly eclipsed as the U.S. stock market continued to grow in value and volatility.

The aftermath of Blue Monday and Happy Tuesday is as important as what happened to the market on those days. The change in circuit breakers most likely took the market from one bad system to another, but at least the new circuit breakers would take much longer to trigger. Even if we ignore the fact that any type of circuit breaker is likely to be counterproductive regardless of how it is structured, as technology stocks continued their unprecedented climb, the Dow was becoming less representative of the dangerously volatile part of the market. Indeed, on several occasions in 2000 and 2001, the Dow would move strongly higher on many days where the Nasdaq and S&P (Standard & Poor's) averages plummeted. The Dow had become a *safe haven* for the rest of the market and so investors could sustain enormous losses without their being reflected in the Dow.

The other fallout from Blue Monday was that the SEC, almost a year after the incident, produced a report indicating that the system worked while grudgingly admitting that the circuit breakers likely contributed to the rapid decline through their *magnet effect* rather than abating it. Still, they gave the overall concept of circuit breakers a clean bill of health even though they had provided no hard evidence to support this conclusion.

Step into the Wind Tunnel

It is instructive to compare the collapse of a market with its counterpart in the physical world. Although Wall Street ends at the East River, those wishing to continue across need only look to the north and there, less than half a mile away, is that monumental feat of engineering—the Brooklyn Bridge. This legendary structure of the nineteenth century, frequently sold to the unsuspecting and the subject of the first Ken Burns documentary, gave the world a glimpse of what might be possible in the twentieth century. But the frenzy of bridge construction that the Brooklyn Bridge inspired had to be reconsidered when engineers eventually pushed the limits of the physical world.

As engineerng failures go, the 1940 collapse of the Tacoma Narrows Bridge ranks among the most visually arresting. When it was unveiled in June 1940, the bridge was the third-longest suspension bridge in the world. It did not stay open for long, however, because the bridge's inclination to sway violently in the wind soon became apparent and so all traffic was banned from its roadway. This penchant for twisting in the wind was so pronounced that it earned the bridge its sobriquet—Galloping Gertie.

On November 7, 1940, Galloping Gertie did more than just sway; hit with a brisk 42-mile-per-hour wind, the bridge galloped into the waters of Puget Sound below. The popular reason given for the collapse was that the sustained gales caused the bridge to resonate (like a tuning fork) until it shook itself to bits. Such problems with bridges have been known since ancient times; indeed, soldiers have long been trained to break step when marching across a bridge to prevent it from resonating with their collective footsteps.

It is fortunate both that no one was injured in the collapse and that a camera crew was present to capture the event on film. This amazing footage has become the classic example of an engineering blunder; indeed, many engineering students must have the pleasure of viewing it several times in the course of their education as an object lesson.

Although the collapse of the Tacoma Narrows Bridge was a multimillion-dollar embarrassment, it led to improvements in bridge design that have helped prevent any further wind-induced collapses. The key improvement, which is now standard engineering practice, was to test the aerodynamic properties of the bridge during the design process by placing a model of the bridge in a wind tunnel. (Engineers at the University of Washington had already started wind tunnel testing of a modified bridge; however, Gertie collapsed before any of their fixes could be applied to the bridge.) Using powerful fans to create a sustained breeze, the wind tunnel provides a controlled, simulated environment in which to subject a bridge to the conditions that it could encounter out in the "real world," only on a much smaller scale. The wind tunnel works because the tendency for a bridge to resonate in the wind is approximately the same at both the small scale of the model and the large scale of reality.

As long as the scale-model bridge captures the essential aerodynamic features of the real bridge, what we learn from placing the model in the wind tunnel can be applied to the bridge in its natural setting because the same physical laws apply to both. For the purposes of wind tunnel testing, the model bridge does not have to be an exact replica of the proposed bridge. Only those *salient* features that contribute significantly to the aerodynamic properties of the bridge need to be included in the model. In addition, many of the finer details of the bridge, such as the electrical and drainage systems, can be omitted. Finally, because even scale-model bridges are costly, wind-tunnel tests are designed not to destroy the model, only stress it. This type of testing is far more convenient and cost effective than building the real bridge and hoping that the right gust of wind comes along to provide an adequate test of stability prior to its opening.

In general, the type of model that we should construct is dictated by what we expect to learn from it. A wind tunnel model is likely to be very different from an architect's display model, where physical appearance rather than structural stability is the reason for building the model.

Luckily for those of us who cross bridges, the government did not just issue a report saying that despite Gertie's collapse, suspension bridges were fundamentally safe, and then suggest some minor changes in their construction. Without testing a bridge before constructing it, one could only guess as to whether any recommended changes in engineering specifications would have the desired result. Although wind tunnel testing, like any simulation procedure, has its limitations, it provides an inexpensive way to avoid costly, and even life-threatening, mistakes.

It is natural to wonder why, if wind tunnels and related simulation methods work so well in the physical world, something like them cannot be used for markets, which after all provide a bridge between buyers and sellers. The economic cost of a crash in a major financial market can be trillions of dollars and the human cost is immeasurable. With that much on the line, it would seem that something well beyond a standard bureaucratic response is appropriate.

One need not spin conspiracy theories in order to find a reason why experimentation has taken so long to appear on the radar screens of many economists (and has yet to appear on the screens of some). For the bridge, the transition from blueprint to model and then on to the real world is quite smooth. The universality of physical law ensures that the basic properties of the blueprint bridge are manifested in the model.

Only occasionally will the nuances of the physical reality of the model differ significantly from the idealized world of physics. Indeed, engineering as a discipline is mainly concerned with the issues that arise when going from the scientist's theoretically perfect world to the real world that we inhabit. The next transition—from model bridge to real bridge—is smoother still. Except at transgalactic and subatomic scales, physical law applies consistently. The amoeba and the elephant dance to the same tune.

While Newton's laws and the everyday physical world form a near-perfect match, the same cannot be said for economic laws. Even the most zealous advocates of the market system are careful to distinguish between the abstract virtues of markets and their real-world manifestations. While engineers have been able to attribute apparent differences between theory and practice to ancillary forces, most notably friction, there appears to be no simple way to reconcile such discrepancies in the economic world. Given that the match between theory and reality is already tenuous, there would seem to be little to gain from interposing a model between them.

This book shows how creating markets in a laboratory setting not only serves as a useful way to model markets, but also helps to narrow the gap between economic theory and practice. Advances in technology are already narrowing this gap as electronic trading in real-world markets makes them more like the markets run in computerized economics labs. While there are many aspects of the global economy, including the actions of governments and central banks, that cannot be faithfully reproduced in a controlled setting, the basic mechanisms that underlie the market for all assets, not just financial ones, are ideally suited to the laboratory.

Physical scientists must be content with discovering the rules that nature presents to them; social scientists have the ability to make their own rules, or at a minimum to attempt to influence those who make the rules. Laboratories provide economists with the ability to test several alternative sets of market rules before they are unleashed on the economy.

Isolated from the noise of real-world markets—or *naturally occurring markets* as we will call them following the convention of experimental economics—the fundamental character of economic law is easily examined. In particular, within the laboratory we can adjust the parameters of the market mechanism, such as the mandated circuit breakers on U.S. stock markets, and determine their effect on market performance. By refusing to consider the market mechanism as merely the black-box abode of the invisible hand, but rather as a sophisticated computational device whose programming determines its performance, we take the first steps along the path to making markets fulfill their potential.

Our Road Map

The events of Blue Monday are not just an interesting story of regulatory folly; they provide a useful reference point for the contents of this book. Although the end-of-millennium bull market still had years to run, on December 5, 1996, Fed Chairman Alan Greenspan pondered: "How do we know when irrational exuberance has unduly escalated asset values, which then become subject to unexpected and prolonged contractions?" Translated into everyday English, Greenspan was signaling to the financial markets that he was concerned that the U.S. stock market was in a *speculative bubble* and that he might be forced to do something about it. Although Chairman Greenspan's remarks initially dampened spirits in the market, the effect was short-lived and the run-up in stock prices soon resumed. Nonetheless, many viewed the more than 1,000-point decline in the Dow during the following October as evidence of a market bubble that was beginning to deflate. Furthermore, the problems experienced by the U.S. market could be traced to a more obvious bubble in Asian securities markets. What no one could know then is that the real bubble in the U.S. had only begun to form. The bubble was not so much in the Dow as it was in the high-technology stocks on the Nasdaq (National Association of Security Dealers Automated Quote [System]).

A speculative bubble is said to occur when the price of an item, usually a financial asset, is driven *substantially* above its *intrinsic value*, which is its value determined by an objective procedure. In a bubble, buyers are willing to overpay for an item in hopes that a *greater fool* will emerge who is willing to pay an even higher price. When the supply of fools dries up, the price falls, often quite rapidly. The collapse of a bubble in one market can be contagious, precipitating declines in other markets, regardless of whether or not they are also in a bubble.

Bubbles are a controversial topic within the economics profession. Some economists, led by the late Merton Miller, a Nobel Prize–winning economist who taught at the University of Chicago, believe that the inherent efficiency of markets precludes the existence of speculative bubbles. Indeed, there are even articles that argue that the famous bubbles of history, such as the Dutch tulip mania, were not really bubbles. On the other hand, a growing group of economists, including Richard Thaler (also at Chicago) and Robert Shiller (at Yale), have conducted research on the behavioral aspects of economics and finance that provided the scholarly support for Chairman Greenspan's irrational exuberance remark.

Given that engineers can build defective model bridges and watch them twist inside a wind tunnel, might we also be able to create our own market bubbles and crashes in the laboratory? While such a laboratory bubble would not constitute proof that any specific naturally occurring market was experiencing a bubble, it would demonstrate that bubbles are possible in certain market settings. Indeed, part of the problem with determining whether any given market is in a bubble (aside from agreeing on the precise definition of a bubble) is that we cannot know an asset's intrinsic value with any degree of certainty. In the controlled laboratory setting, we can know its value because we are able to induce it.

In the preface, we noted that the first market experiments, which are described in Chapter 2, were conducted using index cards in a Harvard classroom in the 1940s. It was not until the 1980s that the first bubble experiments were run in a computer-based market laboratory at the University of Arizona. In Chapters 3 and 4, we will embark upon the 40-year voyage necessary to develop the techniques of experimental economics, apply them to a variety of market settings, and determine the parameters under which bubbles are formed, so that they can be replicated at will in laboratories around the world.

The beauty of being able to create market bubbles and crashes in the controlled environment of the laboratory is that we can then alter the environment in an effort to see what measures might prevent bubbles from forming in the first place. While there are several ways to avoid or reduce bubbles by educating the subjects in our experiments—something that may not be practical in naturally occurring markets—it turns out that bubbles can also be mitigated by allowing trade in securities whose value is derived from that of the assets that we wish to keep from entering into a bubble. Such securities, known as *derivative securities*, have sometimes been viewed more as a bane of the market than its salvation. Indeed, as we shall see in Chapter 5, the kind of derivative security that has shown some success at reducing bubbles in the laboratory was banned from U.S. exchanges in 1982 and only recently legalized.

The next part of this book explores the role of derivative securities in the proper functioning of the market mechanism. Chapter 6 explores Black Monday, the climactic day of the stock market crash of October 1987. Although stock prices were certainly high by historical standards and objective valuation measures coming into Black Monday, the crash appears to have been caused not so much by market excesses as by the widespread use of a certain kind of *portfolio insurance*. Although stock portfolios can be easily insured using stock index options, a type of derivative security that came into common use in the 1990s, these options, although legal in 1987, were not easy to trade—that is, the market for them was *illiquid*. Large institutional investors, concerned that stocks were in a speculative bubble but unable to use stock index options as insurance against a downturn, embarked on computer-driven trading strategies that became sufficiently widespread to exert a destabilizing influence on the stock market.

Black Monday can be viewed as an unintended consequence of a financial system that had temporarily become too sophisticated for its own good. The confluence of revolutionary financial theories, inexpensive computational power, and relaxed government regulation transported the markets from the white-shoe world of the gentleman banker to a high-tech universe of fast deals and programmed trades. The new sophistication was most apparent in the explosive growth in options and derivative securities that began in 1973 and continues to this day as options pervade the financial markets. Chapter 7 examines how options work and how to compute their value.

The pivotal chapter of this book is Chapter 8, where we see that the pervasiveness of options extends to the market mechanism itself by influencing *price discovery*, the process by which markets determine prices. While the price discovery process that takes place in most financial markets is too complicated to model satisfactorily, the behavior of auction markets, similar to those that have appeared on the Internet, has a large body of economic theory to help explain them. We examine how an auction's rules can affect its performance.

The second part of this book concludes with a general look at liquidity in markets. Chapter 9 examines those instances where inadequate information can seriously impair markets, sometimes leading to total market failure as buyers refuse to buy any item that a seller is willing to sell for fear that it is a "lemon." In contrast, Chapter 10 provides a brief examination of money, a derivative security that is liquidity in its purest form.

Before we discuss the final part of the book, it is worth remarking on what happened to financial markets in the year that followed Blue Monday. Although the U.S. stock market recovered nicely, going on to make higher highs in the months that followed, the inability of Russia to make the interest payments on its outstanding bonds the following August led to a financial crisis unlike any that had preceded it. At the center of the storm was Long-Term Capital Management (LTCM), a hedge fund with more than 60,000 positions that controlled over $100 billion of assets with an investment of $2.3 billion. LTCM made its money by doing some of the invisible hand's work; when the prices in related markets would get out of line, LTCM would profit by buying the underpriced assets and selling the overpriced assets and would then wait until the prices got back in line so that it could exit the position, a procedure known as *arbitrage*.

LTCM was the acknowledged master of its universe and its partners were the dream team of the financial world. The most visible partners were Nobel laureates Robert Merton and Myron Scholes, who first appear in this book in Chapter 7 as the inventors (with the late Fischer Black) of a revolutionary new method for pricing options. But LTCM's bench was just as impressive, if not as well known. Many of them had already been stars on Wall Street working for the legendary John Meriwether, LTCM's chairman, at Salomon Brothers.

With vast computer power at its disposal, LTCM could quickly scour the global markets to catch arbitrage opportunities as they arose. Over time, LTCM (and the Wall Street firms that emulated it) exhausted the easy opportunities for arbitrage, and so computers became even more critical to finding ever-more-convoluted ways in which it could squeeze arbitrage profits from the market. After superlative performances in 1996 and 1997, LTCM started to lose its touch in 1998.

By September 1998, it became clear to the financial markets that Meriwether and LTCM had been dealt a losing hand that it could not fold. In the wake of Russia's financial difficulties, financial markets no longer snapped back in line as LTCM had counted on, but drifted farther out of whack. LTCM had found itself at the center of what could best be described as financial gridlock. Because of the way in which the financial markets were interlinked, LTCM lacked the resources (capital) necessary to exit its positions. Its over 60,000 positions alone appeared to exhaust the available liquidity of the market. As with an automobile stuck in traffic gridlock, outside intervention was necessary to extricate LTCM.

Portfolio insurance, which destabilized financial markets on Black

Monday, and the LTCM's arbitrage activities, which shook them nearly 11 years later, are examples of *program trading*, the implementation of trading strategies with computer programs. In both instances, these strategies were initially profitable because they served to fill holes in the market system. With portfolio insurance, the holes came from the absence of critical markets for stock index options; for LTCM, missing links between markets created the holes that facilitated arbitrage.

The alternative to leaving the task of perfecting the market to private parties who fly the flag of the invisible hand but may unwittingly destabilize markets is to program the market mechanism itself. Markets that are programmable in this way are known as *smart markets* or *intelligent markets*. (Of course, programming alone does not make a market smart. Circuit breakers constitute a simple market program, and as we saw on Blue Monday, they were anything but intelligent.)

The third part of this book examines the linkages between markets and how to create more of them and keep them in better shape using smart markets. Building on the lessons introduced in Chapter 11 from the example of LTCM, Chapter 12 explores some smart market mechanisms, how they can help stabilize markets and prevent gridlock, as well as some of their limitations. Then, in Chapter 13, we look beyond financial markets to examine how specialized smart markets are starting to be deployed in other places in the economy as smart versions of the auction markets introduced in Chapter 8. One of the first institutions to experiment with smart markets was a government facility with several wind tunnels of its own, the Jet Propulsion Laboratory (JPL), which is jointly run by NASA and Caltech. Another government entity, the Federal Communications Commission (FCC), has not only tested smart markets for use in its auctions of the electromagnetic spectrum; it is working to deploy them. To both JPL and the FCC, institutions steeped in physics and engineering, the process of designing and testing a market in the laboratory before putting it into service is just common sense, and not a radical new approach to economics and markets. In Chapter 14, we go behind the perfection of the market mechanism itself and examine the challenges posed by the imperfections of the political processes by which markets are implemented.

2

Bargain Hunting

T he SEC's official report on the events of Blue Monday and Happy Tuesday is notable for the scant attention it pays to Nasdaq stocks; its over 100 pages of narrative, charts, and tables focus on the Dow Jones Industrial Average and the S&P 500 to the virtual exclusion of other indexes. As the 1990s rolled on, Nasdaq would become more difficult to ignore. In 1995, the Nasdaq Composite Index first topped 1000 and then with only occasional blips steadily rose until it briefly breached 5000 in March 2000. As Nasdaq ascended, it became a fixture on the evening news, and a weekly chart of its fortunes was featured in *Barron's*, an honor usually reserved for the stock averages compiled by its corporate parent, Dow Jones.

Nasdaq started out as low man on the Wall Street totem pole. Nasdaq market makers traditionally dealt in stocks that could not meet the requirements for listing on the American Stock Exchange (now merged with Nasdaq) or the New York Stock Exchange (NYSE), aka, *the Big Board*. Nasdaq became more respectable in the 1980s as companies like Microsoft and Intel found no reason to jump through the NYSE's hoops, remaining on the Nasdaq long after they could have qualified for Big Board listing. These companies became such an integral part of the stock market that they were the first Nasdaq stocks included in the Dow Jones Industrial Average. With newfound status and low entry requirements, Nasdaq had become the preferred habitat for high-technology companies.

After peaking in March 2000, the Nasdaq Composite began a long, steady decline following a pattern that many analysts consider typical of a bear market—a sequence of sharp plunges punctuated by quick, abortive rallies. While the financial media had been reluctant to deem the climb in Nasdaq to be a speculative bubble, once the decline was well under way, the bubble bandwagon took off. Companies that built their businesses around the Internet were the first Nasdaq stocks to have the bubble label slapped on them.

Shares of Internet companies, most having minimal sales and no realistic expectation of profits in the future, became speculative favorites as these shares could not only literally double overnight, they could repeat the feat seemingly at will. Indeed, by 1999 it became possible for entrepreneurs and venture capitalists to make a billion dollars with two magic syllables: *dot* and *com*. A prime example of this phenomenon is priceline.com. Just a month after going public at $19/share in March 1999, priceline.com skyrocketed to $162/share, giving the outstanding shares a value of over $28 billion. As a company that sold airline tickets (and eventually other items) using its patented *name-your-own-price* model, priceline's stock had become far more valuable than that of any airline.

Although the company received a great deal of media attention with catchy commercials featuring actor (and shareholder) William Shatner, priceline.com was entirely at the mercy of its suppliers: the airlines. Any time they wanted, the airlines could stop selling their excess tickets to priceline and sell them directly to the public. The high value that the market placed on a company with such a questionable business plan was evidence to many that the company's stock was in a bubble of vast proportions. Nonetheless, stock analysts flocked to priceline's defense, arguing that one had to understand the so-called *new economy* in order to value its stock properly. Some elite investment banks with no direct involvement in priceline's initial public offering hopped on the bandwagon by touting the company just as its stock price was peaking.

After the excitement wore off in mid-1999, priceline.com stock trended down over the next year as concerns about the profitability of all Internet companies surfaced. Although priceline.com initially escaped with only minor bruises, in September 2000 negative publicity about priceline's business practices sent the stock plummeting. As investment banks finally downgraded the stock to *market perform* or *hold* after the horse had left the barn, it dropped at one point to just above $1/share. (Although investment banks can issue *sell* recommendations, they rarely do this, as they do not want to make enemies of any potential future clients. While this tactic may have worked when it first caught on in the 1990s, investors have since cracked the code and even a straight *buy* recommendation—as opposed to *strong buy* or *recommended*—can spook them.) Many other dot-com companies that never achieved priceline.com's staggering market capitalization, but were still worth billions at their peak, went under completely.

With benefit of hindsight, priceline.com stock at $162/share was almost certainly in a bubble. It is difficult to know—even in retrospect—when a speculative bubble has formed because an objective valuation of most financial assets is virtually impossible. Honest differences of opinion about the future prospects of a company can lead to vastly different valuations for the same shares of stock. While it is quite possible that a few of the hundreds of Internet companies that the market bid up might one day justify their high valuations, there was no foolproof way to separate those firms from the numerous failures, even though some analysts claimed that they could. In the face of such overwhelming uncertainty, each firm should be treated as if its shares were lottery tickets on the future of the Internet and not as if they had already won the lottery.

We start by introducing the methods of experimental economics so that we can demonstrate that speculative bubbles truly exist by creating them under the controlled conditions of the laboratory. There, we have the benefit of knowing the value of every asset because we determine it by design. In order to understand bubble experiments, which are among the most sophisticated market experiments conducted to date, we must first consider the fundamentals of markets and economic experimentation.

Capturing the Human Element

As we noted in the previous chapter, engineers make use of wind tunnels because even though the test environments they create may not be *real*, they capture enough reality for their intended purposes. Economic experimentation aspires to attain similar results, embodying the salient features of economic interactions within a controlled environment in order to test alternative market designs and the economic theories on which they are based.

The major difference between experimental economics and the rest of economics is that it uses living, breathing human subjects. Standard empirical analysis in economics avoids dealing directly with humans by using statistical methods to infer their behavior from market data. The shunning of human interaction by economists is not just a manifestation of their introverted nature; instead, it is a rational response to the difficulties associated with using human subjects. Humans make costly and inconvenient subjects and their participation in experiments is strictly regulated in the United States and other countries.

Experimenting on humans rather than on computerized models of them might appear unnecessary and even extravagant. Indeed, engineers have largely abandoned real-world wind tunnels for computerized testing because it is cheaper and easier to place a computer model in a computer-simulated wind tunnel than to place a scale model in a real wind tunnel. But engineers have the advantage that the properties of bridges, automobiles, aircraft, and so on, are much easier to model than the complexities of human behavior. Human behavior has some quirks in it that could have a real impact in the marketplace, yet may not be captured in a simulation. The antics of Commander Data, the android character in *Star Trek: The Next Generation* who has difficulties with the finer points of human interaction, vividly illustrate just how large a gap remains between idiosyncratic human behavior and the most accurate simulation that can be plausibly imagined using the nascent technology of *artificial intelligence*. In particular, Commander Data is designed to be perfectly rational, while many human idiosyncrasies that can affect markets may involve departures from rationality.

Rationality and Induced Value at Your Corner Grocer

It may be impossible to create a completely faithful model of human behavior, but it is still important to have at least a basic model in mind as a guide for constructing experiments. A useful insight for modeling human behavior is to view it as consisting of two parts: *universal* and *individual*. The universal part of human behavior is that behavior that is uniform and consistent from person to person. Clearly, there are some aberrant individuals whose actions deviate so much from the norm that they do not conform to any reasonable notion of universal behavior. These *outliers*, as statisticians call them, are small enough in number and influence to be considered as a special case, or ignored completely. In contrast to the consistency of the universal part, the individual part of human behavior can vary greatly. This part includes what economists refer to as *preferences*, the relative value individuals place on items, both alone and in combination with other items.

When a subject arrives at an experiment, he or she brings both the universal and individual aspects of behavior with him or her. Because universal behavior is truly universal, it stays with the subject wherever he or she goes, including during the time spent in an experiment. Even though individual behavior is difficult to model, the experimenter can often control certain aspects of it with relative ease. The primary way to establish this control is to alter the incentives that the subject faces.

A simple example will illustrate how an experimenter can "reprogram" individual behavior. Suppose that I came up to you in a grocery store by the peanut butter display and announced that I'd pay you $20 for a jar of peanut butter. If you did not immediately walk away, wondering what I was really up to, I could then explain to you that I would let you select any jar of peanut butter from the shelf. Then, showing you a $20 bill, I would explain that I would give you the $20 minus the price displayed on the shelf (saving you the bother and risk of checking out with the jar first). Hearing this, and still wondering about my sanity, you might then look though the display and possibly ask me if I wanted smooth or chunky or even cared at all about what kind you got. I would tell you that it did not matter, as long as it was a jar of peanut butter. At this point, you might find a jar for $3.50, give it to me, and I would give you $16.50—the difference between $20 and the $3.50 marked on the jar. You might then look at the $16.50 in your hand, still in disbelief, and ask if I needed some jelly, too. Then I would just walk away (before the manager of the store would ask me to leave once he found out what I was doing) and the experiment would be over.

As economists generally view individual choice, rationality is the universal part of behavior and preference is the individual component. Coming into the store, you brought your own personal preferences for peanut butter. A quick, objective view of those preferences can be captured in the amount that you would be willing to pay for a single jar. By approaching you with a $20 bill, I can provide the necessary incentive to override your initial valuation (which you are still free to act upon after I leave) and instead I induced a value of $20 for the jar.

The normal response to this situation is for people to search the shelves for the lowest price, pick up a jar with that price, hand it to the experimenter, and collect the difference between $20 and the price. Given no expressed desire for a larger jar, a name brand, or anything else, it makes no sense to get a more expensive jar. Furthermore, if somehow all the jars cost more than $20, then it makes sense to refuse the deal entirely since you would lose money. This behavior is also rational. If this incident took place in a laboratory (most economics laboratories are just special classrooms equipped with computers for each subject) rather than in a grocery store, nothing fundamental would change; I could still induce a value of $20 for the jar of peanut butter merely by offering to pay you that amount for it.

Notice that the potential for manipulating preferences is considerable. If I wanted to induce a higher or lower value than $20, I could do so by raising or lowering the price I offered for the jar. Furthermore, going beyond the single jar of peanut butter, I could induce preferences that were even more elaborate. For example, the textbook economic phenomenon of diminishing marginal value can be induced by offering $20 for the first jar, $15 for the second jar, and so on. Different types of peanut butter—smooth, chunky, and so on—can also be given different values. Finally, values can be placed on bundles of items; for example, introducing jelly as a second item, which might also have a value of $20 alone, but could be worth $50 in combination with the peanut butter.

We must be aware of the possibility that a subject with particularly strong preferences concerning peanut butter may be willing to forgo some money in order to express those preferences. However, as long as the buyer perceives the payment as being sufficient compensation for his time and trouble, the payoff will tend to dominate any prior associations that he brings to the market. Furthermore, to eliminate any feelings—positive or negative—or any possible allergic reactions associated with peanut butter, jelly, or any other product, in actual laboratory experiments it is referred to simply as an "item" (or similar neutral word) that is never actually seen by either the buyer or seller. In the early days of market experimentation there was even concern that the use of the local currency—dollars in the United States—would influence subjects, and so an artificial currency was used. The conversion rate from the artificial currency to dollars was announced at the beginning of the experiment and subjects were paid the appropriate dollar amount at the end of the experiment.

Now that we see how existing preferences can be overridden using the appropriate monetary incentives, let us move on to rationality, the universal part of human economic behavior. It is worth noting that the economic meaning of the word *rational* differs from its standard usage. In normal conversation, when we refer to someone as rational, we mean that his actions are reasonable and appear to be the result of a logical thought process. In contrast, irrational people are wild; their behavior cannot be understood (rationalized) by others. Economists, however, view rationality as something more along the lines of an internally consistent greed. The cornerstone of economic rationality is a logically consistent desire for an improved state of economic well-being. In essence, a rational economic person knows what he wants, knows that he wants more of it rather than less, and knows that he wants it sooner rather than later.

In general, the economic notion of rationality does a good job of capturing the essential universal aspect of human economic behavior, although, as we shall see later, it is not the entire story. Most economic choices do have a certain logical consistency. For example, if someone prefers corn flakes to shredded wheat and prefers shredded wheat to oatmeal as well, it is reasonable to conclude that he will prefer corn flakes to oatmeal. This property of preferences is known as *transitivity*. Experiments on pigeons and lab rats have shown that basic economic rationality, such as transitivity, is not limited to humans; other animals exhibit internally consistent greed when placed in a controlled setting.

The key element of rationality that economic experiments exploit is that, all things being equal, people prefer more money to less money. The offer of money for the jar of peanut butter would not be meaningful to someone who has no desire—and may even harbor an absolute distaste— for money. The intensity of this desire for money, as indicated by what a person would be willing to do for it, does indeed vary considerably from individual to individual, but the presence of that desire is virtually universal. Most people who would fail to meet any noneconomic criteria for rationality are still self-interested enough to satisfy this minimally demanding notion of rationality.

The universal part of human economic behavior, because it is hardwired into almost everyone, cannot be induced within an experimental setting. As the peanut butter example illustrates, there are aspects of individual behavior that can be manipulated using the appropriate incentives; however, some preferences are difficult, if not impossible, to induce. The most important of these preferences is the subject's attitude toward risk. This attitude, which is now thought to have significant biological roots, is a basic personality trait: Some people are big risk takers; others are quite risk averse.

For example, suppose that instead of paying you $20 for the jar of peanut butter, I flipped a coin and gave you $30 if the coin came up heads and $10 if it came up tails. Assuming that I can convince you that the coin flip was fair—with heads and tails equally likely—this new, uncertain payoff would be worth somewhat less than $20 to most people. (Economists use the terms *risk* and *uncertainty* nearly interchangeably; however, uncertainty concerns not knowing the payoff and risk concerns the possibility of an adverse payoff.) The problem is that the amount of the discount that one places on facing uncertainty is an individual preference. With uncertainty entering the picture, I can no longer induce an unambiguous value in my subjects. Furthermore, there is no simple way to make individual adjustments so that all subjects would assign that gamble an equal value, for example, $18.

There are two practical ways to deal with the problem of risk and uncertainty. The first is that if the risks are small enough—for example, if the flip of the coin determined that the value would be just 30¢ or 10¢—it is safe to assume that most subjects would have a value close to the expected value of 20¢, which splits the difference between the two payoffs. The other way to deal with risk is to design experiments so that the actual induced value under uncertainty becomes irrelevant, only the fact that this value will be less than or equal to the expected value for most subjects, a property known as *risk aversion*, is used. Although risk aversion cannot be considered a universal economic property, studies show that the vast majority of people tested are risk averse. The occasional individual who is not risk averse can be detected through the administration of a simple questionnaire before the experiment begins and can then be reassigned to another experiment. Because uncertainty is an essential feature of financial markets, experiments that explore the properties of these markets must be carefully designed.

Risk poses a problem not only because it is more difficult to control than other preferences, but also because some experimental subjects appear to have difficulties making consistent choices and using information properly when faced with risk. Hence, the universal aspect of their behavior may contain elements of irrationality. Although this limited form of irrationality does not come into play in most markets, we will consider it later as a factor in the development of market bubbles.

Let's Make a Deal

The old saying goes, "it takes two to tango," and so the ability to control the value a buyer places on an item is pointless without having a *real* seller to sell to him. It is no more difficult to create sellers in a controlled environment than it was to create buyers. The only difference is that while buyers are motivated by the valuation they place on the item, sellers are motivated by the cost of producing the item. Let us return to the grocery to see how sellers work.

For the buyer, our challenge was to override any preferences for peanut butter that he brought to the store with him by our offer of $20. Although we tampered with the buyer, the seller of the peanut butter remained the same; the grocery store determined the price, which in turn determined what the buyer could keep as a profit from the transaction. For the grocery store, the principal determinant of the price of the peanut butter was its cost, which would be how much it paid the wholesaler for the peanut butter plus any other costs associated with its sale. Except in special circumstances, such as for *loss leaders* that serve as a marketing device to attract business, the store needs to offer the peanut butter at a price above its cost to earn any profit. Of course, the store takes the chance that it will fail to sell its peanut butter if it sets the price too high. In the world outside the grocery store, buyers have other ways of acquiring peanut butter and even within the store there are products that consumers may be able to substitute for it.

With the underlying economics of the grocery store beyond our control, we must accost another shopper to fill the role of the seller. We explain to her that she will be selling a jar of peanut butter to the buyer that we have already cornered and that her only way of obtaining a suitable jar of peanut butter to sell to the buyer is to buy it from us for $10. If she can sell the peanut butter for more than $10, which is the cost that we have induced in her, she gets to keep the difference. For example, if the seller is able to sell the peanut butter for $15, she gets to keep $5 as her profit. In this new setup, we no longer allow the buyer to get his own peanut butter from the grocer's shelves; instead, the only peanut butter for which we will pay the buyer the $20 is the jar sold by our designated seller. In addition, we do not let the seller know what we are paying the buyer for the jar and the buyer will not get to know what the jar cost the seller.

We now have a seller with a cost of $10 and a buyer with a value of $20. What remains is to determine the setting and ground rules under which trade occurs. The simplest way to conduct this basic experiment is to give them a time limit by which each must privately submit a written price for the peanut butter to the experimenter. If the two prices match, a trade has been successfully negotiated and the seller receives the price minus the cost and the buyer receives his value minus the price. If either party fails to submit a price or if the prices do not match, then there is no transaction and so neither party receives any money. No matter what happens, the jar of peanut butter is returned to the grocer's shelf.

Of course, we do not need the grocery store as a setting for conducting this experiment; we can perform it in virtually any controlled environment. (Indeed, with many external stimuli that are uncontrollable, a grocery store does not really constitute a controlled environment.) We can then have buyer and seller transact face-to-face, on the telephone, or over a computer network.

Whatever the setting, the buyer and seller usually spend much of the allotted time haggling over the price. The buyer may initially offer to buy for $1 and the seller might respond by offering to sell at $50. Depending on the behavior of the buyer and seller, an agreement in the range of $10 to $20 may come quickly, it may come right at the deadline, or it may not come at all. Trades outside this range, which would cause one of the parties to lose money, are quite rare—usually the result of a misunderstanding—so it is standard procedure in this type of experiment to prohibit either party from trading at a loss.

The deals that a buyer and seller can strike are illustrated with the *payoff table* given in Table 2.1. Although trades are possible at any price from $10 to $20, this table simplifies matters by only showing the payoffs for multiples of $1. The rows give the price submitted by the buyer and the columns give the price submitted by the seller. Each entry in the table shows the buyer's payoff followed by the seller's payoff. For example, the entry where both buyer and seller submit a price of $13 is (7, 3): $7 for the buyer and $3 for the seller. We can check this entry by noting that the buyer buys from the seller for $13 and sells to the experimenter for $20, while the seller buys from the experimenter for $10 and sells to the buyer for $13.

Notice that positive payoffs only appear on the diagonal of the payoff table. Any other entry in the table has a payoff of (0, 0) because a transaction occurs only when the prices match. Also, as we would expect, the buyer and seller payoffs along the diagonal always sum to $10. The sum of the buyer's payoff, which economists call *consumer's surplus*, and the seller's payoff, which economists just call *profit*, is known as the *(total) surplus*.

Table 2.1 **Payoff Table for a Symmetric Two-Person Bargaining Game
with the Nash Equilibria Highlighted Along the Diagonal**

		Seller										
		$10	$11	$12	$13	$14	$15	$16	$17	$18	$19	$20
	$10	(10,0)	(0,0)	(0,0)	(0,0)	(0,0)	(0,0)	(0,0)	(0,0)	(0,0)	(0,0)	(0,0)
	$11	(0,0)	(9,1)	(0,0)	(0,0)	(0,0)	(0,0)	(0,0)	(0,0)	(0,0)	(0,0)	(0,0)
	$12	(0,0)	(0,0)	(8,2)	(0,0)	(0,0)	(0,0)	(0,0)	(0,0)	(0,0)	(0,0)	(0,0)
B	$13	(0,0)	(0,0)	(0,0)	(7,3)	(0,0)	(0,0)	(0,0)	(0,0)	(0,0)	(0,0)	(0,0)
u	$14	(0,0)	(0,0)	(0,0)	(0,0)	(6,4)	(0,0)	(0,0)	(0,0)	(0,0)	(0,0)	(0,0)
y	$15	(0,0)	(0,0)	(0,0)	(0,0)	(0,0)	(5,5)	(0,0)	(0,0)	(0,0)	(0,0)	(0,0)
e	$16	(0,0)	(0,0)	(0,0)	(0,0)	(0,0)	(0,0)	(4,6)	(0,0)	(0,0)	(0,0)	(0,0)
r	$17	(0,0)	(0,0)	(0,0)	(0,0)	(0,0)	(0,0)	(0,0)	(3,7)	(0,0)	(0,0)	(0,0)
	$18	(0,0)	(0,0)	(0,0)	(0,0)	(0,0)	(0,0)	(0,0)	(0,0)	(2,8)	(0,0)	(0,0)
	$19	(0,0)	(0,0)	(0,0)	(0,0)	(0,0)	(0,0)	(0,0)	(0,0)	(0,0)	(1,9)	(0,0)
	$20	(0,0)	(0,0)	(0,0)	(0,0)	(0,0)	(0,0)	(0,0)	(0,0)	(0,0)	(0,0)	(0,10)

In this example, all $10 of the available surplus is appropriated whenever a deal is struck. Deals such as these, where all surplus is extracted by the subjects, are considered to be *allocatively efficient*, or simply *efficient*. While efficiency appears unimportant in the context of simple bargaining because any deal that can be consummated is efficient, it is less easy to achieve in other situations.

Games and Strategies

Economists and other social scientists refer to this bargaining situation and similar strategic interactions between individuals as a *game*. John von Neumann and Oscar Morgenstern invented *game theory* in the 1940s as a way to understand the theory behind games such as chess and poker and then generalized their theory to handle economic interactions. The bargaining situation that we created in the previous section is known as a *two-person bargaining game*.

Like most economic situations, this game has both *cooperative* and *noncooperative* aspects to it. To get on the diagonal of the payoff table, the buyer and seller must cooperate so that they will submit the same price. Once they are on the diagonal, however, the game reduces to determining how to split the $10 of surplus between them. Such situations where one party's loss is the other party's gain are popularly known as *zero-sum games* (although they are technically *constant-sum games*).

A great deal of economic policy hinges on whether certain situations are zero-sum games. If the economy viewed as a whole is just one gargantuan zero-sum game, producing whatever it is destined to produce regardless of the policies the government decides to pursue, then the pleasure and pain of redistributive government policies is limited to those directly targeted by the policies. On the other hand, to the degree that the economy is not a zero-sum game, then the reactions of the victims of redistributive policies can spread to the economy at large. This will—to use an economic cliché—reduce the size of the pie.

The best reason for having a theory, such as game theory, is for its predictive capacity. Unfortunately, in bargaining games, game theory cannot predict very much. The natural, even obvious, prediction for this game is that the buyer and seller will gravitate to the center of the payoff table. Here, the buyer and seller agree to a price of $15 and each receives a payoff of $5. Although this split is a common outcome, there is a nearly universal tendency for the price taken over many trials to average several cents less than $15. This seems to happen because most people have more experience as buyers than as sellers, and so they are better at bargaining for lower prices rather than higher prices.

Furthermore, the transaction price in simple bargaining experiments is often widely dispersed around the average, reflecting the fact that there is no unique solution to this game; indeed, every diagonal payoff (as well as the fractional dollar payoffs that are not on the table) is a legitimate solution to the game. Indeed, the only meaningful prediction of the theory is that the buyer and seller—unwilling to let their differences stand in the way of receiving $10 to split between themselves—will ultimately agree upon a price.

The negotiated price in this game is largely determined by three factors: the rules that govern the negotiations, the information given to each party, and the relative bargaining skills of the buyer and seller. If the rules of the negotiation somehow allow one of the parties to present the other party with an ultimatum, the party who presents the ultimatum is likely to receive a greater share of the $10. In general, the rules for experimental bargaining games that do not intend to study ultimatums are carefully arranged to prevent them from being given. For example, if the seller can publicly write her price on a piece of paper and present it to the experimenter at any time as her final offer, then the buyer is in the position of either taking or leaving the price. Of course, the seller should do this only after the negotiations are well under way to minimize the chance that she chooses a price higher than the buyer's value.

As far as bargaining is concerned, knowledge is truly power. If the seller knows the buyer's value but the buyer does not know the seller's cost, then the seller can set the price just below $20. Conversely, the buyer can use any information he has about the seller's cost to his advantage. The enormous value of information in bargaining is why car dealers always start by asking how much a prospective buyer is willing to spend for a car and why educated buyers always do research to determine almost precisely what the dealer paid for a car before entering the showroom or web site.

The bargaining power a seller gains from any information she can obtain about a buyer's redemption value is the reason that the name-your-own-price policy of priceline.com was not as consumer-friendly as it might otherwise appear. Being forced to name a price first in a bargaining situation puts the buyer at a strategic disadvantage because the bid price establishes a minimum possible level for his redemption value.

Any set of individual payoffs that sums to $10 can be viewed as an *equilibrium* allocation for the bargaining game. The notion of equilibrium is something that economics has borrowed from physics. An economic equilibrium is a situation where opposing forces are in balance; in this case, the force of the buyer pushing the price down is balanced by the force of the seller pushing it up. One notion of equilibrium for a game, known as a *Nash equilibrium* after John Nash who shared the 1994 Nobel Prize in Economics for its discovery, carries over to the concept of a *competitive equilibrium* in a market, which we will introduce in the next chapter.

Like many fundamental discoveries, the idea behind the Nash equilibrium is enticingly simple. Consider a buyer who knows that the seller is submitting a price of $13. The natural choice for the buyer is to also submit a price of $13. Any other price will create a mismatch, giving him nothing, while a price of $13 will yield a payoff of $7. Similarly, a seller who knows that the buyer has submitted a price of $13 will also feel compelled to submit a price of $13, as any other choice will also yield nothing. What makes this a Nash equilibrium is that the buyer is doing the best that he can given the seller's actions, and vice versa, a feature that holds for any price match between $10 and $20. An important aspect of the Nash equilibrium is that the consideration of alternatives never leads to an observable action; instead, it is a type of thought experiment. (The father of the thought experiment and an occasional character in this book, Albert Einstein, was at Princeton University when John Nash came up with his equilibrium concept as the basis for his doctoral dissertation. Unfortunately, Einstein and Nash found no way to work cooperatively.)

Shortly after coming up with his equilibrium concept for games, Nash looked for a way to solve the bargaining problem, reducing the continuum of Nash equilibria that lie between $10 and $20 to a single price. Although the results of this investigation are intellectually satisfying and continue to be cited and refined in the academic literature, they have limited predictive power. If everyone in the world had identical preferences, an even split would be the obvious solution to the bargaining problem. The difficulty is that everyone is not equal and there is no adequate way to measure these differences. (This leads to other problems, as well, when we look at the issue of aggregation later on.) For example, suppose that the seller is extremely thirsty, has no money, and knows that there is a soda machine around the corner that sells cans of soda for $1 each. This creates an *aspiration level* of $1 in the seller's mind and so the first dollar has much greater value to her than the successive dollars that she might get out of any bargain. When faced with a normal buyer, this seller will stand tough in getting the first dollar of profit, but be more willing to make concessions after that.

The fact that people do not value each additional dollar that they receive equally has a significant impact on the results of bargaining experiments. Fortunately, most market interactions do not depend on such relative valuations. Indeed, the bare bones of individual rationality, that more money is preferred to less, is all that is needed to drive most markets. The overall intensity of that preference does not come into play.

In the bargaining experiment, both the buyer and the seller possess accurate information about the value and cost of the item, respectively; however such information is frequently incomplete or inaccurate. In these cases, the market process itself may provide additional information about an item's value. As we shall see, this is especially true in auctions where a single seller sells to several competing buyers. Each buyer in an auction carefully monitors the actions of the other buyers, both to get a better idea of the item's value and to gauge the depth of the resale market for the item should the buyer decide to sell the item at a later date.

All market interactions can be viewed as an extension of what goes on in a two-person bargaining situation. The institutions that facilitate or impede this interaction help determine the market's outcome. Although humans, as social animals, originally performed all the functions of the marketplace through direct, face-to-face contact—the technology to do otherwise was not yet invented—computers increasingly play an intermediary role in this contact and appear well on the road to becoming the universal market medium.

Market participants are continually learning from what transpires in the market, so how they are able to communicate becomes critically important in determining market outcomes. Negotiations that proceed smoothly in the informationally rich environment of close, personal interaction may break down completely if attempted over a computer network, such as the Internet. On the other hand, the limitations of computer-mediated interaction may actually help to bring focus to certain types of transactions, eliminating some of the distractions of direct communications.

Much of the stated opposition to the automation of the few organized financial markets with live trading floors that remain, such as the New York Stock Exchange and the commodities futures pits in New York and Chicago, is that the trading floor provides an informationally richer environment than does a computer. (It is more plausible, however, that this opposition stems from the desire of members to maintain privileged market access that automation would eliminate.) Traders in these environments believe that the overall ambiance of the trading floor—the sounds, the sights, and even the smell of the traders' perspiration—provide valuable information on the state of the market. Trading floors are laid out with a keen awareness of how the relative positions of the pits will influence the flow of information. Although there is no immediate prospect that the richness of the experience of being on a trading floor can be re-created using computers, the environments that can be created have the potential to convey even more information to the trader than he or she receives on the trading floor. For all the joys that the trading floor brings to our proud gladiators of capitalism, which include the crushing feet and stabbing pens of their adversaries, cost considerations alone have put the trading floor on the financial endangered species list.

It Came from Harvard

The first experimental market was conducted far from the bustle of Wall Street, in the peaceful setting of a Harvard University classroom in Cambridge, Massachusetts during the 1940s. This experiment, which was conducted by Professor Edward Chamberlin, is recognized as not only the first market experiment, but also the first economic experiment of any kind. Because computers were still primitive, expensive, and noninteractive, the experiment was conducted entirely by hand. It was originally intended as a classroom exercise designed as an informal test of Chamberlin's theories, but he found the results interesting enough to write up and submit to the *Journal of Political Economy*, where they were published in 1948.

Edward Chamberlin has never experienced the widespread acclaim of his contemporary, John Maynard Keynes, but he was a commanding figure in the world of economic theory. Even before Keynes (Alfred Marshall's star student) revolutionized economics with ideas that would become the basis for the new field of macroeconomics, Chamberlin had been challenging the prevailing economic view of how firms competed in markets. Before the 1930s, economists largely viewed markets as either competitive or monopolistic. In competitive markets, individual firms were small relative to their markets and so they were unable to influence prices. In monopolistic markets, a monopoly or cartel had the power to set prices and would do so in a way that maximized profits.

In a brilliant stroke, Chamberlin saw that markets could simultaneously have elements of both competition and monopoly, and he called this situation *monopolistic competition*. Monopolistic competition is like competition in that there are sufficiently many firms competing that none can control prices; however, each firm's product is somewhat differentiated from the rest, giving it a *local monopoly*. Coming after the advertising boom of the Roaring Twenties, an economic theory built around product differentiation was only natural. It took over 40 years for economists to develop the necessary analytic methods to examine Chamberlin's theory rigorously. Still, the idea that the structure of an industry could influence its economic performance led to the development of a new field of economics, *industrial organization*, which studies how market structure affects industry performance, from which many of the concepts of experimental economics are derived.

Professor Chamberlin's experiments closely paralleled the bargaining example given above; however, instead of a single buyer and a single seller, he employed several buyers and sellers in equal numbers to maintain a balance of power on either side of the market. Of the 46 experiments he conducted, he reports complete results for only a single experiment that involved 62 subjects from his economics class: 31 buyers and 31 sellers. Each subject was given a card with a letter and number on it. For example, Card B–30 indicated that the subject who received it was a buyer and valued the item at 30. No monetary units were assigned to the numbers and neither were the students paid based on the outcome of the experiment nor did it count toward their grade in the course. To eliminate the possibility of the subjects sustaining unbounded losses, buyers were forbidden from buying above their assigned value and sellers from selling below their assigned cost. After receiving their cards, students were instructed to mill about the classroom to make deals with their counterparts. As each deal was consummated, it was reported to a transactions desk where the price of the deal would then be written on a blackboard. A warning was given shortly before the close of trading so that any last-second deals could be consummated before time ran out.

Table 2.2 shows the buyer values and seller costs for this experiment. Notice that only even numbers were used and that there are occasional gaps in the values. Professor Chamberlin dealt the cards out from a large deck and the random gaps were a result of making the experiment *double-blind*, so that even the experimenter did not know the exact cards that students were given for the experiment.

The results of this experiment appear in Table 2.3. The trades are listed in the order that they occurred. As one would expect, buyers with higher values found it easier to make a deal, as did sellers with lower costs. Note that the highest unmatched buyer value was 58 and the lowest unmatched seller cost was 66. This indicates that it was impossible for the buyers and sellers who remained to complete any additional deals. Despite this encouraging outcome, the overall results might unsettle those who believe that the market is efficient.

A hallmark of an efficient market is that goods flow from the lowest-cost sellers to the highest-value buyers. Although this experiment leans in that direction, there are some notable mismatches. For example, Buyer 58 does not trade even though Buyers 44, 48, 52, 54, and 56—all with lower values—were able to purchase items. Hence, even though as the experiment ends there are no qualified sellers left to transact with Buyer 58, if it had been permitted, any of these five buyers could have profited from reselling the unit they had bought to Buyer 58. (Allowing Buyer 58 to buy from another buyer is known as *recontracting*, a concept that comes up again in the next chapter. Most market experiments do not allow recontracting because

Table 2.2 **Buyers' Values and Sellers' Costs for the Original Chamberlin Market Experiment**

Buyer Value	Seller Cost
104	18
102	20
94	26
90	28
86	30
84	32
82	34
80	36
76	40
74	42
72	44
68	46
66	50
60	52
58	54
56	58
54	62
52	64
50	66
48	68
44	70
38	72
34	74
32	78
30	80
28	82
26	84
24	88
22	90
20	98
18	104

Adapted from Chamberlin, 1948.

Table 2.3 Trades (in Time Order) as Reported by Chamberlin

Trade	Buyer	Seller	Price
1	56	18	55
2	54	26	40
3	72	30	50
4	84	34	45
5	44	44	44
6	102	42	42
7	80	20	40
8	60	28	55
9	48	40	45
10	76	36	45
11	94	52	55
12	68	58	62
13	66	46	55
14	82	32	58
15	90	72	72
16	104	54	54
17	52	50	50
18	86	64	64
19	74	62	69

Adapted from Chamberlin, 1948.

it is not possible in most naturally occurring markets.) Trade 5, where Buyer 44 and Seller 44 trade at a price of 44, is particularly disturbing because a low-cost seller is taken out of the market without generating any tangible benefit (other than the joy of trading) to either himself or his buyer.

Another notable deviation from what one might expect in an efficient competitive market is a significant fluctuation in prices over the course of the experiment. The apparent eagerness to make deals, such as Trade 15 between Buyer 90 and Seller 72 at the high price of 72, kept the price from settling down to any one level. Indeed, if the subjects were concerned with trading rather than making money, which was not real money after all, one might expect some degree of pairing off by buyers and sellers with similar values and costs. Such behavior, as occurs to varying degrees in Trades 5, 9, 15, and 17, would lead to a dispersion of prices rather than convergence to a single price.

An objective way of measuring the performance of this experimental market can be derived from the concept of surplus that was introduced earlier in this chapter. Recall that in the bargaining example in which the buyer had a value of $20 and the seller had a cost of $10, the available surplus was $10—the most money that the buyer and seller together could extract from the experimenter in payoffs. The surplus that subjects receive as a percentage of the available surplus is a measure of the efficiency of the market. For the bargaining experiment, the efficiency was either 100 percent ($10 out of $10), if a deal was reached, or 0 percent ($0 out of $10), if they failed to agree.

With 31 possible buyers and 31 possible sellers, things get considerably more complicated. We can determine the total available surplus using the schedule of buyer and seller values. We do this by forming pairs of buyers and sellers that can extract as much money from the experimenter as possible. The first obvious pairing is Buyer 104 with Seller 18, which generates a surplus of 86, the difference between 104 and 18. The actual price of a hypothetical transaction between them is unimportant; just knowing that they agreed on a price tells us that they will split 86 in surplus. Moving down the table, we can pair Buyer 102 with Seller 20 and get a surplus of 82. Continuing down the table, we can create 15 profitable pairs of buyers and sellers—ending with Buyer 58 and Seller 54—who generate a surplus of 4. The next row of the table does not provide any further surplus, because Buyer 56 cannot trade with Seller 58. Similarly, all the rows below it cannot contribute a positive amount to the available surplus. The total available surplus produced by these 15 pairs of buyers and sellers is 644. While different pairings of the 15 buyers and sellers can generate the same total surplus, there is no set of deals that yields greater overall surplus.

An *efficient allocation* in this market is one in which the buyers and sellers together appropriate 100 percent of the 644 in available surplus. Matching the best buyer with the best seller and so on down the first 15 rows of the table is only one way to achieve efficiency. Indeed, any set of 15 trades involving the first 15 buyers and the first 15 sellers will appropriate the full surplus of 644.

One might think that the allocation that Chamberlin observed, with 19 total trades, would be an even better allocation than the 15 trades involving the top 15 buyers and sellers; however, purely from an efficiency point of view, it is not. The injection of these additional buyers and sellers reduces the overall surplus. The total surplus in the market that Chamberlin created was 584, which yields 60 less than the available surplus of 644. The ratio of 584 to 644, which is a little below 91 percent, is a measure of efficiency in this market. This is a clear indication that the market is not completely efficient; however, with the benefit of hindsight, 91 percent efficiency is not particularly bad, especially when one considers that no monetary or other real payoffs were used. Chamberlin did not compute the surplus or efficiency for any of his experiments; indeed, it would be 30 years before experimenters would report such information.

Chamberlin never really analyzed the data from his experiments; he merely presented the results and observed that they refuted the prevailing economic theory of Alfred Marshall. Chamberlin expressed obvious pleasure that the results of these experiments supported his theory of monopolistic competition—showing markets to operate in what seemed to be a most imperfect manner—but it also appears that he did not take them particularly seriously. Although he continued using experiments as a pedagogical tool, he never published any further results and rarely referred to his experimental work in any later articles or books. Nonetheless, even though economists would ignore this work for years, it would not be forgotten. Because Professor Chamberlin had performed his experiment on so many students and because it was so easy for any of them to run their own experiments, it seemed inevitable that experimentation would not simply end in a Harvard classroom. (The reader should feel free to join in as well, either by winging it based on the descriptions given here or by referring to the many articles cited in the notes.) In the next chapter, we will see the surprising results that one of Chamberlin's subjects, Vernon Smith, got as he tried to improve on this imperfect market.

3

A Tale of Two Smiths

It is not surprising that a Caltech engineering graduate, Vernon Smith, would give experimental markets a new life while teaching economics at Purdue, a university so steeped in engineering that its athletic teams are called the Boilermakers. Indeed, it was an engineer, Jules Dupuit, who conceived the idea of surplus, which we used as a gauge of the efficiency of Chamberlin's maiden experimental market. As France's inspector general of bridges and highways, Monsieur Dupuit's interests went beyond paving roads and keeping bridges from collapsing. Dupuit examined the fundamental economic question of how to determine which of the many roads and bridges proposed for construction it was in society's interest to build. He came up with the idea of computing the surplus attributed to the construction project as a measure of its benefit, which could then be compared with its cost to see whether the project was worthwhile.

Dupuit's method for computing benefits was just one of several steps involved in developing the Marshallian theory that Chamberlin's experimental market sought to discredit. The process started in Scotland several years before the birth of Adam Smith, and would take two roundtrips across the English Channel before finding its ultimate resolution at Oxford with Alfred Marshall's formulation of the *Law of Supply and Demand*.

Progress in many disciplines is driven by efforts to resolve a particularly thorny problem that resists solution by existing methods. In economics, the *diamond/water paradox* of John Law, a Scottish rogue entrepreneur, gave the first economists fits. In his famous 1705 pamphlet,

Money and Trade Considered, Law observed that diamonds commanded a higher price than water even though water was a necessity and diamonds were a luxury. Law was unable to provide a satisfactory resolution to this paradox and it would continue to vex economists for nearly 200 years.

John Law was not only responsible for formulating the central question of economics; he was ahead of his time in other ways. Like contemporary globetrotting economists, who are keen to test their theories on any country willing to take them in (and perhaps be "taken in" in the process), Law took his radical idea for establishing a bank that issued paper money to France after the Scottish government rejected it. King Louis XIV also declined, but on his death in 1715 the throne passed to his five-year-old son, Louis XV. Acting on the child king's behalf, the Duke of Orleans granted John Law the charter for a central bank.

Everything might have worked out fine for Law's new bank; however, it became involved in a scheme involving France's Louisiana land claims. This *Mississippi scheme*, as it was known, generated such speculative interest that it expanded into the *Mississippi bubble*. When the bubble ultimately burst, the financial crisis that followed helped bring about the French Revolution many years later.

The French Revolution was not just about money; it was more the product of the French Enlightenment, an intellectual revolution concerning man's place in the universe. While this movement is popularly associated with Voltaire and Diderot, it counted one very significant economic thinker among its ranks, François Quesnay, an advisor to the adult Louis XV and personal physician to the notorious Madame Pompadour. As a physician, the circulation of the blood—William Harvey's 1628 discovery that used experimental evidence to secure its universal acceptance—fascinated Quesnay. He created the first economic flowchart, his *Tableau Économique*, which showed how goods circulate through the economy much as blood circulates through the human body.

The economic school of thought that Quesnay founded, known as the *physiocrats*, developed in opposition to the reigning school, *mercantilism*, of which John Law was an early critic. Mercantilists viewed precious metals (gold, silver, etc.) as the source of a nation's wealth and they advocated restrictive trade policies that would help create a surplus of these metals. Physiocrats, however, saw economic value as flowing from the land and so the mercantilists' interference in the flow of trade was both unnatural and deleterious. The best economic policy was to leave things alone so that nature could take its course, a doctrine that the physiocrats called *laissez-faire*, literally "allow to do" in French.

This is where Adam Smith, another Scotsman, enters the picture. Adam Smith traveled to the great salons of Paris to confer with Quesnay and the other shining stars of the French Enlightenment. Although Smith disagreed with Quesnay on several points, laissez-faire served as the foundation for the comprehensive economic theory the Scottish philosopher published in 1776 under the title: *An Inquiry into the nature and causes of the Wealth of Nations* (commonly known as *The Wealth of Nations*). In dealing with fundamental economic questions, such as why the price for diamonds greatly exceeded that of water, Smith imagined an invisible hand orchestrating the market so that the "natural price" of each good would arise from competition. Smith clearly had high aspirations for markets—the word *perfect* in various forms (perfection, imperfect, etc.) appears over 100 times in *The Wealth of Nations*.

While Smith saw a link between prices and the cost of production, especially the labor component of that cost, the details—especially the invisible hand itself—were left to the reader. Although Adam Smith acknowledged John Law's diamond/water paradox and alludes to the Mississippi scheme, speculative bubbles were sufficiently anomalous in the eighteenth century that they receive no mention in *The Wealth of Nations*. While Adam Smith was concerned with the threat that government and monopoly posed to free markets, he does not to appear to have viewed bubbles as posing a similar threat.

The hundred years following the publication of *The Wealth of Nations* saw a long string of philosopher/scientist/economists working to fill in the details of the theory outlined by Adam Smith. The first wave of elaborators included the *classical* economic theorists, who continued Smith's mostly philosophical approach to economic problems. By the middle of the nineteenth century, however, the flow of ideas from the physical sciences into economics that had begun in the previous century started to bear fruit. A second wave, the *neoclassical* economic theorists, used increasingly mathematical methods to advance the classical philosophy of Adam Smith. While the classical economists had the field largely to themselves, the neoclassical economists stood in opposition to Karl Marx and his followers. Marx had turned the idea that the value of an item was wholly determined by its labor content, put forth by David Ricardo in his refinement of Smith's theories, into an argument against the laissez-faire policies of the economic mainstream. In order to counter what might be viewed as the fuzzy thinking of their Marxist adversaries, the neoclassical economists abandoned mere philosophizing and looked to make economic analysis more rigorous.

It took a second circuit of the English Channel to get free-market economics back on track. Building on advances by two Frenchmen, Jules Dupuit and Leon Walras, as well as on advances by some British colleagues, Alfred Marshall had all the pieces of the perfect market assembled by 1890. In his *Principles of Economics*, the first modern economics textbook, Marshall provides a brilliant synthesis of all the classical and neoclassical economics that preceded it.

Marshall's role in economics is similar to that of Beethoven in music. Beethoven not only provided the culmination of all the classical music that preceded him; by elevating that music to new heights, he also set the stage for everything that followed him. Similarly, Marshall, intent on transforming *political economy* (as the field of economics was then known) into *economic science*, constructed a comprehensive theory of economic interaction patterned after natural law. While the textbooks before his contained "political economy" in their titles, Marshall's *Principles of Economics* envisioned an economic universe that operated without specific regard to politics. As our story develops, we will find that Marshall's separation of political motivation from economic motivation discarded important information required to understand markets.

The Law of Supply and Demand

The cornerstone of the Marshallian synthesis was the definitive statement of the Law of Supply and Demand, which finally provided the resolution of John Law's diamond/water paradox. Before Marshall, economic theorists concentrated mainly on how the value of an item was determined by the circumstances of its production, which only influences its supply. By giving demand equal weight in the determination of prices, Marshall would paint a complete and objective picture of how markets arrive at them. In a famous analogy from his *Principles*, Marshall views supply and demand as similar to the two blades of a pair of scissors, neither of which can cut without the other.

Edward Chamberlin designed his pioneering experiments to test the Law of Supply and Demand. We can show how this theory works by turning Chamberlin's index cards into a Marshallian picture of supply and demand. We first consider demand, which is derived from the values that buyers place on the item. Referring to the values assigned to buyers in Table 2.2, the highest price that any buyer is willing to pay is 104, so demand will be 0 at any price higher than that. At a price of 104, that highest-value buyer appears, so demand becomes 1 at a price of 104. To entice a second buyer into the market the price must drop to 102, so demand stays at 1 between the prices of 102 and 104, but increases to 2 at a price of 102. The next buyer can enter at a price of 94, increasing demand to 3, and so on down the table, with demand reaching its maximum of 31 when the price falls to 18. Having exhausted the pool of 31 buyers, any further reduction in price, even down to 0, will not raise demand; so, it remains at 31 for all prices between 0 and 18. Note that by determining demand in this manner, a buyer's willingness to pay for an item is exactly the amount given on the index card; no allowance is made for any effort expended in purchasing the item or for any "profit" that the buyer might expect to receive.

The path that demand takes as it increases from 1 unit at a price of 104 to 31 units at a price of 18 is shown using a *demand curve*. (Economists use the term *curve* in the formal mathematical sense of any connected line, including not just curved lines, but straight and jagged lines as well.) The table of buyers' values produces a demand curve (Figure 3.1) that is similar to the textbook picture of demand that appeared as one of the many footnotes that contained the formalities of Marshall's *Principles* and has graced economics textbooks ever since. The only difference is that while textbooks usually show demand as either a straight line or a smooth curve, this demand curve looks like a staircase, reflecting the limitation of purchases to discrete units. Although most of the steps are the same size, the unassigned index cards create several larger steps.

Analogously, we can construct a *supply curve* (Figure 3.2) from the unit costs assigned to sellers. The price must be at least 18 for the first seller to enter the market. At any price between 0 and 18, there are no sellers, and so supply is 0. A second unit is supplied when the price rises to 20. As the price rises further, additional units are supplied until the price reaches 104, at which point the entire supply of 31 units is exhausted. Additional price increases beyond 104 will result in no additional units from sellers, and so the supply curve becomes vertical there. As was the case for demand, the supply is determined directly from the sellers' index cards.

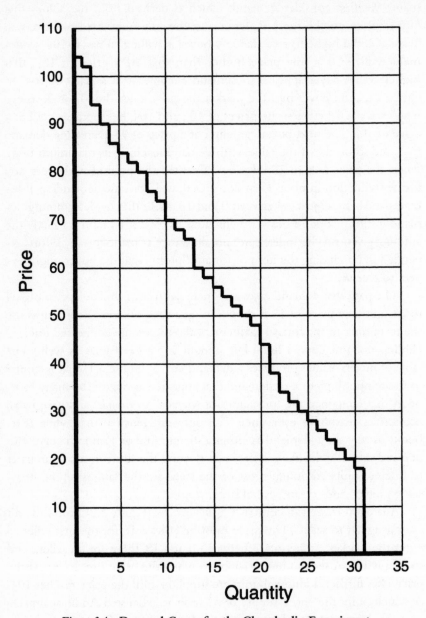

Figure 3.1 Demand Curve for the Chamberlin Experiment

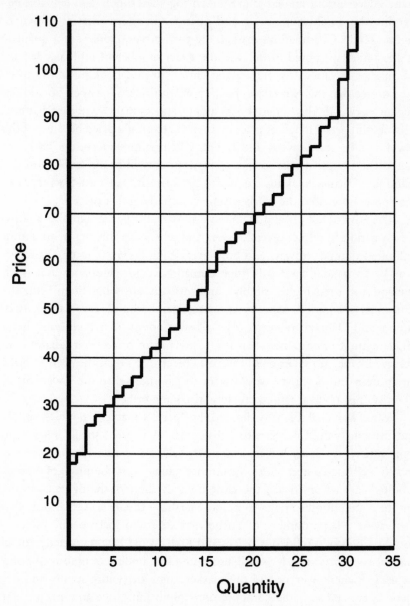

Figure 3.2 **Supply Curve for the Chamberlin Experiment**

Marshall's crowning achievement was integrating the supply and demand curves into a single picture. Taken together, supply and demand determine the equilibrium price and quantity in the market as shown in Figure 3.3. In Chamberlin's market, the two curves intersect at a quantity of 15, which we noted earlier was the exact number of units needed for the market to efficiently extract the entire surplus. Looking at the price axis, we see that the two curves overlap when price is between 56 and 58. For any price in this range, both supply and demand will be 15 units. Chamberlin gets a range of prices rather than a single price because of the way his index cards were distributed. Chamberlin's successors have designed their experiments so that a single price will bring supply and demand into balance, making it easier to perform the statistical tests that can determine how close the market came to achieving that price.

The Law of Supply and Demand is remarkable because it takes a complex situation in which several buyers and sellers can interact in an almost unlimited number of ways and boils everything down to an exact prediction. It can handle diamonds (high demand and low supply), water (high demand and even higher supply), and virtually any other item with the same ease. In addition, contrary to what Chamberlin observed, the Law of Supply and Demand reinforces the classical notion that each good has a single, natural price rather than the scattering of prices that Chamberlin observed. Since no seller would want to receive less than the highest price for an item and no buyer would want to pay more than the lowest price, all units must trade at (approximately) the same price.

Alfred Marshall formally defined the "perfect market" in which supply and demand would come into balance as: "A district, small or large, in which there are many buyers and many sellers all so keenly on the alert and so well acquainted with one another's affairs that the price of a commodity is always practically the same for the whole of the district." In order for competition to reign supreme, Marshall's theory had to assume that there were a large number of buyers and sellers so that no one of them could significantly influence prices and each would have knowledge of all available opportunities. Marshall also noted that under conditions of *perfect knowledge*, where everyone in the market knew the entire supply and demand curve and so could compute the equilibrium price and quantity for themselves, the market price should immediately converge to where supply and demand crossed.

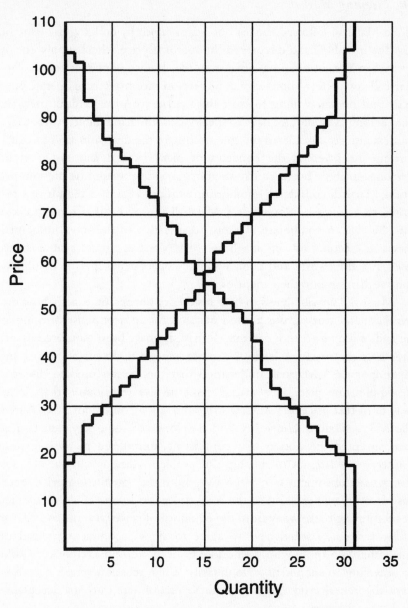

Figure 3.3 **Supply and Demand Determine Equilibrium**

Adapted from Chamberlin, 1948.

The Groping Market

Alfred Marshall followed the lead of Adam Smith by dodging the issue of how the invisible hand discovered the uniform price where supply equals demand in a realistic setting—that is, in the absence of perfect knowledge. Marshall saw perfect knowledge as unnecessary for markets to operate perfectly and he was willing to trust the market to Adam Smith's invisible hand as long as he did not have to specify how the hand did its work. Marshall extensively considered the role of time in the determination of equilibrium—he invented the concepts of *short run* and *long run* used in economic analysis; however, like the physicists from whom he drew inspiration, Marshall considered equilibrium without regard to the process required to achieve it. Nonetheless, Marshall was aware that some process must be able to equilibrate markets because two of the most influential neoclassical economists upon whose work Marshall's grand synthesis was based, F. Y. Edgeworth and Leon Walras, incorporated a specific equilibration mechanism into their theories.

Marshall's unwillingness to have his theory depend on exactly how the invisible hand worked was a good decision for an economist working at the end of the nineteenth century. (It may also have been motivated by his unwillingness to acknowledge the importance of the contributions of his contemporaries.) Marshall understood that the process used to discover the equilibrium price in a market must involve transactions that occur away from that price. F. Y. Edgeworth, who was a contemporary of Alfred Marshall at Oxford University and developer of some key neoclassical ideas, invented the notion of recontracting, introduced in the previous chapter, in an attempt to sidestep this problem. Although it was obvious that transactions might take place away from the equilibrium price, once this price became revealed in the marketplace, everyone could recontract by substituting trades away from the equilibrium price with trades at it. Of course, everyone would have to agree to allow recontracting ahead of time; otherwise, those who would lose from the recontracted price would be unwilling to submit to it voluntarily. While recontracting is a convenient theoretical crutch, it is difficult to incorporate into any acceptable market mechanism.

Leon Walras, who worked independently of Edgeworth and Marshall in Lausanne, Switzerland and was largely ignored by them, was the first economist to posit an explicit mechanism by which prices could come into equilibrium. Walras envisioned an auctioneer, now known as the Walrasian auctioneer, who would state a price and then elicit from buyers and sellers their demand and supply at that price. If supply exceeded demand, the auctioneer would lower the price and repeat the auction; if demand exceeded supply, he would raise the price. This process, known as *tâtonnement*—the French word for *groping*—would continue until a price was announced at which supply and demand were equal. Then, all transactions would be consummated at this price.

The Walrasian approach to determining prices is worth noting because a variant of it, known as a *call market*, is used by some securities exchanges, including the Paris Bourse (stock exchange) from which Walras appropriated his notion of *tâtonnement*. In most cases, call markets are used to supplement existing continuous markets. For example, stocks on the New York Stock Exchange are opened for trading, both at the beginning of the day and after trade has been halted for pending news, using a call market run by the specialist on the floor of the exchange. The *early indications* and *order imbalances* reported by the financial press for specific stocks traded on the exchange are disseminated by the specialist as he works to find the market-clearing price for each of his stocks. A similar call market is also conducted just before every day's close.

The *tâtonnement* process is not restricted to a single market; it can be applied to several related markets simultaneously. Note that Chamberlin's experiment involves only a single market that is isolated from the influence of other markets. This simplified view of markets in which each is considered by itself is known as the *partial equilibrium* approach.

In order to examine asset markets (and the anomalies, such as bubbles, that may occur in them) we must introduce not only the element of time, but also how time links markets together. A broader approach to markets that incorporates these linkages is known as *general equilibrium* theory. Indeed, Walras was able to derive the set of equations needed to solve for the equilibrium price and quantity simultaneously in an arbitrarily large number of markets. Although we will be sticking with partial equilibrium in this chapter, in order to conduct experiments on asset markets we will move on to a general equilibrium framework in the next chapter.

The trading institutions used by Chamberlin in his market lie on the opposite end of the spectrum from recontracting and *tâtonnement*. Chamberlin's buyers and sellers are given a single shot at transacting and are limited in their ability to learn from each other's actions. Naturally occurring markets operate somewhere between the extremes of the idealized world of theory and the artificial environment that Chamberlin had created. In the next phase of market experimentation, a modern Smith explored the happy medium between these extremes.

New Market Rules

A few years after Vernon Smith participated in one of the Chamberlin experiments, he found himself at Purdue University faced with the prospect of teaching introductory economics for the first time. He reflected on the experiment and toyed with using it in his course. Unable to sleep one night in the fall of 1955, he was suddenly struck by the idea that he might be able to make an even stronger case against the Law of Supply and Demand than Chamberlin had if he changed the way he conducted the experiment. In reinventing Chamberlin's experiment, Smith used the floor of the New York Stock Exchange as his model. Smith performed this new market experiment on his introductory economics class in January 1956.

Buyers and sellers in the Chamberlin experiment had to connect with each other in the classroom and so it was likely that many potential interactions were missed. This failure to interact, and not some intrinsic flaw of the market, may have caused the market to miss the competitive price and quantity. Rather than have buyers and sellers mill around the classroom looking for deals, Smith structured his market more like a stock exchange and used the blackboard at the front of the classroom as a central order book where buyers and sellers could submit bids and offers. This order book was like the one that specialists on the NYSE floor maintain, but with two major differences: Its contents were public knowledge and trading by the order taker was prohibited.

As noted above, Marshall's notion of a perfect market required buyers and sellers to be aware of all other prices available in the market. While Chamberlin's decision to post these prices on the blackboard after each transaction might have been in the spirit of a Marshallian perfect market, it did not go far enough. Because each buyer and seller could deal in only a single unit, once Chamberlin posted a transaction price the actions that the remaining buyers and sellers could take were limited. Using an open order book, Smith's design was closer to Marshall's ideal.

In working out his version of the market experiment, Vernon Smith repeated the market several times to see if the results changed as the subjects figured out the rules and how the market worked. He wanted to make sure that Chamberlin's results did not merely reflect a misunderstanding on the part of subjects rather than any fundamental problem with the market. This repetition was designed to perform the same function as recontracting or *tâtonnement* without the complications required to implement these procedures. (Like Chamberlin, however, Smith allowed only a single direct transaction between each buyer and seller so that once a unit changed hands it could not be traded again in that period.) By allowing the market to adapt, this experiment was a better test of Marshall's neoclassical theory of supply and demand. Marshall never claimed that in the absence of perfect knowledge markets would work well enough that they could bring supply and demand into equilibrium immediately, but rather that price and quantity would tend toward equilibrium over time. Smith was confident that even with his Marshall-inspired modifications, Chamberlin's results would continue to hold, providing even stronger evidence of the failure of the Law of Supply and Demand.

Like Chamberlin, Smith divided his class into an equal number of buyers and sellers; however, Smith had only 22 students (11 buyers and 11 sellers), many less than Chamberlin's 62. It was unclear whether this was a large enough group to constitute a truly competitive market, but it was all that Smith had available to him. The market was arranged as a *double oral auction* with Smith filling the role of auctioneer. The auction was *double* because buyers and sellers participated on equal terms, and *oral* because orders were communicated orally to the auctioneer so that every student could hear them.

Buyers expressed their willingness to buy through bids. A buyer willing to pay 1.00 for an item would bid 1.00 and it would be written on the blackboard. Similarly, sellers expressed their willingness to sell with offers. A seller willing to sell for 3.00 would offer 3.00 and that too would go on the blackboard. Trades were consummated when either a seller accepted a buyer's bid or a buyer accepted a seller's offer. These acceptances were made openly and the unit was circled on the blackboard to show that it was no longer available for trade. (Anticipating making cash payments to subjects in the future, Smith used manageable dollar and cent amounts in his experiments in contrast to Chamberlin's purely abstract whole-number units.)

Figure 3.4 contains a typical blackboard display for a double oral auction similar to the one used by Vernon Smith. The bids and offers are recorded in the order that they were made and the identification number of the buyer or seller precedes the amount. In this example, the bidding starts with a bid of 0.50 by Buyer B3—the line through that bid indicates that it was subsequently canceled. Next, Seller S4 offers a unit at 4.50. Then Buyer B4 beats B3's bid with a price of 1.20, which is followed by a lower bid of 0.80 by Buyer B8. Notice that this bid does not improve on the previous bid; however, if B4's bid were accepted, it would become the

Bids	Offers
~~B3 0.50~~	
	S4 4.50
B4 1.20	
~~B8 0.80~~	
(B3 1.75 S7)	
	~~S8 3.00~~
	S1 2.00
	S8 2.00
	S8 cancels 3.00
	S7 takes B3
B3 cancels 0.50	
B5 1.90	
	(S8 1.95 B8)
B8 takes S8	
B8 cancels 0.80	
B4 1.92	

Figure 3.4 **Sample Blackboard for a Double Oral Auction**

best bid. Then, Seller S8 offers 3.00, Seller S1 undercuts him at 2.00, and S8 matches him, canceling his earlier offer immediately to avoid the possibility of selling the same unit twice. Seller S7 then accepts B3's bid of 1.75, which is then circled on the blackboard to indicate a trade. On completion of this purchase, B3 cancels his other (outstanding) bid at 0.50. Buyer B5 bids 1.90 and this bid is followed by an offer of 1.95 by Seller S8, which is immediately taken by Buyer B8. This example ends with B8 canceling his bid at 0.80 and Buyer B4 bidding 1.92. A double oral auction can require dozens of bids and offers in order to consummate a handful of transactions.

In order to give the market its best shot, Vernon Smith not only introduced the double oral auction mechanism, he repeated the auction market several times in rapid succession, with students having five to six minutes to trade in each *period*. At the end of each period, the market was completely reset with the values assigned to buyers and the costs assigned to sellers remaining unchanged. The units that buyers were unable to buy and that sellers were unable to sell disappeared at the end of each period; they could not be carried over to the next (or any later) period. At the beginning of a period, every buyer and seller received a new opportunity to trade.

Figure 3.5 shows the supply and demand diagram for a typical double oral auction experiment and Figure 3.6 graphs the trades (in time order) that occurred in each of the first four periods. Notice that Smith designed his experiment so that both the equilibrium price ($4.65) and quantity (15) would be uniquely determined. Like Chamberlin's experiment, the early prices are below the equilibrium level; however, prices are less volatile than what Chamberlin found. By the third period, many trades are at $4.65, the equilibrium price, with the deviations from equilibrium being minor. The equilibrium quantity of 15 is reached in the third period. Finally, in Periods 3 and 4, the market was 100 percent efficient, with all available surplus captured by the buyers and sellers.

The results of the double oral auction experiments stunned Vernon Smith. He was trying to build the strongest possible case against the Law of Supply and Demand and instead he ended up showing that it worked even better than Marshall could have imagined. In both Chamberlin's original market design and Smith's revision of it, buyers and sellers not only lacked the perfect knowledge that many economists at the time thought that markets required, they had only the minimum information needed to trade in the market—their own value or cost. In addition, Smith got his results

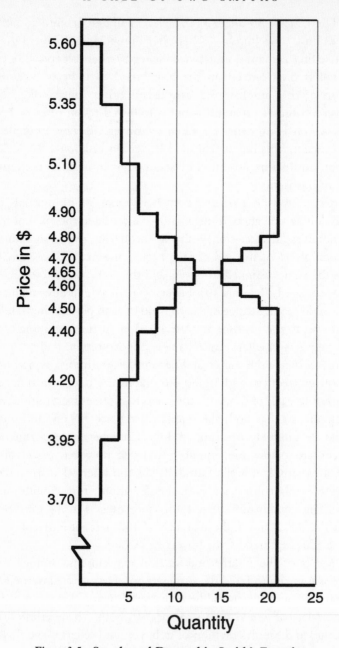

Figure 3.5 **Supply and Demand in Smith's Experiment**

Adapted from unpublished charts provided courtesy of Vernon L. Smith.

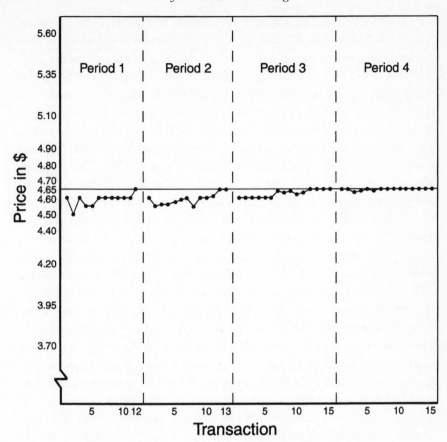

Figure 3.6 **Market Results with Prices Converging to $4.65**

Adapted from unpublished charts provided courtesy of Vernon L. Smith.

without the large number of buyers and sellers thought to be necessary for perfect competition. Later experimentation would show that even fewer participants were required for competition to occur. Market experiments are now routinely performed with as few as four buyers and four sellers.

Perfect Without Knowledge

Vernon Smith discovered that the market mechanism could serve as a remarkable computing device that could take the private information of buyers and sellers and aggregate it into a single efficient price and quantity. These results confirmed F. A. Hayek's view of market mechanism as a superior aggregator of information, an idea that was introduced in the Preface. Openly combining each individual's private information was all that was required to achieve the perfect market result—100 percent efficiency. The ability of markets to aggregate information without buyers or sellers having to reveal it indicated that markets could allocate resources at least as well as a centrally planned economy, which would likely have difficulty extracting the needed information from buyers and sellers. The postulate that markets can allocate goods efficiently when bids and offers are the only information traders exchange is known as the *Hayek hypothesis*.

Smith's results would likely have pleased neither Chamberlin nor Hayek. For Chamberlin, the reason for this displeasure is obvious—Smith's experiments showed that the Marshallian view of markets could survive experimental scrutiny. Hayek's displeasure would have been more subtle. While Smith's results were a vivid illustration of how, as Hayek theorized, spontaneous order could arise from the market mechanism, Hayek was strongly opposed to the use of the scientific method in economics. To Hayek, it was not only impossible to see the invisible hand; its presence could not be discerned by any scientific means. Hayek's opposition to "scientism" in any form, which made him an outcast in an economics profession that was increasingly using mathematical models, was rooted in the abuse of "science" by the Fascists and Communists of the time. That one market mechanism might perform better than another would also not be news to Hayek; the spontaneous process by which markets evolve would have led any inferior mechanisms to be rejected automatically.

Smith ran his experiments several more times under a variety of conditions—changing the shapes of the supply and demand curves and the number of periods—and each time he got the same basic result: convergence of price and quantity to the competitive equilibrium with efficiency approaching 100 percent in the final periods. Smith submitted an article with these results to the *Journal of Political Economy*, which had fallen under the influence of a new generation of free-marketeers of the Chicago School soon after the publication of Chamberlin's article in 1948. This group, led by Milton Friedman, thought the results of Smith's experiment were obvious and uninteresting (despite the fact that the *Journal* under previous management had published Chamberlin's paper reaching the opposite conclusion). Furthermore, it is likely that Chicago found experiments to be unnecessary and even dangerous tampering with the market, its most sacred of social institutions. Nonetheless, the *Journal* finally published the paper in 1962, but only after it had been subjected to four independent reviews.

Smith continued to run variants of his experiments throughout the 1950s and 1960s. During this period, his approach to experimentation was influenced and reinforced by economist Lawrence Fouraker and psychologist Sidney Siegel, whose game theory and bargaining experiments refined the methods of experimental economics and extended them outside the context of competitive markets. (A third line of economic experimentation, studying the rationality of individual choices, was also emerging at this time.)

Taking note of these experiments and his own experiences running experiments, Smith made two fundamental changes to his experiments. First, following the practice of Fouraker and Siegel, he made his markets more realistic by using cash payoffs either from government grants or out of his own pocket. This change was critical to making the experiments salient, so that subjects would face the same economic incentives as in naturally occurring markets by inducing values in the same way as in our grocery exploits of the previous chapter. When "funny money" is used— as in Chamberlin and Smith's original experiments—it is possible that the entertainment value of participating in the experiment could dominate the economic incentives that one is attempting to induce in subjects. Second, because he found that buyers and sellers tended not to transact merely for the fun of it, Smith paid buyers and sellers a "commission" of five cents for every unit that they traded. This commission was gauged so that it was small enough not to alter the supply and demand curves significantly, but large enough to encourage trade of the unit where supply and demand intersected. This last unit was problematic because it generated no profit for either the buyer or seller. The addition of the token commission provided them with some compensation for the effort required to consummate that last trade.

Smith's new experiments on Marshallian supply and demand replicated the efficiency of the market in a controlled environment. In addition, Smith found more evidence that market organization affected market performance. His double oral auction mechanism, where the blackboard at the front of the room served as an open central order book, generated the greatest market efficiency. Not only was the Chamberlin market without a central order book less efficient, so were other market mechanisms where bids and offers were not immediately made public. In particular, the use of sealed bids and offers, which is common both in traditional auctions and in those that take place on the Internet, is usually less efficient than the double oral auction mechanism.

Vernon Smith was not the only one to replicate the results of his double oral auction market experiment. This experiment has been run countless times around the world in every imaginable setting and with a wide variety of subject pools. Furthermore, it has become a standard first-day exercise in many economics courses. With only rare exceptions, the markets in these experiments rapidly converge to the competitive equilibrium. The path to equilibrium and the rate of convergence may vary from experiment to experiment, but the basic result is virtually always the same. Even the occasional confused or "irrational" subject has minimal effect on the results; he or she ends up being overwhelmed by market forces.

Smith's experiments provided a valuable proof of concept for the markets and the Law of Supply and Demand that no amount of abstract theory or government data could match. Although the elegance of Smith's experiment is rooted in its simplicity—it captures the essence of the market mechanism with the fewest possible moving parts—the question arises as to whether the virtues of the market extend to situations that might be more representative of naturally occurring markets.

4

Bubbles in the Lab

T
he demonstration that experimental markets obeyed the Law of Supply and Demand was monumentally important. A related result, of almost equal importance, also emerged from Vernon Smith's experiments. The competitive equilibrium achieved with the double oral auction was a stable equilibrium. This meant that price and quantity approach the equilibrium in an orderly manner and once equilibrium is reached, the market would remain near it for the remainder of the experiment. Any minor deviation away from equilibrium is quickly corrected, with the market returning to equilibrium rather than careening away from it. Smith's market was not only perfect, it was dull.

Given that experiments could re-create the attractive features of the market mechanism in a controlled setting, the question remained as to whether the market's most unattractive feature—the infrequent, but traumatic, appearance of speculative bubbles and the crashes that followed them—could also be reproduced in the laboratory. Of particular interest was the possibility that bubbles, like those experienced in the U.S. stock market, could be created in a controlled setting and replicated at will. In order to provide the opportunity for bubbles to appear, experiments had to incorporate a new dimension into their design: time.

Cycling Through Time

Time is something that has confounded scientists of all stripes—physical and social—in their efforts to create orderly theories of the world around them. Einstein showed that the temporal dimension of the physical world was integrally woven into the three spatial dimensions to form a unified space-time continuum. The classical notion of a single clock that kept time throughout the universe was replaced by a virtual infinity of clocks—one at every location in the universe. Placing time on the same footing as space changed physics forever, opening up new areas of research for physicists and new plotlines for science fiction writers.

The economic world does not yet need to be concerned with the deep mysteries of the space-time continuum; dealing with simple New-tonian time is sufficiently challenging. The mechanism that brings markets into equilibrium, Adam Smith's invisible hand, must do its work while the clock is ticking. As we saw, the basic Marshallian view of markets is static; it does not explicity show how supply and demand might change over time and the path that prices and quantities would take in response to those changes. Edgeworth's recontracting and Walras's *tâtonnement* were conve-nient fictions designed merely to patch theoretical holes rather than ex-plain how markets actually worked.

Alfred Marshall was keenly aware of the importance of time to mar-kets. He saw time as being linked to flexibility—in the long run, firms could vary technology and resources that were taken to be fixed in the short run. (To Keynes, knowing that things could adjust in the long run provided cold comfort to him. Indeed, the most famous of his many apho-risms is: "In the long run we are all dead.")

Time is a critical ingredient in any market because the adjustments re-quired to reach equilibrium cannot be made instantaneously. If the flexi-bility of the market is inherently limited, making the invisible hand an imperfect guide, the fine-tuning necessary to reach equilibrium might not be possible. For example, sellers usually respond to high prices for an item by increasing their production of it. Although this response may be rational for individual sellers, when they are considered in aggregate, the ensuing flood of goods onto the market will cause prices to drop. Then, the realiza-tion of lower prices will cause sellers to cut back production.

It is easy to see that if this process repeats itself, the market can become caught in a vicious cycle, with periods of surplus and low prices followed by periods of scarcity and high prices. In the throes of such a cycle, equi-librium will never be attained. Since many important physical phenom-ena—from the swing of a pendulum to the phases of the moon—are cyclical, it should come as no surprise that economists would be alert to the possibility of cycles not just in single markets, but also in the economy as a whole. These obvious swings in the economy—where boom begets bust begets boom, ad infinitum—became known as the *business cycle*.

In the nineteenth century, it was common knowledge that the business cycle came from outer space—from the surface of the sun to be more precise. One of the first things that Galileo saw when he pointed his telescope skyward was a group of black spots on the sun that had been invisible to the naked eye. Over time, astronomers observed that the activity of these *sunspots* followed a regular cycle. Working with scarce raw data, it was natural for economists to imagine that sunspots must somehow be linked to the cycles experienced by the economy. The sunspot theory of the business cycle was not an entirely crackpot one; sunspots were believed to influence the weather, and so they could affect crop yields. At a time when agriculture still dominated the world's economy, it seemed reasonable that sunspots could induce cycles in the economy. In the end, however, the sunspot theory was just an early example of the evils of *data snooping* or *data mining*—the indiscriminant digging through all available data until evidence to support a pet theory is found. In the twentieth century, similar excavations would uncover spurious links between the performance of the original NFL teams in the Super Bowl and the stock market.

Pure coincidence led economists to the sunspot theory of business cycles. The renowned astronomer and planet finder, Sir William Herschel, discovered that sunspot cycles had a period of 10.45 years, meaning that the peak of sunspot activity would occur every 10.45 years. Some years later, William Stanley Jevons, a neoclassical economist whose work on marginal analysis and the demand curve contributed to Alfred Marshall's neoclassical synthesis, calculated that the cycle of commercial activity had a period of about 10.46 years. This coincidence of the cycle periods led to the conclusion that sunspots caused the business cycle. (At least no one thought that the causality might go the other way, with commercial activity creating sunspots!) This theory was taken seriously in the latter part of the nineteenth century, and went out of fashion only when a careful recomputation of the periods for the two cycles showed that their lengths differed by more than a year.

Recently, sunspots have staged a comeback, not because sunspots are once again believed to affect the business cycle, but because economists have developed a notion of equilibrium, the *sunspot equilibrium*, in which the mere belief by enough people that something completely irrelevant like sunspots might have an effect on a market serves as a *self-fulfilling prophecy*. (Sociologist Robert K. Merton—the father of economist Robert C. Merton, who enters this book later—developed the modern notion of a self-fulfilling prophecy.) The possibility of sunspot equilibria is not confined to natural phenomena; the use of *technical analysis*, with its support levels, trend lines, and so forth, by enough traders in a market can significantly influence certain markets in ways that makes it self-validating.

Economists have noted a phenomenon known as an *information mirage* in which traders ignore their own information and instead look to "follow the herd." This type of behavior is self-reinforcing and has been produced in laboratory experiments. In an information mirage, also known as a *reverse information cascade*, an individual trader (lemming) who can be certain that his or her own information is reliable is likely nonetheless to head for the cliff with the other traders (lemmings) even if he or she knows that everyone else does so based on bad information. As we shall see, such behavior may play a role in bubble formation.

The early failure of the sunspot theory did not keep the study of business cycles from becoming a dominant theme in economics. Because Marshall's neoclassical theory contributed little to the subject, the search for a meaningful theory of the business cycle motivated many advances in economic thought, even if it also triggered additional data mining expeditions that were ultimately counterproductive. Not everything associated with business cycles has turned out badly. The National Bureau of Economic Research, a leading center of economic thought, was founded in 1920 by Wesley Mitchell, the father of modern business cycle research, primarily to investigate the business cycle. Although the business cycle has frequently been left for dead, the Business Cycle Dating Committee at the National Bureau continues to make the official determination of when each U.S. recession begins and ends.

Austrian-born economists were especially fascinated with the business cycle; however, they preferred to theorize about cycles rather than traipse through forests of data. F. A. Hayek, following the lead of his fellow Austrian Ludwig von Mises, developed a monetary theory of business cycles that had attracted renewed interest at the end of the twentieth century. A central tenet of this theory is that the monetary actions taken by central banks tend to induce cycles in the real cycle. Lax monetary policies lead to excesses that misallocate capital and that can only be resolved with tight policies that trigger recession (or worse). A logical consequence of this view is that longer booms create longer busts, leading some economists to worry that the long boom of the 1990s might lead to a proportionately long bust in the following decade.

Another Austrian economist whose ideas experienced a popular renaissance is Joseph Schumpeter, a Harvard contemporary of Edward Chamberlin who invented the concept of *creative destruction* to help explain the business cycle. This theory, which has become a mantra to venture capitalists and high-tech entrepreneurs, puts forth that economic fluctuations are caused by the introduction of new technology that destroys the value of existing investments built on old technology. Schumpeter took this line of thinking further and foresaw that the creative process of capitalism itself "sows the seeds of its own destruction."

It is ironic that the technology mavens who were the biggest proponents of Schumpeter's theory, using it to justify investments in new technologies, also subscribed to the view that the business cycle—the logical consequence of innovation to Schumpeter—is now dead and that the capitalist system had begun to experience a long boom of indefinite duration. In striking contrast, Schumpeter boldly pronounced that capitalism itself would be the ultimate victim of creative destruction as successive waves of innovation would leave what little profits remained in the economy in the hands of a few large corporations. Unlike the other Austrians, Schumpeter saw the problems of capitalism as inherent to the system and not confined to the actions of central bankers.

Doubtless, Joseph Schumpeter would have agreed with the general assessment of Harvard graduate students of his time that Professor Chamberlin's experiments were "silly." It mattered little what happened in a single market when the entire capitalist system was doomed. Although Schumpeter, like Malthus and Marx before him, was at least temporarily wrong in his dismal forecasts, it is important to be aware that markets do not exist in a vacuum but as part of a dynamic sociopolitical system. The author does not wish to alarm the reader; however, this is an important point that we will revisit toward the end of the book.

Most theories of the business cycle are *macroeconomic* in nature, focusing on the economy as a whole rather than on the conditions in individual markets and the linkages between them—the prevailing *microeconomic* approach of Marshall's neoclassical synthesis. The development of a general theory at a macroeconomic level by Keynes was motivated by his perceived need to go beyond Marshall to find an explanation for the

business cycle. Instead of focusing on individual markets, macroeconomics lumps all markets together with the exception of those for money
and investments, which are treated separately because they serve as time's
connective thread. Even though talk of macroeconomic phenomena—
Gross Domestic Products, fed funds rates, and so on—permeates the financial press, most economists believe that macroeconomic theory has
yet to produce reliable predictions of economic activity. Indeed, the expectation that the chaos of individual markets would somehow sort itself
out when they were considered in the aggregate was a giant leap for
Keynes to make and one that his friend Hayek was among the first to
find both unpersuasive and ill-advised.

An obvious limitation of experimental methods is the difficulty that
they have modeling the aggregate behavior of an entire economy within
the confines of the laboratory. Some of the problems that have prevented a
truly useful theory of aggregate economic behavior from developing may
be traced to the primitive state of existing markets, which makes it impossible to know what the economy is doing at the aggregate level until
months after the fact. Technological advances in the market system that experimental methods can be instrumental in facilitating might someday
help to put macroeconomics on a sounder footing. Nonetheless, informational problems alone can make many types of economic aggregation impossible. Although none of this theory had been developed when Hayek
voiced his disapproval of Keynes's general theory, Hayek's doubts were
clearly rooted in his profound understanding of information and markets.

Fortunately, we can explore simple economic cycles without the need
to examine the entire economy; in fact, we can create a cycle in a single
market. The standard trick for creating a theoretical market that cycles automatically is to require producers to commit to production before bringing their goods to market. If sellers base their production solely on the
prevailing price from the previous period, they will always be off the mark.

Figure 4.1 shows how this process, which we alluded to earlier in this
chapter, might proceed over time. (Demand and supply are taken to be
straight lines to simplify the diagram; however, the process applies to any
supply and demand curves with reasonable shapes.) Sellers start by bringing a quantity of the good to market, at which point the demand from
buyers determines the price. Sellers then assume that this price will prevail in the next period, so the new amount they bring to market is determined by the supply curve. This process repeats, with consumer demand

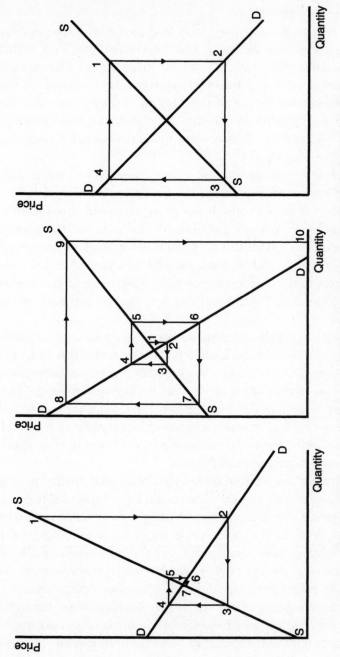

Figure 4.1 The Three Types of Cobwebs: Converging (left), Diverging (middle), and Looping (right)

determining the new price that—in turn—determines the quantity supplied in the next period.

This *lagged adjustment process* can lead to one of three possible outcomes, as Figure 4.1 illustrates. The best course of events is that the market is stable, with each adjustment bringing the market closer to equilibrium, so that it ultimately converges. The diagram on the left shows a rapid convergence to equilibrium, tracing a path that starts at Point 1 and approaches equilibrium at Point 7. The resemblance of this trail to a spider's cobweb has caused this model of price adjustment to be called the *cobweb model*.

Convergence of this process is not assured. The middle diagram, in which demand is steeply sloped and supply is relatively flat, shows an unstable market with a cobweb that diverges, moving from its origin at Point 1 to the ultimate collapse of the market at Point 10, where buyers bring so much to market that no price is low enough to sell everything. Only when supply and demand are perfectly aligned will the market cycle forever, as the diagram on the right illustrates with the market going from Point 1 to Point 2 to Point 3 to Point 4 and back to Point 1 indefinitely.

If one picks supply and demand curves at random, convergence and divergence are the two most likely outcomes. A market that cycles perpetually not only is highly unlikely to occur, but it is very delicate: Any small change to the market will lead it to either converge or diverge. Furthermore, there is nothing that makes it more likely that the supply and demand curves will lead to stability rather than instability, so if the cobweb model or anything like it is an accurate picture of how markets adjust over time, the market mechanism is doomed.

In order for any of these three cycles to develop, market participants must be exceptionally myopic. One would hope that individuals trapped in a web would notice the cycle and adapt their behavior to it, which is enough to terminate the cycle. People who are able to recognize that the market is looping must possess rationality that goes beyond the basic notion of rationality discussed earlier, which required only consistent choices and a desire for greater material wealth. This more refined rationality requires an understanding of the market mechanism itself, so that each individual learns from the past behavior of the market and bases his or her future expectations of the market on what has been learned.

The extension of economic rationality to expectations, which was first proposed in the 1960s, is known as *rational expectations*. Rational expectations picked up where the Marshallian notion of perfect knowledge left off. People who form their expectations rationally do not blindly follow rules of thumb, such as "the price next period is the same as the price last period"; instead, they form their expectations by constructing the proper economics models in their heads.

The broad application of rational expectations theory, pioneered by University of Chicago economist Robert Lucas in the 1970s, not only rids the market of cobwebs, it can be viewed as undermining the Keynesian theory of macroeconomics when Keynesian policies work by creating illusions. Although this work earned Lucas a Nobel Prize in 1995, it remains controversial as it creates as many questions as it answers.

In looking at a single market, experimental economists have found no tendency for markets to either cycle endlessly or become unstable. Even when experiments are run using supply and demand curves that would be highly unstable in a cobweb world, these markets readily converge to the competitive equilibrium. The ongoing feedback provided by the bids and offers in the double oral auction helps the market to adapt to changing circumstances, promoting its stability.

The Seasonal Shift

The cobweb model provides only one explanation for the cyclical behavior of markets. Some cycles occur because of seasonal shifts in supply, demand, or both. In the United States and most other developed countries, for example, gasoline prices are usually higher in the summer months, when consumption surges in connection with vacation travel. This cycle persists even though drivers, petroleum companies, and commodities traders are aware of it. One might think that the cycle would eventually vanish as gasoline supply is shifted from winter to summer, either by changing the production schedule or by storing gasoline produced in the winter for sale in the summer. Despite the fact that every effort is made to shift supply from winter to summer, the cycle persists because it is so costly to store gasoline. For one thing, the volume and weight of gasoline is high relative to its price, which is substantially less than most bottled water in the United States. Furthermore, it is extremely flammable, so that special

facilities are required to store it safely. The cost and danger of storing gasoline make it impractical for ordinary consumers of gasoline to hoard much
more of it than their vehicles' gasoline tanks can accommodate.

The partial equilibrium (single market) picture of supply and demand
is inadequate to capture the complexity added by seasonal shifts; however,
a simple general equilibrium model that links the two seasons readily accommodates these shifts. Applying techniques developed by John Williams
in the 1930s, Paul Samuelson was able to illustrate how seasonal markets
work by placing two sets of supply and demand curves back-to-back. Figure 4.2 shows a two-season market in which a low-demand season is followed by a high-demand season. Units can be carried forward in time
from the low-demand season to the high-demand season by incurring a
storage fee. The supply and demand diagram for the low-demand season is
elevated by the cost of storage, which is assumed to be the same for each
unit stored.

A joint equilibrium for these two markets does not occur when
supply equals demand in each separate market. Instead, equilibrium for
the two markets considered jointly is reached when the amount stored
in the low-demand season, known as the *carryover*, is consumed in the
high-demand season. Figure 4.2 shows the equilibrium amount of carryover. Notice that by elevating the low-demand season by the unit carryover cost, c, we are imposing the condition that the price in the
high-demand season, p^H, must exceed that in the low-demand season,
p^L, by exactly the carryover cost. This is a basic form of a condition
known as a *no-arbitrage condition*.

As this problem is set up, the equilibrium price in the high-demand
season will never exceed the equilibrium price in the low-demand season
by more than the carryover cost. If this ever occurred, it would be profitable
to carry more units over to the high-demand season. The additional carryover from the low-demand season will push that price up and the additional carryover to the high-demand season will push that price down. This
adjustment will continue until profitable arbitrage is no longer possible.
Hence, the prices in the two seasons, p^L and p^H, are jointly determined so
that the amount *stored* in the first season is equal to the amount *used* (from
inventory) in the second season as shown in Figure 4.2. At this *intertemporal
competitive equilibrium*—with supply and demand in balance when both seasons are considered together—as at the competitive equilibrium in a single
market, all possible surplus from the two markets is captured.

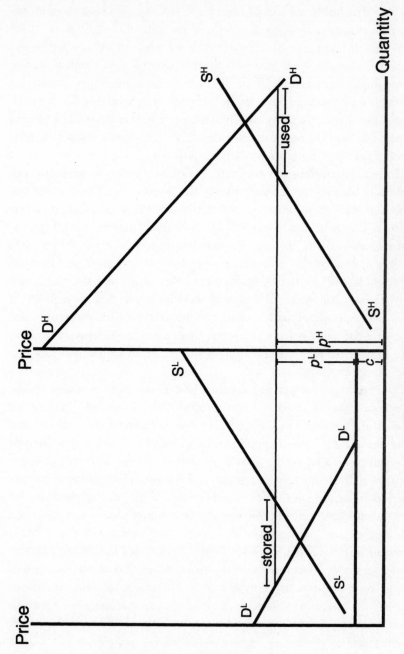

Figure 4.2 Equilibrium in a Two-Season Market with Carryover

This two-season market is an example of a general equilibrium model. The glue that holds this model together is that the two seasons taken together constitute a *closed system* because we can ultimately account for every unit that was stored. (If units can spoil while in storage, we would still have a closed system in which there was a risk that a unit placed in storage might not be available in the high-demand season, effectively increasing the unit storage cost.) Whatever units materialize for the high-demand season are allocated by adjusting the price in that season. The general notion that "supply creates its own demand" is known as *Say's Law*, after French classical economist Jean-Baptiste Say.

To general equilibrium theorists, Say's Law appears as an innocuous accounting identity that mathematically shows how an economy with any number of markets, not just the two in the above example, is a closed system. Say's Law is necessary to solve for the equilibrium prices and quantities in every market—an exercise first performed by Leon Walras. Say's Law was critical to the advancement of classical economics and to Marshall's neoclassical synthesis. John Maynard Keynes, however, did not view Say's Law as a harmless mathematical technicality; he saw an inability of demand to meet supply as the central problem of modern economies and as the fatal flaw in Marshall's economic theory. Keynes left it to his followers to find a consistent general equilibrium model in which Say's Law was somehow violated.

The technique of placing supply and demand in two markets back-to-back can also be used to analyze other linkages; indeed, economists first used this technique to study international trade, which is where Paul Samuelson got the idea of applying it to speculation. Markets separated by space, rather than by time, work in an analogous way: The cost of transportation replaces the cost of storage and the possibility of travel in both directions must be considered. Furthermore, if the two markets are located in separate countries, differences in consumer tastes and production technologies may cause supply and demand to vary across the markets. Moreover, any tariffs that are levied must be included in the cost of transporting an item between the two locations. When two markets are linked through time or space, any activity in one market can influence the other, sometimes in surprising ways. Because time is an essential element of financial markets, general equilibrium methods should be used to analyze these markets.

Building on the financial market theme, it is important to notice that hiding within the two-season market system is a third market. During the time when the good is in storage awaiting sale in the high-demand season, it becomes an asset for its owner. The market for this asset, which is purchased in the low-demand season and sold in the high-demand season, is the third market. Its sole function is to link the two seasonal markets. This asset market is fundamentally different from the other two markets; it is impossible to participate in this market without incurring some risk. Because the future value of the asset is unknown when it is purchased in the low-demand season, the buyer must wait until the high-demand season to see what it is worth. Although the tendency of markets to move toward a stable intertemporal competitive equilibrium may reduce the risk, it can never be eliminated.

In many markets, neither buyers nor sellers may want to bear the risks involved in moving goods between seasons, and that is where speculators enter the picture. Once the seasonal disparity in prices, and the arbitrage opportunity it presents, becomes evident, speculative demand for the good in the low-demand season will work to bring the two markets into intertemporal equilibrium.

The actions of speculators, however, may do more than aid the invisible hand as they help bring markets into intertemporal equilibrium. In naturally occurring markets, when people search for the culprits behind erratic or extreme price movements, their attention naturally turns toward speculators—whether in the form of Wall Street professionals, hedge fund managers, or day traders. Because speculators profit only when prices fluctuate, they are often suspected of destabilizing markets. However, without someone to transport goods through time, markets can become very inefficient.

While this potential trade-off between stability and efficiency is difficult to test in naturally occurring markets, it is an ideal topic for an experimental study. The incorporation of the various elements—seasons, speculators, carryover, and so on—needed to link markets requires some new machinery. Once this machinery is in place, we can then study many types of asset markets in a controlled environment.

Speculators Enter the Laboratory

The double oral auction mechanism of Vernon Smith's early market experiments may have been inspired by the floor of the New York Stock Exchange, but it would be several years until experiments that explored asset markets and speculation were developed. From the time of Chamberlin's first experiments in the 1940s and on through the 1960s, market experimentation involved only partial equilibrium market settings—a single market with fixed supply and demand.

Things started to change in the early 1970s, however, when Vernon Smith returned to the California Institute of Technology where he was reunited with an old Purdue colleague, Charles Plott. The two of them, along with many of Caltech's other social scientists, soon turned Caltech into a hotbed of experimentation on how groups made decisions. These new experiments were not limited to markets, but extended into the political realm. They examined the behavior of subjects acting as voters or committee members who would receive monetary payoffs based on group decisions. Although some of this work built on prior experimental work in game theory, much of it was completely original.

In their early collaborations, Plott and Smith worked out the finer details of experiments on Marshallian supply and demand, most notably using Marshall's notion of surplus to measure the efficiency of experimental markets. It may seem surprising that it would take over 25 years for experimental economists to use an obvious measure of market efficiency, but technical difficulties with Marshallian surplus formed the basis for parts of the new mathematically rigorous approach to microeconomics that Paul Samuelson developed at the same time and place that Chamberlin was running his experiments. While Samuelson provided valuable insights that demonstrated why Marshall's surplus could be a flawed measure of efficiency, by the 1970s evidence was mounting that the error introduced by using surplus was normally quite small. The resurrection of surplus as a measure of efficiency came at just the right time for experimental economics.

Charles Plott and Vernon Smith, having solidified the foundations of experimental economics, began to look for new venues where they could use experimental methods. As part of their search, they jointly taught a seminar course in experimental economics in the spring of 1974. As one of the few students enrolled in their course, the author was interested in how speculative markets worked and was eager to find any possible avenue to explore them.

Experimental economics may have been in its infancy in the 1970s, but research of any kind into how speculation affects markets was still in the womb. The only dent that speculation had made on the economic literature related to the question of whether speculation would stabilize or destabilize markets. That literature had a strong "how many angels can dance on the head of a pin" flavor to it. Speculators themselves never appeared as actors in these theories; they simply exerted a force on the market and how this force might affect the market depended on a raft of assumptions.

Edward Chamberlin was among the staunchest advocates of the position that speculation destabilized markets. In the work that established his reputation, *The Theory of Monopolistic Competition*, Chamberlin examines the role of speculation in markets and reaches the following conclusion: "Indeed, it seems more likely that speculation would cause more and greater fluctuations [in the market.]" Given several years to reflect on his experiments, Chamberlin wrote in the final footnote to the reprinted version of his 1948 article that appears in his collected essays, *Towards a More General Theory of Value*, that his original experimental results support the view that speculation was destabilizing.

Vernon Smith's work on double oral auctions had demonstrated that experimental markets could obey the Law of Supply and Demand. In order to introduce speculation into an experiment, one needed to go beyond the existing theory and convert speculators from an abstract force into a human presence. By introducing a third type of subjects into experiments to play the role of speculators, one could test their ability to destabilize the market.

We can examine how speculators influence both the stability and efficiency of a market by performing two experiments—one with speculators and one without them—and compare the results. Smith's double oral auction design contained most of what was needed to have a meaningful speculative market, but the element of time was missing. Although one could designate some subjects as speculators by giving them neither redemption values nor costs but allowing them to trade for their own account, the time in which they traded was purely artificial. The key to getting *real* time into the market was to create the simplest intertemporal market possible—one based on the Williams two-season model.

Seasons were incorporated into experimental markets by dividing each period into two seasons. The first season (with low demand) was called the *Blue Season* and the second season (with high demand) was called the *Yellow Season.* The colors were chosen to evoke mental images of spring (Blue) and autumn (Yellow), while avoiding colors like red and green that could have other connotations. Just as the items used in experiments were kept generic, the use of actual season names was thought to be too suggestive.

This new experimental market was run as a sequence of identical two-season periods. As in earlier experiments, periods were completely independent, preventing any carryover from period to period; however, carryover from the Blue Season to the Yellow Season within a period was allowed. In the experiment with speculators, who were given the more neutral designation of *traders*, only they were authorized to carry units over. In the experiment without speculators, only buyers could carry units over, and then only to redeem them in the Yellow Season. Furthermore, there was no charge levied for carrying a unit over from the Blue Season to the Yellow Season. As a result, in an intertemporal competitive equilibrium the price is the same in both seasons.

The two-season experiments were designed so that it was riskier for traders to carry units over from the Blue Season to the Yellow Season than it was for buyers. When a buyer carried a unit over that he bought in the Blue Season, he knew exactly what he would receive by redeeming it in the Yellow Season. The only uncertainty that he faced was whether the unit might be available at a lower price later. Traders, on the other hand, had no direct information about either supply or demand; all they could do was watch the bids, offers, and trades and react accordingly.

The two-season experiments turned out to be far more complicated than any that had preceded them despite every effort to keep them simple. Chamberlin and Smith had performed their early experiments as a classroom exercise, and so their experiments could run for at most an hour. The additional details of the two-season experiments made running it in a single hour impossible. Everything about the new experiment took more time—the rules were more complicated, each period was twice as long, and more periods were necessary to see if the markets converged. Requiring well over two hours each, these experiments tested the limit of how long subjects could be expected to participate in an experiment at a single sitting.

Figure 4.3 gives the supply and demand in each season and shows the

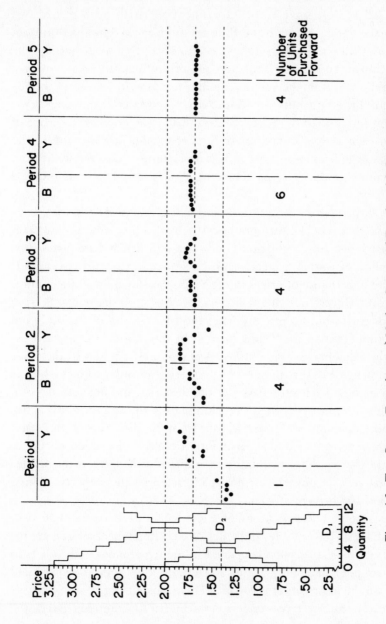

Figure 4.3 **Two-Season Experimental Market Setup and Results with Buyer Carryover**

Reprinted with permission from the *Quarterly Journal of Economics* (Miller, Plott, and Smith, 1977). Copyright by MIT Press Journals.

results for the experiment run without speculators, where buyers could carry over units from the Blue Season to the Yellow Season. Six buyers and six sellers were used in the experiment and each of them had two units apiece to buy or sell. If the Blue Season is viewed in isolation from the Yellow Season, a situation that economists refer to as *autarky*, the equilibrium price is \$1.40 and the equilibrium quantity is 5. Similarly, for the Yellow Season, the autarky equilibrium price is \$2.00 and the autarky equilibrium quantity is 9. With zero carryover cost, allowing carryover from the Blue to the Yellow Season leads to an equilibrium price of \$1.70 in each season. Carryover suppresses equilibrium demand in the Blue Season to 3 units and expands it to 11 units in the Yellow Season. With 7 units produced at equilibrium in each season, 4 units must be carried over.

The surprising result of this experiment is that despite its complexity, the market mechanism continues to work efficiently; it just takes somewhat longer to equilibrate. The increase in demand from the Blue to the Yellow Season predictably causes the price to rise during Period 1. Given the uncertainty of prices in the Yellow Season, only a single unit is carried over. Buyers, noticing that prices are higher in the Yellow Season, then proceed to bid up prices during the Blue Season of Period 2 and carry 4 units over to the Yellow Season. In the process, the price overshoots the equilibrium price of \$1.70, reaching \$1.85, and so the price collapses below \$1.70 at the end of the period in order to bring buyers into the market. Each successive period, the price and quantity close in on equilibrium, although the price plummets at the end of Period 4 because too many units were carried over from the Blue Season. In Period 5, the final period of the experiment, virtually every trade occurs at \$1.70 and the equilibrium number of units is traded. As in the single-season markets, all possible surplus is extracted by the subjects, making the market 100 percent efficient.

The second experiment follows the same basic design but with slightly different buyer values and seller costs. (Although all subjects are instructed not to discuss what happened in the experiment with others in the subject pool, different price parameters are used in every experiment just in case the information leaks out.) The major difference is that buyers cannot carry units over; two traders perform that function. Altogether, the market had six buyers, six sellers, and two traders, and none of these subjects had participated in the first experiment. Traders were allowed to buy

units in the Blue Season and sell them in the Yellow Season. As noted earlier, traders differed from buyers in that they did not have a guaranteed
price at which they can sell to the experimenter in the Yellow Season; in
fact, if they were unable to sell a unit that they carried over, they would
forfeit the entire price they paid for it. This additional risk is compounded
by the fact that traders receive no private information about either supply
or demand, while buyers and sellers are aware of their personal demand or
supply in each season.

Figure 4.4 shows the results of the second two-season experiment. It is
similar to the first experiment but with two minor differences: Prices
within a period are less variable and the market is still slightly away from
the competitive equilibrium at the end of the experiment because the
traders consistently carried over one excess unit. Nonetheless, the key result of the second experiment is that the presence of speculators does not
destabilize the market, which was contrary to the conventional wisdom of
the economics profession at the time. Both buyer carryover and speculative
carryover increase market efficiency and neither introduces instability into
the market.

That the market mechanism could allocate goods efficiently between
markets separated in time was a very powerful result that inspired further
research, if only because the results of this experiment seemed incredible.
Smith and Plott, working with several colleagues, performed similar experiments in the coming years and the efficiency of intertemporal market allocations was replicated under a variety of conditions. It was one thing to
get to a competitive equilibrium in a single market; now we could achieve
it in three markets simultaneously with speculators thrown in the mix to
boot. As later research showed that the real source of interest was not the
two seasonal markets, but rather the *asset market* connecting them, experimental economists developed methods to study asset markets directly. In
addition, the role of speculators was limited to carrying units over for buyers because a way to let them trade for their own account—and put their
own money at risk—had yet to be invented.

Behold the Bubble

In the standard supply and demand experiments, units are traded because
subjects have different costs and values. The act of exchange creates surplus
by transferring the unit from where its cost or value is lower to where it is

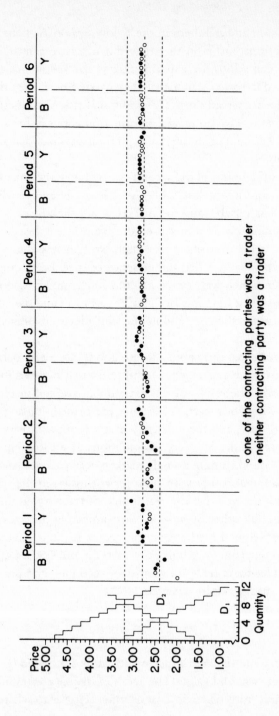

Figure 4.4 **Two-Season Experimental Market Setup and Results with Speculator Carryover**

Reprinted with permission from the *Quarterly Journal of Economics* (Miller, Plott, and Smith, 1977). Copyright by MIT Press Journals.

higher. On the other hand, assets, which are goods used in the production process, are purchased for the returns that they generate for their owner at one or more future dates. (*Securities*, such as stocks and bonds, are pieces of paper or electronic entries that are *secured* by one or more assets. Although there are times when the distinction between an asset and a security is important, the choice of which term to use in a given situation is largely determined by convention, which we follow in this book. In general, securities may always be considered as assets but assets do not have to take the form of securities.)

In asset markets, exchange is not driven by differences in costs and values; rather, it is motivated by differences in the subjects' attitudes toward risk and their assessment of the future value of the asset. Economic theorists have long grappled with the problem that the level of trade seen in real-world asset markets requires more heterogeneity in the economy than can be easily accommodated within a mathematical model. In experiments, motivating trade through such individual differences presents a challenge because factors that affect a subject's valuation of an asset are difficult to control.

It is easy to construct a market experiment in which there is no apparent reason for subjects to trade units. For example, consider an experiment in which there are nine subjects; each is given a unit and is told that at the end of the trading period the experimenter will pay $3.60 for the unit. Then there is no incentive for the subjects in the experiment to trade their units and, if they do trade, the obvious price is $3.60. One could complicate matters by dividing the experiment into 15 periods and paying a dividend of 24 cents at the end of each period. This asset would then be worth $3.60 in the first period, which is the sum of all the payments to be received during the course of the experiment. In the second period, after the first dividend of $0.24 had been paid, it would be worth $3.36. This would continue until it should trade for $0.24 in the fifteenth and final period. (As it turns out, even though the value of the asset is obvious and uniform, subjects will trade in it anyway, but we will return to that point later.)

The way to create an incentive for trading this asset, while maintaining control over the value of the asset, is to inject some uncertainty into its value. For example, suppose that instead of paying a dividend of $0.24 each period, the dividend was randomly drawn with equal probability (25%) from four values: 0 cents, 8 cents, 28 cents, and 60 cents. (To assure the subjects that the choice is completely random and not rigged in any manner, it may be necessary to use a mechanism, such as balls drawn from a bingo cage, that the subjects can observe for themselves.) These four possible dividends add up to 96 cents, so the average dividend will be 24 cents—the same as before. The expected value of the asset is also the same, declining from $3.60 in the first period to $0.24 in the final period; however, there is now an incentive for more risk-averse and/or pessimistic subjects to sell the asset for cash. Subjects more willing to take risk or with a more optimistic view of the payoffs would be willing buyers of the asset at the right price. Of course, both the attitude toward risk and the optimism that subjects bring to an experiment is beyond the control of the experimenter.

Asset market experiments evolved from the cyclical speculative markets to a pure asset market in the late 1970s and on into the 1980s. Charles Plott continued to run experiments at Caltech, while Vernon Smith moved to the University of Arizona to begin the construction of an experimental economics laboratory in 1975. Plott, working with a range of collaborators that included Robert Forsythe, Thomas Palfrey, and Shyam Sunder, worked out many of the critical details of asset market experiments, including the payment of dividends and the randomization of payoffs. Meanwhile, in Arizona, Vernon Smith and Arlington Williams continued to experiment with asset markets and took the major step of moving market experiments onto computers. Using a computer network system designed for educational instruction (PLATO), Williams took the basic mechanism of the double oral auction and other auction mechanisms and created their automated counterparts. The importance of the computer to experimentation was the increased control that it provided to the experimenter. Now, all forms of communication between subjects could be controlled and monitored. The personal computer explosion of the 1980s and the development of network software to run experiments by Arizona, Caltech, and other universities, sparked the global spread of computer-based laboratories for experimental economics.

Building on the new work in asset markets and the computerization of experimental markets, Vernon Smith, along with Gerry Suchanek and Arlington Williams, performed several computer-based asset market experiments between 1982 and 1986 to study the formation of speculative bubbles. Their experiments used several versions of the 15-period asset market described above. Each trader received an *initial endowment* that was a combination of dividend-paying shares and cash. Traders with more shares were given less cash and vice versa. As in previous experiments, traders received only their own private information; they were not told anything about the initial endowments of other traders. To ensure that traders' actions were not the result of simple mathematical errors, at the beginning of each period, traders were told the minimum possible value, maximum possible value, and expected value of a share, including both the remaining dividend payments and any final payment.

The finer details of the experiment were the same as in the speculation experiments except for a few minor twists. First, there were no limits on the number of trades that a subject could make in a period and the *commission* was dropped so that clever traders would not execute a series of *wash trades* with the intention of extracting commissions from the experimenter. Second, to speed up the trading, an *improvement rule* was instituted that required that each bid be at a higher price than the previous bid and that each offer be at a lower price.

Figure 4.5 shows the results from one of these experiments, which are typical of the results they found. In the first period, the asset trades consistently below its expected value of $3.60. Prices do rise through the period and this rise continues into the second period, where all but one of the units trade at above the expected value. The increase in prices continues through the fourth period. Then, prices begin to decline, but remain well above the expected value of dividends to be paid. Finally, in Period 9, bids for shares almost completely vanish and the price crashes to below the expected value, where it remains until near the end of the experiment. Most market analysts believe that this tendency for the collapse to overshoot an asset's value on the way down is typical of crashes in naturally occurring markets.

This runup in prices clearly constitutes a bubble, as subjects begin to trade based on the expected future price of the asset and not on the value determined from expected future dividend payments. (The experimenters verified this by polling the subjects at the end of each period on what they thought the asset was worth.) In fact, it is common in bubble experiments for the asset to trade at so high a price that even the maximum possible stream of dividends could not cover it.

To the extent that one can place a formal definition on a market bubble, it is a situation where the price of an asset is determined by its trading value rather than its intrinsic value. An asset that is experiencing a bubble

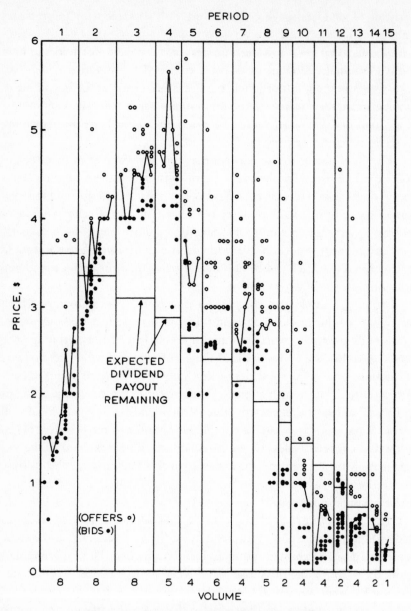

Figure 4.5 **Experimental Asset Market Bubble**

Reprinted with permission from *Econometrica* (Smith, Suchanek, and
Williams, 1988). Copyright by the Econometric Society.

becomes a kind of hot potato that is passed from trader to trader with each successive holder of the asset hoping to find a buyer at a higher price and not become stuck with the asset. While the repeated two-season market of the first market with speculators did not give the bubble sufficient time to develop because the day of reckoning was always close at hand, the one-shot 15-period asset market provided ample opportunity for bubbles to develop.

On the Origin of Bubbles

Smith, Suchanek, and Williams replicated this pattern of a bubble followed by a crash using a variety of experimental parameters. The only way that they could reliably prevent a bubble from forming was to have the same subjects back to participate in the same bubble experiment three times; a single repetition of the experiment was often insufficient to prevent a bubble from forming. There is also preliminary experimental evidence showing that subjects with experience in non-bubble-market experiments may also serve as a calming influence on the market.

Previous asset-market experiments had shown markets to be surprisingly efficient, but these new experiments showed the ease with which bubbles could be produced. In fact, these experiments were initially designed to be control (or baseline) experiments because Smith and his colleagues thought that a more complicated experimental design would be necessary to produce a bubble.

Subsequent experiments conducted by Gunduz Caginalp, David Porter, and Vernon Smith can help us understand the ease with which bubbles form. For example, changing the random payment of dividends, which served to provide a rationale for trading, to a fixed dividend of $0.24 per period does not affect bubble formation. So even though this simple experimental design was never seriously considered at first, not only did subjects trade units, but essentially the same bubbles formed as with uncertain dividends.

These follow-up experiments also uncovered two factors that contribute to the formation of bubbles. The first factor is momentum. In virtually every bubble experiment, the price in the first period is significantly below the expected dividend payout of $3.60. The movement of the price toward the fundamental value of the share from below creates *upward momentum* in the market that then continues to carry the price further upward and into a bubble. Shares then take on the attributes of a hot potato that no one wants to be left holding at the end of the experiment. The combination of the downward forces of the declining dividends and the conclusion of trading halt the upward momentum of the market and ultimately bring about a crash.

Experiments that have mitigated the initial momentum of the market by controlling the prices paid for the asset in the early periods have been able to reduce or eliminate the bubble altogether. It is clear that in the controlled environment of the laboratory, witnessing a rapid increase in prices will sufficiently distract all but the most experienced subjects so that they temporarily ignore the fundamentals of asset valuation.

The second factor that affects the formation of bubbles is the availability of cash. Clearly, without any cash at all in the market, shares could not trade and so bubbles would never form in the first place. In general, making more cash available to traders increases both the likelihood and size of market bubbles. While one must be careful not to infer too much from experimental results, it is interesting that runaway prices in naturally occurring asset markets are often fueled by the *easy money* policies of governments and central banks that facilitate the lending of the money that buyers need to drive up asset prices.

The tendency of bubbles to form so readily is matched by their tendency to pop rather than slowly deflate. As in naturally occurring markets, the bursting of a bubble is not instantaneous; deteriorating market conditions usually precede it. As bids dry up, prices stabilize or even decline, interrupting the upward momentum. Eventually, the few buyers who continue to bid are only willing to buy at prices that sellers consider absurdly low. The unwillingness of buyers to participate in a slow deflation of the bubble with an orderly price decline leads to its precipitous collapse, taking it back below the expected dividend payout, where it will remain for the rest of the experiment. While the same set of subjects will likely repeat the bubble-and-crash phenomenon in a second (though rarely in a third) run of the experiment, one bubble per experiment is all that can be expected. The downward momentum of the crash appears to preclude the formation of a new bubble in the remaining periods in the experiment.

Just as the convergence to the competitive equilibrium in Smith's original double oral auction has been replicated under a variety of conditions worldwide, so has the formation of market bubbles. (As in other disciplines that involve human responses to external stimuli, the earliest published results in experimental economics tend to suggest rather than prove the existence of an observed phenomenon.) Vivian Lei, Charles Noussair, and Charles Plott have even gathered evidence that the possibility of speculative gains may not be necessary to create a bubble in the laboratory. When placed in an experimental design with no economic incentive to trade, subjects may trade nonetheless and generate a bubble as a result of their trading. While such a result may be viewed as an *artifact* of the experimental process (much like the placebo and Hawthorne effects found in other types of experimentation involving human subjects), the human desire to trade is very evident outside the laboratory and could ultimately emerge as a central cause of market bubbles. When we examine smart markets later in this book, we will see how this desire to trade or even gamble might be redirected away from the capital markets.

Few economists were interested in bubbles when the original bubble experiments were conducted. Future stock market crashes were thought to have been precluded by the market reforms enacted after the 1929 Crash. All that changed when Black Monday hit in October 1987. The article on experimental bubbles by Smith, Suchanek, and Williams was quickly (by economics journal standards) published in response to the renewed interest in bubbles and crashes.

The interest in bubble experiments did not spill over to the government regulators who oversaw the stock market. They imposed circuit breakers on the U.S. stock markets without conducting a single experiment on their likely effect on the markets. Fortunately, one government agency, the National Science Foundation, provided a research grant to Vernon Smith and Arlington Williams to study several aspects of speculative bubbles, including the efficacy of circuit breakers. In collaboration with Ronald King and Mark van Boening, they found that circuit breakers generally made bubbles worse and certainly did not eliminate them. Apparently, the false sense of security imposed by the downside limits of the circuit breakers causes the bubble to grow even faster.

A similar false sense of security was felt in the market during the Nasdaq/Internet bubble. Although the stock market circuit breakers are not triggered by moves in the Nasdaq Composite Index, traders and investors felt the Fed's actions after the 1998 LTCM crisis indicated that Alan Greenspan stood ready to bail out the stock market if necessary. The protection that the Fed Chairman supposedly offered the market was known as the *Greenspan put*, after a type of stock option that plays a critical role later in this book.

Nonetheless, the Black Monday crash of October 1987 cannot be viewed as merely the popping of a bubble—its root pathologies were far more subtle and complex than its great predecessor. Still, the first experimental bubbles contained a clue as a general source of market instability that would encompass both typical bubbles and the atypical situation that arose in 1987. Before we pursue this clue and the experimental evidence that leads us to it, we will step outside the lab for a while to look at bubbles in their natural setting.

5

Bubbles in the Wild

Formal theories of speculative bubbles can be mathematically formidable, so we are fortunate that John Maynard Keynes has provided us with an amusing story to explain how valuations can escape reality. Although Keynesian economics may be the topic of endless debate and reappraisal, there is no question that Keynes set the standard for economic storytelling. Adam Smith may have been content to spin yarns that used the process for manufacturing pins to illustrate the division of labor, but Keynes set his gaze on Fleet Street, the home of London's thriving newspaper industry. In Keynes's time, Fleet Street was more circumscribed in how it could appeal to the prurient interests of its readers. Still, in those less-enlightened days, London's newspapers could cultivate their readership by running "beauty contests" in which readers voted for 6 out of 100 women whose pictures appeared in the newspaper. The winner was the woman who received the most votes and all voters who included the winner on their ballot were entered in a lottery that gave them a chance to win valuable prizes.

An economically rational person voting in this contest would not vote for the women that he or she thought were the most beautiful, but rather for those that he or she thought that others would find most beautiful. The story does not end here, however, because if the other voters employ similar reasoning, it makes sense not to vote for the women that the others would find most beautiful, but rather for those that the others would *think* that others would find most beautiful. Of course, this introspective reasoning can go on forever, which was exactly the point that Keynes wished to make about the stock market.

Stocks (and other assets as well) are like contestants in a Keynesian beauty contest. Most are ordinary and have little hope of receiving special treatment by investors. Some stocks, however, are special—we might say that they have "sex appeal." In order for these "sexy" stocks to maintain a price above their intrinsic value, it is important that their beauty lie not only in the eye of their current holder, but in the eyes of potential future holders willing to bid their prices up for the privilege of ownership. The important point of this analogy is that an appealing stock need never have direct appeal to anyone; all its value can come from the expectation of appeal to other investors or the expectation of that expectation, and so on.

The Keynesian beauty contest not only provides an engaging analogy to how a bubble in stock prices might come about, but also can explain how assets could trade at a less lofty premium to their intrinsic value on a continuing basis. Similarly, "unattractive" stocks could trade below their intrinsic value if there were widespread expectations that no one wanted to hold them. Although Keynes did not elaborate on the beauty contest idea with a formal theory—he tells the entire beauty contest story in a single paragraph of *The General Theory*—what it suggested was chilling enough to the notion that free markets were efficient markets. If asset prices were not under the complete control of the Law of Supply and Demand, traders' expectations (or their expectations of expectations. . .) could sway the market enough to generate major inefficiencies.

Asset Valuation and Efficient Markets

The suggestion that expectations could exert a perverse influence on asset prices showed that the Law of Supply and Demand needed to be strengthened if it were to continue to support free markets. This beefed-up version of market efficiency is called the *efficient-market theory* (also known as the *efficient-market hypothesis*). Recall that competitive markets are efficient because the prices and quantities that they generate capture the entire available surplus. As noted earlier, market experimentation has demonstrated that the market tends toward efficiency even when individuals keep their own demand and supply information private, just as F. A. Hayek had hypothesized.

The efficient-market theory as originally formulated by Eugene Fama in the 1960s at the University of Chicago goes beyond Hayek's hypothesis by postulating that markets efficiently aggregate all available information, which includes not only each individual's information about the value of an item to him or her (as we can induce in the market experiments), but also any information that could influence the market in any way. (There are different versions of the efficient-market theory, depending on what one means by "all available information," but such distinctions are unimportant here.)

In an efficient market, the value of an asset is equal to the sum of the value of the (appropriately adjusted) *cash flows* that it generates. (The reader can think of cash flows as just money; in practice, however, they can be more complicated.) Not all cash counts equally; however, cash that is received in the future is worth less than cash received now. Furthermore, the strong tendency toward risk aversion among market participants reduces the value of cash flows that are uncertain to be received. The timing and risk of a cash flow can be taken into account by applying a *discount rate* to it. Discount rates range from zero to infinity; a cash flow with a discount rate of zero is equivalent to cash received now with absolute certainty and a cash flow with a discount rate of infinity is completely worthless. In the bubble experiment discussed earlier, it was safe to assume that the discount rate was close to zero because all cash flows were ultimately received at the same time (the conclusion of the experiment) and the money at risk was small.

Much of the work done in financial economics consists of determining the appropriate discount rate for the various types of cash flows that are possible. Except under unusual circumstances, the preliminary determination of the discount rate for an asset requires nothing more than a glance at the yields of Treasury securities. The creditworthiness of the federal government of the United States is deemed so high that its securities could be considered free of risk that the government would default on its financial obligations. The discount rate implied by the yields of U.S. Treasury securities could then be used as a risk-free (that is, free from risk that the Treasury will fail to pay interest or pay off the security at maturity) benchmark or baseline against which the discount rate for risky assets could be set. (This benchmark became less reliable during the late 1990s when speculation about the retirement of the national debt by the U.S. Treasury appeared to distort yields.)

The easiest assets to value are *plain vanilla* bonds, which provide the bondholder with a series of interest payments. Most bonds pay interest semiannually (every six months) and include the last interest payment with the return of principal. For example, a $1,000 bond with a life of 10 years issued with an interest rate of 10 percent would make 19 semiannual payments of $50 and a final payment of $1,050 ($1,000 principal plus $50 interest). These 20 payments constitute the cash flows generated by the bond.

In an efficient market, one would expect that at the time a bond is issued its price would equal the value of the cash flows to the buyer. (Actually, both to ensure a successful bond offering and to reward the subscribers to the offering, most bonds are issued at a slight discount.) After a bond has been issued, its price is determined by the supply and demand for it in the market. Although the cash flows generated by the bond are fixed at the time that it is issued, its value will fluctuate over time as the discount that the market applies to future cash flows changes. Notice that the bond in the example above costs $1,000 but generates a total cash flow over time of $2,000 ($1,000 interest and $1,000 repayment of principal). The apparent windfall of $1,000 vanishes when one realizes that the cash flows generated by the bond must be discounted because they are risky cash flows received in the future. Using the appropriate discount rate, which is the same as the interest rate of 10 percent per annum, the total value of the cash flows is exactly $1,000.

Valuing stocks from their projected cash flows is more complicated than valuing simple bonds. The big difference is that the uncertainty concerning the cash flows is much greater. Except in cases of financial distress (insolvency, bankruptcy, etc.), the size of the cash flows generated by a bond is known in advance. Bonds, as a form of debt, take priority over stock, which is a form of *equity*. The cash flows that accrue to stockholders are the residue that remains after all other claims on the enterprise are settled. In addition, virtually all bonds have a final maturity date by which time the principal must be repaid to the bondholders, while stocks never mature—the streams of cash flows that they generate theoretically go on for eternity. Two events that can terminate these cash flows before the end of the world are the firm's acquisition and liquidation. Stockholders of a firm that is acquired receive a lump-sum payment for their shares, while those holding stock in a liquidated firm receive whatever might remain after all prior claims have been settled.

The cash flows generated by stocks take the form of dividend payments and increases in the market value of the shares, that is, capital gains.

Until the 1970s, the dividends paid by stocks typically exceeded the interest paid by bonds; however, an increasing awareness of the favorable tax treatment of capital gains relative to dividends appears to have led corporations to pay out less in dividends. Why firms pay dividends and how much they should pay out has been the subject of intense analysis by financial economists; however, one thing is certain—cash legitimately paid out in dividends is no longer available to a company's creditors.

A convenient alternative to the difficult task of projecting dividends and capital gains is to value a company based on its earnings and their projected growth. Because both dividends and capital gains must ultimately flow from future earnings, this is widely used. In addition, some analysts "tweak" earnings numbers in order to compute a truer measure of corporate cash flows that adjusts for depreciation and other accounting distortions.

The considerable latitude possible in computing both the projected earnings for a firm and the discount rates to apply to them means that coming up with a single number for the value of a company's stock by summing up its discounted cash flows is impossible. Nonetheless, the market mechanism, in setting a price for the stock, does exactly this. The efficient-market theory predicts that the market price will correspond to a value based on reasonable estimates of the discount rates and cash flows. This intrinsic value for a stock is often referred to as its *fundamental value*, since it is grounded in the fundamentals that determine the company's worth.

The stocks that appear most susceptible to bubbles are those that have high rates of growth in revenues and/or earnings. Projecting rapid earnings growth into the indefinite future will lead to the untenable conclusion that the value of the company is infinite. An infinite asset value will always result when cash flows are projected to grow faster than the rate at which they are discounted. Should this scenario play itself out, each future cash flow would be worth more than the one before it. If cash flows continue to grow in value (taking discounting into account) without end, then the sum of these cash flows will be infinite.

What keeps assets from having an infinite value despite immediate prospects for rapid growth is that eventually the rate of growth of cash flows declines to where the rate overtakes it, driving the value of cash flows in the sufficiently distant future to zero. Because it is difficult to predict when the inevitable slowdown in cash flow growth will occur, the

potential range of values for a stock can be considerable. Furthermore, analysts who neglect to consider slowing growth may unwittingly base their
price targets for a company on its unbounded value, which can contribute to a bubble in the stock's price. Rather than make their forecasts,
and the unrealistic assumptions behind them, available for public scrutiny,
such analysts will simply announce that conventional valuation methods
no longer apply.

From Noise to Irrationality

The ease with which bubbles can be created in the laboratory suggests that
bubbles are likely to be a common phenomenon in naturally occurring
markets built on similar institutions, for example, financial markets. Although it is easy to refute the efficient-market theory in a controlled setting by creating a bubble, it is more difficult to dismiss the theory when
one can only observe the behavior of the market but not the circumstances of supply and demand that drive it. Despite the limitations of laboratory results, experimental methods are useful for the insights that they
provide into how bubbles and other market anomalies might come about.
Furthermore, experimental markets are *real* and the bubbles that appear in
them are *real*; it is just that the setting in which they are produced is not a
product of nature, but rather is engineered by the experimenter to test a
specific hypothesis.

 An obvious way to refute the efficient-market theory in naturally occurring markets is to show that the value of stocks or other assets does not
equal the value of their expected cash flows. The efficient-market theory
throws two roadblocks in the way of this approach. The first is that the inability to project cash flows with any degree of precision, as noted above,
makes it difficult to know the true value of any asset. It is possible, after the
fact, to determine whether the market had properly valued an asset in light
of the cash flows that it ultimately generated; however, the efficient-market
theory does not require that the market get the future right with pinpoint
accuracy, just that it is right on average.

 The second roadblock erected by the efficient-market theory is the
recognition that noise can enter into asset prices. Just as dust particles will
dance seemingly at random within a ray of sunlight—a phenomenon that
physicists call *Brownian motion*—in the absence of meaningful new information market prices do their own dance, known as a *random walk*. A num-

ber of statistical studies of asset and commodities prices conducted from the 1930s through the 1950s provided a wealth of evidence that commodity and stock prices followed a random walk. The most notable feature of a random walk is that its future path cannot be predicted from where it has been in the past. The statistical work on random walks then served to inspire the development of the efficient-market theory, with Keynes's leading American disciple, Nobel-laureate Paul Samuelson, being the first to provide the advanced mathematics that underlies this theory.

A natural question that arises is: Where does the noise that drives the random walk originate? A definitive treatment of this question appears in an article with the simple title, "Noise," written by Fischer Black—co-inventor of the Black-Scholes option-pricing model around which the next part of the book revolves. Black, building on the work of others, attributes much of the noise in the market to the actions of *noise traders*, who trade without regard to any news that might affect the value of the asset, but rather based on a feel for the market or a trading system. In fact, many of them may be jointly engaged in their own version of the Keynesian beauty contest, riding the upward momentum of hot stocks before they turn cold.

The typical day trader, who trades in and out of companies in an attempt to anticipate immediate market movements, is a prime example of a noise trader. Day traders possess no better information than anyone else in the market; the data feeds that they monitor are available to the public, but they believe that they can interpret this data better than others. The paucity of successful day traders informally shows that most of them cannot outguess the market.

The collective actions of noise traders can potentially lead the market astray. Information mirages, the lemming-like concept introduced briefly in the previous chapter, form more readily in high-noise market environments. Because the transactions of noise traders are not explicitly marked for all in the market to see, other traders can begin to emulate their behavior thinking that they are on to something. The more lemmings that join in, the more real the mirage becomes. In financial markets, sometimes rumors that clearly have no foundation in reality begin to circulate in support of the mirage. In the absence of such rumors, financial commentators might note the large move in a stock's price and comment that it appears unrelated to any news.

In his "Noise" article, Fischer Black deals with the problems that noise creates for the efficient-market theory by adopting a new definition of efficiency. To Black, a market is efficient if the price in the market is between 50 percent and 200 percent of its fundamental value. Some efficient-market theorists propose even larger bands for efficiency. Under Black's definition of efficiency, the price of an asset can instantly plunge 75 percent for no reason whatsoever, going from 200 percent to 50 percent of its real value, while remaining efficiently priced. In this way, Black is able to define away most presumed market bubbles, as few of them are large enough to exceed his noise threshold.

Taking noise into account, the results of Chamberlin's original experiment are entirely consistent with market efficiency even if one does not resort to using Black's broad price bands. Going back to Chamberlin's results, we see that the average price for the experiment was 52.63, which Chamberlin felt was significantly below the predicted range of 56 to 58. It turns out that given the high volatility of that market, which can be measured as a standard deviation of 9.45, the price of 52.63 was not significantly different from either 56 or 58. In retrospect, the results of Chamberlin's experiment did not necessarily refute the Law of Supply and Demand; instead, it may just have highlighted the noise that Chamberlin introduced into his market by the way he organized it.

An alternative approach to demonstrating market inefficiency is to show that when the market is not under the influence of noise traders (for example, when news concerning future cash flows is moving prices) it does not behave in a manner consistent with the efficient-market theory. In particular, there is a growing body of statistical work demonstrating the propensity for stock prices to overreact to news. The standard technique for uncovering overreactions is to create a cash-flow-based model of how asset prices should react to news and then to provide statistical evidence that the actual reactions exceeded what was predicted by the model. In addition, it is possible to demonstrate more generally that stock prices are more volatile than cash-flow models would predict and that they often display *mean-reversion*, so that abnormally high or low returns, a symptom of overreaction, are soon followed by returns that offset them.

The reliance on specific valuation models to demonstrate overreaction gives efficient-market theorists a line of defense, since any evidence of overreaction is only as good as the model used to show it. Excess volatility in markets may simply indicate the presence of noise traders rather than any underlying inefficiency in markets.

To bolster their arguments, advocates of overreaction look to the pioneering experiments of the late Amos Tversky and his colleague Daniel Kahneman, which indicate that some of their subjects do not process information about uncertain alternatives in a way that is consistent with economic rationality. Economists, influenced by the Nobel prize-winning work of Herbert Simon on bounded rationality, had long believed that the computations that individuals needed to perform in order to make an economically rational choice were so costly and complex that they would merely do the best that they could under the conditions or *satisfice*, a term coined by Simon. Economists took Simon's reservations about rationality in stride because they were still consistent with economic rationality when that notion was extended to include the cost of making choices. The results of Kahneman and Tversky's research were more disturbing; they showed that faced with certain choices many subjects were prone to misjudgments and inconsistencies. In particular, their work demonstrated that experimental subjects tend to place too much value on new information that they receive, especially in the face of a large body of older evidence that would contradict this information. Their subjects were especially prone to placing too much credence in convincing anecdotal evidence relayed to them directly by a friend or relative and placing not enough credence in established bodies of scientific evidence based on the results of extensive trials.

The experiments performed by Kahneman, Tversky, and other psychologists were of particular interest to the small group of economists who paid attention to them; however, most of these experiments did not conform to the standards for economic experimentation put forth by Vernon Smith and others. For example, psychologists generally get information from subjects using surveys and questionnaires rather than by providing their subjects with real monetary incentives. Nonetheless, their work has provided the foundations of the fields of *behavioral economics* and *behavioral finance*, which look to extend basic economic and financial theory to deal with the apparently irrational behavior exhibited by some experimental subjects. Caltech social scientists David Grether and Charles Plott conducted experiments in the mid-1970s that examined a simple form of individual irrationality previously discovered by psychologists and replicated it in a controlled economic environment. They were then able to show that the fundamental problem that psychologists had been witnessing was a fundamental violation of economic rationality known as a *preference reversal*. Grether and Plott found that how alternatives were framed led to different choices in situations that economists would view as theoretically equivalent.

It is worth noting that irrationality is not a particularly welcome addition to economic theory. Under the unwritten rules followed by many economic theorists, any argument that relies on individual irrationality to work is not considered kosher. If one builds an economic theory based on the assumption that individuals make irrational choices, then the problem is that anything is possible. By analogy, in pure mathematics, if one takes any logical contradiction, such as $1 = 0$, as mathematical truth, then it is possible to prove anything based on the contradiction. Similarly, in an economic world populated with irrational people, markets can behave in any imaginable way, at least until the economy's collective irrationality brings on its own extinction.

This original prejudice against deviations from irrationality has been softened by the observation that the irrational behaviors documented by economists and psychologists both inside and outside the laboratory are not merely deviations from rationality, but fall into definite patterns. One behavioral economist at the University of Chicago, Richard Thaler (who was not always looked kindly upon by his free-market colleagues there), has made a career of amassing compelling stories that document individual behavior that appears irrational and market behavior that is at odds with the efficient-market theory. While there can be rational disagreement about the importance of these results, the more it accumulates, the harder it has been for economists to ignore. Fortunately, for the survival of our own species, the irrationality found by Kahneman, Tversky, Thaler, and other researchers is far from universal. Many of their more notable instances of individual irrationality are found in less than half of the experimental subjects they test.

Breaking the Bank

Emboldened by the possibility that deviations from rationality could undermine market efficiency, behavioral economists have not only looked for statistical proof of inefficiency in the financial markets, they have set up shop as investment managers to capitalize on their findings. Indeed, the most alluring (and remunerative) way to disprove the efficient-market theory is by developing a technique to "beat the market." If they are able to beat the market using the fruits of their research, these academics can validate their findings and make a fortune at the same time. Indeed, the money made from a successful trading system is far greater evidence of market inefficiency than mere academic scribblings because profits that might appear possible on paper may not be available in the marketplace. Of course, as some academics who have gone into investment management can tell you, the pendulum swings the other way as well. A system that either fails to uncover inefficiency in the market or does not execute properly can bankrupt its authors.

To see what such a successful trading system would be like we can look to another speculative habitat—the blackjack table. Under the rules of blackjack as it was played in the days when Las Vegas was just a small town in a big desert, a player could use a technique known as *card counting* to gain a significant statistical advantage over the house. By tracking when certain cards in the deck were played, a perceptive blackjack player could adapt his play so that, unlike other games in the casino, the odds would favor him. Some early card counters were able to make considerable money using this technique. Even though in its purest form card counting gives the player only a 2 to 3 percent advantage over the house, spread over many hands this advantage becomes sizeable. Casinos caught on to card counting and instituted a variety of measures to discourage those who exploited it at the casinos' expense. It is interesting to note that casinos have tended not to completely close the loopholes in the rules that made it theoretically possible to profit from card counting. A casino can expect to win more money from inept (and unprofitable) neophyte card counters than they can lose to the rare professional, especially when one considers that once a player is suspected of being a professional he or she becomes *persona non grata* and can no longer enter the casino, much less beat it.

Just as casinos love amateur gamblers who think they can beat the house by counting cards, the financial markets are enamored of people who think that they can beat them using a system. The most spectacular market losses come from systems that work for a while, luring their devisers in with bigger and bigger bets, and then suddenly stop working. Indeed, many false discoveries of market inefficiencies are a result of data snooping.

The problem with data snooping is that just as enough monkeys typing long enough would eventually produce all of the works of Shakespeare, if you sift through a large enough body of financial data you will find what appear to be patterns in the data. For example, the performance of the U.S. stock market for many years was closely related to the results of the annual Super Bowl played in late January or early February. Because there is no meaningful causal link between U.S. football and the stock market, this relationship was merely a coincidence that one should not have relied on to have any predictive value. With so many sporting events to choose from, it is likely that one of them would appear to have some bearing on the stock market.

The basic intuition for why asset markets should be efficient is straightforward. Assets that trade at a discount to their fundamental value are like blackjack tables at a casino that allows card counting. Given enough time the value of the asset will revert to its fundamental value, so buyers, like card counters who play blackjack long enough, will be rewarded. On the other hand, assets that trade above their fundamental value also provide an opportunity for profit. The only direct way to reap this reward, however, is by selling the asset *short*, which means borrowing the asset, selling it, and then buying it back later (for return to its owner) at what one hopes is a lower price than one received for selling it. (Conversely, outright ownership of an asset is known as taking a *long* position.) *Short selling* overvalued assets is a more difficult way to make money than buying undervalued assets. For one thing, some assets cannot be sold short because their owners are either unwilling to lend them out for sale or are willing, but assess prohibitively high interest for the privilege.

Assets that can be readily sold short, which include most stocks listed on major exchanges, present still another serious obstacle for those wishing to profit from their being overpriced. The buyer of an asset stands to lose the entire purchase price of the asset. In contrast, the potential loss to a short seller is unbounded; there is no limit to how high the price of an asset can rise. In order to protect the individual from whom the asset was initially borrowed, the short seller is required to put up *margin*, which serves as a kind of security deposit. As the price of the asset rises, the amount of margin is increased. Hence, a short seller can be correct about an asset being overpriced, but can end up bankrupt if the price of the asset rises sufficiently before reverting to its fundamental value and he or she does not have the financial resources to meet the ever-increasing margin requirements. Because short sellers unable to meet a margin call are forced to purchase the asset in order to return it to the individual from whom it was borrowed, they can actually help to fuel an asset bubble rather than bring it under control.

The presence of a large pool of short sellers can serve as assurance to the holders of an asset in which a bubble has developed that they can find a "greater fool" at a higher price, because the short sellers, who are forced to buy the asset (back) if its price goes high enough, will all play the fool. (The possibility that short sellers might help fuel bubbles has been observed when they have been added to bubble experiments. In any event, the presence of short sellers by itself does not prevent bubbles from forming in the laboratory.)

It turns out that buying underpriced assets and selling (short) overpriced assets, while easy enough to do, is not the wisest way to exploit transient market inefficiencies. The problem is that after one has taken a position in the asset, the fundamentals that determine its value might change. A stock that is underpriced could become overpriced not because its price went up, but because changing market conditions caused its value to go down. A better way to exploit any underpricing is to find a similar asset that is either overpriced or properly priced and take a short position in that asset that exactly balances the long position in the underpriced asset.

The strategy of taking positions in mispriced assets and then hedging them to pick off the mispricing is the idea behind the original hedge funds. To avoid regulation by the Securities and Exchange Commission, these funds were not marketed to the public, but only to a small number of high-net-worth individuals and institutions. Now the term *hedge fund* refers to any investment fund organized so that it escapes SEC oversight regardless of the strategy it uses.

The blackjack table is not the only place in the casino that one can use a system. One can also try to beat the house at any game that is nearly a fair bet, such as black and red bets on the roulette wheel (we will ignore the "0" and "00" on the wheel, where the house makes its money, but it is easy to modify this example to take them into account). Suppose you want to make $1,000 at the casino. Simply bet $1,000 on black (red) on the roulette wheel and if the wheel comes up black (red) on the first spin, the house will pay you $1,000 for your bet. If you were wrong, simply bet again, raising your bet to $2,000. If you win on the second spin of the wheel, you will win back both the $1,000 you wagered on the first spin as well as your $1,000 in winnings. If this is not your lucky day, and you lost on the first two spins, simply try again, this time betting $4,000. Eventually, with enough spins of the roulette wheel, you will win your desired $1,000. Unfortunately, if you run out of money (or reach the casino's table limit) first, you will learn why statisticians refer to this game as *gambler's ruin*.

Investment management strategies that are based on exploiting transient market inefficiencies have a gambler's ruin aspect to them that is easy for their managers to overlook. If these markets return toward equilibrium rapidly enough, these strategies not only make money, but also may serve to enhance market efficiency in the process. Alternatively, if the markets move further away from equilibrium for an extended period of time, these strategies will fail, as their managers will exhaust the capital necessary to post the margin that maintains their positions. Managers who do not employ margin to enhance their returns simply lose their capital more slowly, as their underperformance relative to the market will eventually lead to the withdrawal of the funds under their management.

A major problem faced by managers who use systems, based in theory or in fancy, to beat the market is that the system is likely to become unprofitable once its existence and track record becomes known. Indeed, the true power of the market mechanism is the tendency for inefficiencies that develop to be self-healing. The mere action of trying to exploit an inefficiency in the marketplace can sometimes be enough to make it disappear.

The track records of the more visible efforts at beating the market are less than encouraging and lend support to the efficient-market theory. Clearly, no one has yet devised a foolproof system for beating the market. The developer of any such system would be able to increase his wealth without bound, so that he would ultimately own the market. Even the most successful hedge fund operators appear to reach the bounds of their wealth creation potential rather quickly, causing them to close their funds to new money or even to give money back to their existing investors. The most successful hedge funds of the 1990s, Julian Robertson's Tiger Fund and George Soros's Quantum Fund, started to hemorrhage money in 2000 and were forced to liquidate their holdings as it became clear that they could no longer profitably manage their investors' assets. Furthermore, the hedge fund studded with the most stars, Long-Term Capital Management, failed in such a spectacular new manner in 1998 that it is central to the theme of the last part of this book.

Bubbles: Rational or Irrational?

Before proceeding any further, let us recall some of the basic facts about bubbles and market efficiency. Experimental findings show that while markets can achieve high levels of efficiency, it is possible to design a simple asset market in which bubbles consistently form. Even though naturally occurring markets may sometimes be inefficient, even to the point of producing bubbles, systems have yet to be developed to exploit these inconsistencies in a sustainable manner. Finally, although it is not a universal phenomenon, deviations from economic rationality are common when individuals are tested in a laboratory setting. It has yet to be shown that this limited kind of irrationality will survive the rigors and discipline of the market mechanism, but it seems reasonable to entertain the possibility that it could, either in the laboratory or in naturally occurring markets.

Given the current evidence, it is likely that the bubbles created in the laboratory are *rational bubbles*. Subjects are fully aware that they are paying more than the value of the asset's cash flows, but they rationally compute that the reward from the opportunity to resell the asset at a higher price outweighs the risk of being stuck with it. Karl Marx captured the essence of the rational bubble when he wrote: "In every stock-jobbing swindle every one knows that some time or other the crash must come, but every one hopes that it may fall on the head of his neighbor, after he himself has caught the shower of gold and placed it in safety."

Despite the lack of experimental evidence tying irrational human behavior to bubbles, there is a popular belief that bubbles are a manifestation of "irrational exuberance." Fed Chairman Alan Greenspan uttered those fateful words in a speech given in 1996 as the Dow Jones Industrial Average approached 7000. Greenspan's "irrational exuberance" remark temporarily roiled the stock market, as it feared that the Fed would use its power over short-term interest rates to burst the perceived bubble. Nonetheless, the market quickly recovered, resuming the longest bull market in American history.

In later speeches and in testimony before Congress, Chairman Greenspan elaborated, but did not necessarily clarify, his view of market bubbles. In order to elude the frequent question, "Is the stock market experiencing a bubble?" Greenspan stated that it was not possible to know whether you were in a bubble until after it had burst. While such a statement could be true of the bubbles found in naturally occurring markets, it is clearly not true of laboratory bubbles, and especially not those employing subjects who had participated in a previous bubble experiment.

Potholes on Wall Street

The possibility that bubbles, and other market inefficiencies as well, might be caused by either individual or collective irrationality (the "madness of crowds") is disturbing because of the extreme remedies that might be taken for the sake of bringing rationality back to the market. If the evils of the market truly have their roots in the human psyche, then the only cures are either to replace the market with a government-assigned "rational" allocation of goods or to "reeducate" individuals to behave in a rational manner.

Fortunately, there is no rationale for such drastic measures based on experimental results; and, furthermore, the inherent power of market mechanisms such as the double oral auction is so great that it can overcome a considerable amount of irrationality on its own. The double oral auction not only operates efficiently even when individual subjects exhibit signs of irrationality, it can even deal with traders whose bidding behavior is completely random. Dhananjay Gode and Shyam Sunder have run computer-simulation studies showing that in a double oral auction market inhabited entirely by computerized *robot traders* programmed to place (legal) random bids and offers the market will reliably converge to the competitive equilibrium, although not as rapidly or as smoothly as with human traders.

A 15-period asset market, however, is far more complex than a one-period market with prespecified supply and demand. There is mounting experimental evidence that the bubbles in the 15-period market can be traced to a market mechanism that does not provide enough assistance to traders. In the first period of the 15-period asset market, traders are forced to squeeze the events (dividend payments, etc.) of the next 14 periods down into a single market. What they need to help guide their actions turns out to be more assets. Indeed, the absence of markets for these helper assets has a destabilizing effect that makes them akin to potholes in the market.

The term *helper assets* may have a nice, wholesome ring to it, but the helper assets of Wall Street, lacking the proper public relations assault, have come to be known by a name with more ominous connotations: *derivative securities.* Derivative securities are securities that *derive* their value from that of an *underlying asset.* In the case of the 15-period asset experiments, David Porter and Vernon Smith ran a series of experiments in which buyers not only could make the usual immediate (or *spot*) purchases of the asset, but they could purchase a contract for the delivery of the asset in a future period. Such contracts are known as *forward contracts* or *futures contracts* depending on how they are structured. (In this book, we limit our attention to futures contracts, which are standardized contracts traded on an exchange that have explicit margin and settlement provisions.)

Smith and Porter added a single futures market (technically, a forward market because the final settlement of accounts did not really occur until the end of the experiment) to the 15-period asset market. Hence, as trade began in the first period of the experiment, subjects could trade not only in the immediate ownership of the asset, but also in a contract for its future delivery in Period 8. A trader who takes delivery of the asset in Period 8 is entitled to only eight periods of dividends (Periods 8 through 15, inclusive), so the expected value of the futures contract was eight times the dividend of $0.24 paid in each period, or $1.92. In the early periods of these experiments, the futures contracts tended to trade around $1.92, which served to limit, but not eliminate, the tendency for a bubble to form.

That a single futures market would have such a powerful effect indicates that more of them might work even better. The problem with adding more futures markets to this experiment, and especially with providing one for delivery of the asset in each of the 15 periods, is that the complexity of the experiment can overwhelm and confuse the subjects. Furthermore, although we could overhaul the experiment to make it easier for subjects to deal with a complete set of futures markets, it is likely that in order to generate sufficient trading volume in each futures market we would need more subjects. Currently, bubble experiments are typically run with at most a dozen subjects to keep the budget for monetary payouts reasonable; a full set of viable futures markets might entail several times that.

It is not surprising that missing markets might become potholes. In the 1950s, Nobel laureates Kenneth Arrow and Gerard Debreu married John Nash's game-theory concept of equilibrium with Leon Walras's early efforts at a general equilibrium theory to prove that any number of markets could simultaneously come into equilibrium and that the equilibrium they reached was efficient. Interest in general equilibrium was sparked in the 1940s by the development of an input–output model of the U.S. economy by Nobel-laureate Wassily Leontief, who was also at Harvard in Chamberlin's day. His model of how goods flowed through the economy was a refined and greatly expanded version of François Quesnay's *Tableau Économique*, which had influenced economists from Adam Smith to Leon Walras. (Joseph Schumpeter, another colleague of Leontief, was responsible for rescuing Walras from obscurity.)

Critical to the Arrow–Debreu approach to general equilibrium was the assumption of complete markets, where a market would exist for every imaginable commodity or asset. In addition, Kenneth Arrow worked out how to incorporate uncertainty into general equilibrium theory by establishing a complete set of futures markets that spanned every possible future *state of the world*.

It may not be practical for real-world markets to have futures contracts involving everything that could possibly happen, especially given that most states of the world have little economic relevance. It is doubtful that anyone notices the absence of a formal futures market based on the size of geese migrations in North America. However, certain futures markets appear to be critical to the smooth and efficient operation of the market system.

The incompleteness of markets can hamper efficiency in two important ways. First, every market serves as an arena in which the aggregate knowledge of the economy is converted into prices. The joint absence of the aggregation process and its ultimate output—a market price—can deprive other markets of the information required for them to work efficiently. In the early 1980s, experiments designed and run by Charles Plott and Shyam Sunder showed that one could spread the information needed to resolve any uncertainty in the market among several traders, but the ability of the market mechanism to aggregate this information properly and arrive at an efficient competitive equilibrium depended on the completeness of the market system. The second reason that incomplete markets can limit efficiency is that the information from additional markets can serve as a reality check for existing markets. Indeed, some economists including Robert Shiller have advocated the development of *macro markets*, such as futures contracts based on such things as the Gross Domestic Product of the United States, to help financial markets to aggregate information. The U.S. Treasury has already made efforts in this direction by issuing inflation-index securities that allow traders and economists to compute the financial market's expectation of future consumer price inflation in the United States.

In general, new futures markets are relatively easy to establish in the United States. The Commodity Futures Trading Commission (CFTC) regulates futures markets and typically approves any reasonable new futures markets proposed by an existing exchange. Nonetheless, most new futures contracts fail because they lack the necessary trading volume to cover the expense of running the market. Complex asset market experiments run into the same problem; if subjects are faced with choices involving too many assets, market efficiency suffers.

Curiously enough, the futures contract found to be beneficial in the Porter and Smith experiments could not be legally traded on U.S. exchanges until 2001. The Shad-Johnson Accord of 1982, an agreement between the heads of the SEC and CFTC that staked out their regulatory territories, outlawed futures contracts on individual stocks. Jurisdiction over single-stock futures (and futures on baskets containing only a few stocks) was so hotly disputed that exchanges were forbidden from listing them until the turf battle between the two agencies could be resolved. This temporary measure lasted for 18 years until financial economist Lawrence Summers, who was Secretary of the Treasury at the time, intervened in 2000 to work out a settlement between the SEC and CFTC.

The evidence that futures on individual securities could reduce the occurrence of bubbles does not appear to be an artifact of the admittedly contrived laboratory setting in which bubbles were created. Holman W. Jenkins Jr., an award-winning business journalist and member of the *Wall Street Journal*'s editorial board, wrote an opinion piece in the May 31, 2000 issue of the *Journal* that called for the legalization of single-stock futures. Writing as the Nasdaq was recovering from the initial pricking of its bubble, Jenkins argued that the availability of single-stock futures might have prevented the Nasdaq bubble. Mr. Jenkins's comments appear to have been made independent of any knowledge of bubble experiments; indeed, had he been aware of this research he could have made an even more forceful argument in support of single-stock futures.

Next, we will expand our view of the world from a single asset to multiple assets. When we consider multiple securities together with the linkages that bind them together, our focus shifts from individual securities to *portfolios* of securities. Just as the absence of futures contracts created holes through which a speculative bubble could form, with portfolios the likelihood that market imperfections will impair both the efficiency and stability of the market increases. Indeed, the absence of a derivative security for stock portfolios can be directly linked to the stock market crash of 1987, which reached its climax on Black Monday.

PART II

INSIDE MARKETS: OPTIONS, INFORMATION, AND LIQUIDITY

6

Black Monday

Anyone browsing through the *Wall Street Journal* on the morning of Monday, October 19, 1987 saw a pair of graphs, one on top of the other. The baseline graph showed the rise of the Dow Jones Industrial Average over a period of eight years, from a low around 75 in 1922 to its peak above 380 in 1929. Above that graph was one of the Dow for the eight years from 1980 to 1987, showing a similar although not as steep rise from around 750 in 1980 to just above 2700 earlier in 1987. The only major difference in the graphs was that 1929 was history, so the Dow's full-year performance (including the Crash) was available for that year—while for 1987, the future was yet to come.

The 1987 graph bore ominous signs of the beginning of a crash like that of 58 years earlier. Although two graphs in the *Wall Street Journal* cannot be held responsible for the events that transpired that Black Monday, it is difficult to imagine that many traders were unaware of the eerie similarity.

Had the market recovered quickly from the Crash, it would have gone down in history as just one in a string of financial panics going back well into the nineteenth century. Unlike those panics, however, the Great Depression followed it. Apparently, the end of a boom—whether technically a speculative bubble or not—could create a bust so potent that the underlying economy could be threatened. Getting back to equilibrium once you have strayed from it is not automatic. Should the market overshoot its fundamental value, the global financial system might follow it down.

The financial systems of the developed economies were restructured during the 1930s to prevent the recurrence of a Depression. For a long time the neoclassical notion of a perfect market was replaced by the less ambitious goal of simply getting the market to work without collapsing, which was Keynes's research program. A more extreme alternative, advocated by collectivists was to do away with markets completely and replace it with a resource allocation system controlled by a central government. Starting from the events of Black Monday, we will explore the inner workings of the market mechanism and the importance of options and information to its fluid operation. Sometimes, in order to pave Wall Street, you need to save it first.

Peering into the Abyss

The graphs in the *Wall Street Journal* were one of many signs that the stock market was headed for trouble on October 19, 1987. After five years of swift and steady appreciation, the stock market stalled out in the summer of 1987. Unable to sustain another move upward, the market became increasingly volatile. By the week of October 12–16, it was apparent that the market was coming unhinged. At the close on Friday the 16th, the Dow stood at 2246.74, down nearly 500 points from its August high. Earlier, on Tuesday of that week, the Dow set a record for the largest single-day point loss with a decline of 190.58. Friday's market action tacked another 108.35 points onto that. Still, Tuesday's point loss would fall a notch in the record books before the ink with which it was written had dried.

Trade on October 19, 1987 began with a decline that extended Friday's retreat, reflecting sell orders that had accumulated over the weekend. Chaos soon reigned, however, when the computer systems of the stock exchanges became overloaded. Under the burden of an exploding backlog of offers to sell but few bids to buy, the stock market was no longer an orderly exchange where each stock had a well-defined bid and offer price. At any moment in time, such information was not only unknowable; the concepts of bid prices and offer prices had become meaningless. Phone lines were jammed with customers placing sell orders, and those who got past the busy signals might find their brokers unwilling to answer the phone. At the NYSE, the specialists on the trading floor, who are charged with maintaining an orderly market, were themselves placed at grave financial risk. Plummeting stock prices decimated their capital, which they used to hold inventories of shares in the stocks whose books they maintained.

By the time that all of the damage could be tallied that evening, the Dow had plunged a record 508.32 points to 1738.34. The relative decline in the market, 22.6 percent, also set a single-day record—close to the 23 percent that it dropped during the worst two days of the 1929 Crash combined. Furthermore, because of the difficulty of transacting, the true decline in the market was even greater; a seller wishing to liquidate a portfolio of Dow stocks at the close of Black Monday could only have consummated his trades with divine intervention.

The Black Monday crash was far more serious than the 1997 Blue Monday minicrash. The difference between the two was not just quantitative—with the market falling more than three times as far in percentage terms on Black Monday than it did on Blue Monday—the two crashes just felt different. The 1997 plunge, unlike the one 10 years earlier, was orderly; only when the market was between circuit breakers did it go into freefall. Although trading on Blue Monday was heavy, the computer systems of the stock exchanges could handle it: Bids, offers, and trades were reported in a timely manner. Black Monday, on the other hand, was truly a black day for the markets. It was as if someone had turned out the lights at the stock exchanges—stock prices and the status of open orders were anyone's guess.

An even deeper panic faced the market the next day—now known as *Terrible Tuesday*—when many stocks were unable to open for trading because of a massive imbalance in the market. Led by Fed Chairman Alan Greenspan, whose tenure had begun only two months earlier, the world's major financial institutions provided the safety net of capital required to assure the market that no major player would fall into bankruptcy. Given this reassurance, most stocks moved significantly higher when they finally opened as it became clear that a total meltdown of financial markets would be averted. In addition, several companies took the opportunity of the panic selling to buy back their own shares at what, in retrospect, were bargain prices.

Flying in the face of a new rash of newspaper articles drawing what now appear to be spurious parallels between the Crashes of 1987 and 1929, the world economy escaped without falling into another Great

Depression. The 500+ point loss in the Dow was recouped in less than two years and the world economy, despite pockets of weakness, continued to thrive. Governmental commissions, most notably the Brady Commission, were convened to look into the cause of the crash and to find ways to keep it from happening again. The detailed examination that ensued resulted in the institution of circuit breakers and a stringent set of curbs on electronic order submission that even a modest decline in the overall market would trigger.

As with any market debacle, Black Monday appears to have been the result of several factors working together; however, the factor near the top of everyone's list was a financial innovation that came to the market from the University of California at Berkeley: portfolio insurance. Invented in 1976 by a young and accomplished Berkeley professor, Hayne Leland, portfolio insurance used an unfamiliar trading strategy in an attempt to deal with the problem of a missing market—the market for insurance of large stock portfolios.

Unfortunately, in the process of working around one problem, an even greater problem was created—massive market instability. The best way to understand portfolio insurance is to consider it within the context of a broader revolution in finance that had swept the markets in the years before Black Monday. Having established that context, we can then look at how portfolio insurance was supposed to operate in theory and what went wrong.

The Quantitative Finance Revolution

Revolution is a word that is easily tossed around, but there is no better word to describe what happened to both the theory and practice of finance leading up to Black Monday. Before the 1970s, business schools had taught finance using little more than the *firm handshake theory*, as some finance professors now derisively refer to it in hindsight. Major financial decisions were made not so much on the basis of hard numbers and objective analysis, but rather on subjective assessments of personal character, as might be reflected in a firm handshake and the outward trappings of social status. ("Biff's a fine chap, so we can sign off on the ten-million-dollar loan.") While financial decision making continues to involve subjective input that is difficult, if not impossible, to quantify, financial institutions now rely heavily on objective analysis.

The quantitative finance revolution at the end of the twentieth century can be largely credited to a cadre of young upstarts, whose brilliant new insights into finance came during the 1950s and 1960s. While economists through Alfred Marshall spent their time essentially interpreting or disputing what Adam Smith wrote; after World War II a new generation of economists began to blaze altogether new trails. While new concepts in economics had (with the understandable exception of Karl Marx) usually been spawned in universities, a government-sponsored think tank, the RAND Corporation (RAND coming from R[esearch] and D[evelopment]) in Santa Monica, California played a significant role in pushing economics beyond Marshall's perfect world. Nobel laureates Kenneth Arrow, James Buchanan, Paul Samuelson, John Nash, Herbert Simon, Harry Markowitz, and William Sharpe and many other noted scientists were at RAND early in their careers and performed some of their most distinguished research there.

The economists at RAND, working in an atmosphere of interdisciplinary cooperation, with leading scientists, such as John von Neumann, and powerful computers all around them (and with the Pacific Ocean nearby), would explore quantitative methods nearly as sophisticated as those used by physical scientists. While some of their attempts to apply powerful mathematics to economics were disappointing, financial markets, which are readily characterized by numbers, became the obvious area where mathematics could be put to good use. As almost all of the top economists working at RAND went on to teach at university economics departments and business schools, some of their students would find their way to Wall Street.

This reliance on mathematics for solving economic problems, not surprisingly, initially met with considerable resistance from both the academic world and the financial community. Nonetheless, armed with the hottest financial theories and the fastest computers, practitioners who used sophisticated quantitative methods started to wrest the world of finance from the aristocrats at the Houses of Morgan, Chase, and Mellon.

The revolution was aided by the deregulation of financial markets that came with the overhaul of the Securities and Exchange Act in 1975. Coming after years of rigid regulation that benefited stodgy financial institutions at the expense of their clients by setting commissions too high and interest rates too low, financial deregulation sought to encourage competition and make the financial markets more efficient. Although some of the promise of deregulation has never been completely realized, such as the establishment of a National Market System for stocks (further discussed in Chapter 14), reduced regulation was a critical aspect of the environment in which a new wave of financial innovation would make its mark on the Street.

The quantitative ideas that found their way to Wall Street focused on three areas—portfolios, options, and incentives—that had long played second fiddle to stocks and bonds in the financial world. The idea that investors held portfolios and not just individual assets formed the basis of *modern portfolio theory*; the idea that the value of options could be objectively computed formed the basis of *option valuation theory*; and the idea that incentive structures influenced asset values formed the basis of *incentive management theory*. Modern portfolio theory and option valuation theory were able to cope with previously unsolvable problems by assuming the existence of an efficient market in which any portfolio or option could be valued by decomposing it into an appropriate pair of equivalent assets. When incentives enter the picture, however, we cannot always simply assume our problems away. As we shall see later on, when sufficient information in the market is lacking, incentives can be sufficiently skewed that the market will fail altogether.

Modern portfolio theory is based on the simple concept that investors should not make investment decisions one at a time, but rather should consider the effect of each purchase or sale in the context of their entire portfolio of holdings. In particular, investors should take into account the concentrations of risk in their portfolio, looking to add holdings where concentrations are low and reduce them where concentrations are high. While competent investment managers had long been aware of the importance of diversification, before the revolution they lacked the quantitative tools required to properly balance the concentration necessary to generate superior returns with the diversification that would limit overall risk.

In the 1950s, Harry Markowitz showed how one could use information about the relative movements (correlations) of the returns of different assets to construct "optimal" portfolios that could provide a greater return per unit of risk than would be available from any single asset. Computing a truly optimal stock portfolio using Markowitz's full model would not become practical until the 1980s. In the meantime, Jack Treynor, William Sharpe, John Lintner, and Jan Mossin invented a variety of techniques to create portfolios that approximated the optimal one using the limited computational power provided by expensive mainframe computers that had only recently made the transition from military to business applications.

In order to simplify the Markowitz model of portfolio selection enough to make it computationally practical, economists looked at the problem facing the individual investor to determine how competitive market forces might set the relative prices of assets with differing risk/reward profiles. If only certain profiles could make it through an efficient market process, then an investor could consider market forces when building his or her portfolio. Taking Markowitz's basic model and applying the general equilibrium theory of Arrow and Debreu to it, Treynor, Sharpe, Lintner, and Mossin nearly simultaneously came up with their own versions of the *Capital Asset Pricing Model* (CAPM) in the early 1960s. The result of their research turns out to be shockingly simple.

CAPM shows that with efficient markets the expected return from an asset depends only on the risk it "inherits" from the overall market. The amount of market risk that an asset contains is known as its *beta*. Beta is calibrated so that an asset with no market risk has a beta of zero and an asset with the same market risk as the overall market has a beta of one. The beta for stocks loaded with market risk tends to top out around two. Although it is possible to engineer securities so that they have negative betas, securities issued directly by corporations (stocks, bonds, etc.) virtually never have negative betas because market risk permeates every economic endeavor—even gold will become worthless in a sufficiently bad market.

The amount that one is paid for bearing market risk is known as the *equity risk premium*. The size of this premium is related to the overall level of risk aversion in the economy. Greater risk aversion requires a higher equity risk premium to compensate individuals for bearing market risk. The size and nature of the equity risk premium has been a continuing source of controversy. In particular, during a stock market bubble, one way to dismiss the bubble is by claiming that the rise in stock prices was fueled by a decline in the equity risk premium.

An important consequence of CAPM is that the market rewards investors only for the market risk in their portfolio. Investors can eliminate any risk that is specific to an asset through their holdings of other assets (diversification) and so the market will not reward them for bearing those risks. In theory, investors willing to hold diversified portfolios will arbitrage away any premium associated with asset-specific risk. This allows

CAPM to replicate the risk profile of any individual's holdings using just two assets: a portfolio comprised of every asset in the market and the so-called risk-free asset. In the world of CAPM, the optimal portfolio for every individual is a combination of these two assets; less risk-averse investors will hold more of the *market portfolio* and investors that are more risk-averse will hold more of the risk-free asset. Although CAPM, like the rest of modern portfolio theory, has serious problems when taken as a literal description of financial reality, the basic idea of using an arbitrage argument to determine asset prices drives much of the financial revolution.

Modern portfolio theory could handle not only stocks, but also any asset whose fundamental value could be computed using the discounted cash flow methods introduced earlier. As future projected cash flows and discount factors would fluctuate up and down, so would the values of these assets.

Some securities, however, were designed to adapt their cash flows to market conditions and so their movements were more complicated. Chief among them are derivative securities. While futures contracts are usually easy to value because all they do is delay the receipt of the cash flows until a specified time in the future when the underlying security is delivered, other derivatives are more complex. In particular, derivative securities where cash flows are not automatic, but are provided at the *option* of either the holder or issuer, are far more difficult to value.

It takes a separate theory of valuation built on the foundations of the efficient-market theory and the Capital Asset Pricing Model to value options. Options can appear in isolation or as a feature of other securities, such as *convertible bonds*, which are bonds that give their holder the option to convert them into stock. A special theory that deals with options is more important to finance than it might seem because options are embedded in almost every asset.

Option valuation theory works using the same basic trick as CAPM. In order to value an option, we need to decompose it into two assets: the asset that underlies it and the risk-free asset. The one complication is that this decomposition is not static; as conditions change or time merely passes, the balance between the two assets must be constantly adjusted. In order for this continuous *rebalancing* to be implemented, markets must operate with a perfection that exceeds even that required by the efficient-market theory. (Optimized asset portfolios can need to be rebalanced as well, though much less frequently.) That no market even approaches the ideal assumed by option valuation theory was the crux of Black Monday.

Economic theory did not stand still while financial economists were squeezing the last drop out of the efficient-market theory. Although the general equilibrium theory that lay behind CAPM did an excellent job of linking related markets, its failure to deal explicitly with time and uncertainty made it irrelevant to the study of asset markets, including the one that most fascinated John Maynard Keynes—money.

Kenneth Arrow, keenly aware of the limitations of general equilibrium, began a research program that piece-by-piece plugged uncertainty into a general equilibrium framework. Although Arrow saw what was necessary to handle simple kinds of uncertainty, demonstrating the importance of complete markets to efficiency in the process, he discovered a major obstacle that continues to plague economists.

The smooth and efficient operation of the market mechanism relies heavily on the assumption that information is distributed symmetrically. If everyone knows everything there is to know about the economy, then things work just fine and if everyone is kept equally in the dark—as in the original market experiments—that is fine, too. What Kenneth Arrow and his fellow researchers discovered is that critical problems arise when information is asymmetrically distributed, as it is in almost every naturally occurring market. These informational problems, which are ideally suited to experimental examination, can poke major holes in any market system. Foremost among informational problems are those that relate to incentives, the third major concept in the quantitative finance revolution.

In a typical Marshallian economic transaction, the buyer and seller agree upon what they are trading. On the other hand, when information is asymmetrically distributed, one side of the transaction, usually the seller, will know more about the good or service being sold than the other. This inability to reach a meeting of minds can create a substantial hole in the market. For example, consider the relationship between workers and the companies that employ them. In an economic world of perfect information, the contribution of each employee to the firm's profits would be observable, and so his or her wages could be directly pegged to them. In reality, even imperfect monitoring is costly, especially for workers in management positions, and so compensation can only be loosely linked to a worker's contributions. How workers are compensated matters, because they make numerous choices that trade their own well-being off against that of their employers. In essence, workers are granted valuable options on how they perform their jobs because their bosses cannot be omniscient.

An interesting partial solution to this incentive problem involves granting employees another kind of option: one in their employer's stock. Such options help align the incentives of workers with their employers' profitability because they now share in those profits. Still, this solution to the incentive problem is not entirely satisfying because most of the factors that influence the value of a worker's stock options are beyond his or her control. Furthermore, those things that are under the control of a typical worker have little bearing on the employer's profits. In general, perfect solutions to incentive problems are impossible.

For all their limitations, options remain a useful tool for aligning the interests of workers with their employers, especially when compared with giving them a direct ownership stake. Options cost significantly less than the equivalent amount of stock and they have value only when the value of the company's stock rises. Any decline in the stock's price, no matter how great, provides the identical outcome to the optionholder: the options expire worthless. Still, up until the moment they expire, options provide insurance against a sudden loss, no matter how improbable it might be. The insurance side of options is what made them, or rather their absence, such an integral part of the market's plunge in October 1987.

It's There Until You Need It

Portfolio insurance, the designated villain in the 1987 Crash, began as one of the most clever ideas to come out of the financial revolution. In the heady stock market of the 1980s, investors wanted to lock in their existing stock market gains but still benefit from any further rise in the market. In essence, they wished to purchase insurance on their stock portfolios that would offer protection against a decline in stock prices. While any fees charged for this insurance would reduce the overall returns from owning stock, buying insurance rather than liquidating at a profit would facilitate participation in whatever remained of the bull market.

Those who desired portfolio insurance, mostly investment managers at large institutions such as pension funds, wanted the same type of downside protection provided by stock options, such as those granted to employees or those traded on exchanges. In each case the goal was the same: participation on the upside and protection on the downside.

The problem that institutional portfolio managers faced was that they were prohibited from converting their stock portfolios into option portfolios. Fortunately, they could obtain portfolio insurance without the need to swap their stock for options; instead, they could *overlay* an options strategy on top of their stock portfolio using *put options*, which are the opposite of standard stock options, also known as *call options*.

A call option gives its holder an option to *buy* the stock at a fixed price, known as the *striking price*. For example, an employee might receive options on his company's stock with an exercise price equal to the current stock price of 50. If the stock goes up, he can exercise the option to buy at 50 and then sell at the market price for a profit. If the stock goes down, the options simply become worthless, and so just the premium paid for them is lost.

Put options, on the other hand, are options to *sell* at a fixed exercise price. The value of a put option increases as the stock price falls, and so when it is held in combination with the stock it provides insurance that "pays off" in the event of a decline. Ignoring some minor technicalities, overlaying an existing stock position with (an equal number of) put options converts the position into (an equal number of) call options. The equivalence between one share of stock and the combination of one call and one put with the same exercise price and expiration date is known as the *put-call parity* relationship.

Insuring a stock portfolio by overlaying it with the appropriate set of put options looked great in theory; however, the options markets of the 1980s were insufficiently developed to make it a practical solution for most portfolios. Indeed, until the middle of the 1970s, trade in options was quite limited. Except for a small number of *warrants* (options issued by companies to raise capital), stock options were not publicly traded. Independent dealers of questionable repute who worked from ads placed in the back pages of financial newspapers usually sold those options available outside the warrants market at unfavorable prices.

The establishment of the Chicago Board Options Exchange (CBOE) marked a new era for options. The CBOE opened for business in 1973 listing options on only a few dozen stocks. Although the options markets expanded rapidly, their availability was still spotty well into the 1980s.

A superior alternative to insuring each stock in a portfolio with a separate put–option overlay is to insure the entire portfolio with a single put option based on the portfolio's aggregate value. That securities based on entire portfolios could trade as separate financial instruments was a major innovation of the 1980s that flowed naturally from the Capital Asset Pricing Model. In that model, investors are not compensated for bearing the risk of holding individual assets, so that each optimal portfolio includes a *market basket* of assets. It was only natural that Wall Street would begin to market both the baskets themselves as well as derivative securities based on those baskets. (Although the terms *portfolio* and *basket* are used interchangeably, portfolio has a more active connotation.)

The first stock market index funds were offered in the 1970s, but they were slow to catch on with anyone outside of a handful of daring institutional investors. It took nearly 20 years of underperformance by the typical stock-picking mutual fund to make the virtues of index funds apparent. In the meantime, the real breakthrough for basket trading arrived on April 21, 1982 with the introduction of the futures contract on the Standard & Poor's 500 (S&P 500) Composite Stock Price Index. This contract, which traded on the Chicago Mercantile Exchange, was pegged to $500 times the value of the S&P 500 on a specified delivery date. For example, with the S&P 500 expected to be at 1500 on the delivery date, a single futures contract would be for the delivery of stock worth $750,000 (1,500 times $500). Trade in these contracts—nicknamed *spoos* (or *spooz*) after the symbols for the September and December contracts (SPU and SPZ, respectively)—caught on immediately and remain a favorite of the financial markets.

Futures, like options, are popular with speculators because they provide leverage. The payment for the item under contract—from stock market indexes to pork bellies—is not due until delivery. Before then, all the buyer of the futures contract must do is put up a margin payment, generally 5 to 10 percent of the contract's value. The only potential hitch is that any adverse move in the price of the contract before the delivery date will require the immediate posting of more margin to protect the position. In dealing with futures—and certain option positions as well—it is not enough for a speculator to be correct about where prices are going; he needs to have sufficient capital to maintain the margin for his position through any interim volatility.

The S&P 500 Index futures contract was fundamentally different from any futures contract that preceded it. In particular, it used a new method to settle accounts when the delivery date arrived. When the futures contract for a physical commodity reaches its delivery date, the seller is required to deliver the commodity to the buyer. Although fanciful television and film depictions of this process show the hapless buyer who has neglected to liquidate his futures contract prior to the delivery date having tons of soy beans or eggs dumped on his front lawn, in practice, delivery is made in the less spectacular form of a warehouse receipt. Because most buyers and sellers of commodity futures contracts do not wish to either take or make delivery, they liquidate them before the delivery date, often rolling them over into a later contract. Because of the difficulty of delivering all 500 stocks of the S&P 500 Index in their proper proportions, settlement of these and many other *financial futures* is done in cash. For example, suppose you purchased an S&P 500 Index futures contract at 1500 in February for delivery on the third Friday in March, if the index traded at 1510 on the settlement date, your cash profits would be $5,000, which is the increase of 10 in the index times the $500 multiplier for the contract.

The settlement dates for the S&P futures play a special role in the global economy. These four days—the third Fridays in March, June, September, and December—have come to be known as *triple witching days*. These four triple witching days are also the expiration days for stock options and stock index options, which is where the *triple* comes from. Despite regulatory efforts to adjust the settlement process to limit manipulation of these markets, fluctuations around triple witching time can be extreme.

Futures contracts on the S&P 500 Index were an instant success and so put and call options on them were soon established. Although these options would eventually become as popular as the index futures themselves, during the 1980s, trade in them was still erratic enough that enormous gaps between their bid and offer prices were common. The holdings of large institutional investors were usually sufficiently diversified that the purchase of put options on the S&P 500 Index would provide reasonable insurance against a downturn in the market. The thinness of the market for those options coupled with the increasing volatility of the stock market in the mid-1980s, however, gave them such a high premium that they were often too expensive to be used as portfolio insurance.

Programmed to Trade

The futures contract on the S&P 500 ultimately provided the inspiration that—along with a good dose of high-powered economic theory—made portfolio insurance possible. That inspiration took the form of program trading, the use of computer programs to guide trading strategies. Although mainframe computers had sometimes been used to value and trade financial instruments, their expense and inconvenience made them attractive to only a small number of technology enthusiasts living on the fringes of the financial world. Computer-based trading expanded with the arrival of the minicomputer (particularly the PDP family of machines produced by Digital Equipment Corporation), which was not only far less expensive than the mainframes that preceded it, but facilitated direct interaction through a computer terminal. The real boom, however, came with the arrival of personal computers, which combined the capabilities of the computer and terminal in a single package. Personal computers were priced so that most traders could purchase them without the numerous sign-offs required for larger capital expenditures. High-powered traders had also begun to use computer workstations that were targeted to the computational requirements of scientists and engineers, but which spread like wildfire through Wall Street in the 1980s.

The first major killer application for program trading was *stock index arbitrage*. As we saw in Chapter 4, arbitrage is an important manifestation of the invisible hand; when prices in related markets get out of line, traders engaging in arbitrage across those markets bring them back into balance. Stock index arbitrage is designed to exploit discrepancies between the price of stock index futures and the individual stocks that make up the index. For example, if the price of the futures contract is high relative to the stocks in the index, selling the futures contract and buying the stocks will generate a profit when the market returns to equilibrium. Conversely, if the price of the futures contract is too low, it will pay to buy the futures contract and sell the stocks; however, the strategy in this direction is complicated by rules that limit the selling of a stock that one does not own (*short selling*) to *upticks*—upward movements in the price of the stock. These discrepancies can be quickly discovered with computers, which can then be used to submit the orders electronically to generate an almost instantaneous profit.

The ease with which stock index futures can be traded relative to their component stocks means that any substantial movement in the stock market will appear in the futures contracts before it is reflected in the *spot* (or *cash*) index—that is, the value of the index computed from the last reported prices of all its components. This tendency of the futures to lead any move is part of a larger issue known as *nonsynchronicity*, where prices of different securities are fixed at different times.

If one looks at a snapshot of prices in the market, such as on a trading monitor or as reported in a newspaper, the prices are not completely comparable because they usually just record the price at the last (or closing) trade, and those trades could have taken place minutes, hours, or even days, apart. The cash value of a stock index is a weighted average of the current price of the stocks in the index and so it will often lag its theoretical true value when the overall market is moving. This discrepancy can become quite large, as it has in all modern stock market crashes, when major components of the index cannot trade either because of a trading halt or an order imbalance.

Viewed with a conspiratorial eye, traders in stock index futures can appear to be moving the market against its will. Sizeable movements in stock index futures, regardless of their basis in fundamentals or the whims of the market, will induce sympathetic movements in the stocks that constitute them. Program traders, looking to exploit the inertia of the market, submit orders that both profit themselves and help to "resynchronize" the market by bringing the price of stocks back in line with the futures.

A more dynamic approach to valuation lay behind the second major killer application for program trading: portfolio insurance. As noted above, the idea for portfolio insurance came from Hayne Leland. Professor Leland enlisted a Berkeley colleague, Mark Rubinstein, and a marketing expert, John O'Brien, to found the investment advisory firm of Leland O'Brien Rubinstein Associates, which developed the first computerized portfolio insurance strategies. Their portfolio insurance program exploited the concept at the heart of option valuation theory, the ability to replicate put options by suitably adjusting one's holdings in the underlying assets and a risk-free asset, usually U.S. Treasury bills. In the case of a stock portfolio, the insurance provided by owning a put option against the portfolio can be replicated by selling some of the portfolio whenever it drops in value and buying more (from one's reserves of Treasury bills) whenever it increases in value. Using the option valuation theory of Black, Scholes, and Merton, one can compute the precise amounts that need to be bought and sold to replicate the put option.

Intuitively, this technique should work well at providing insurance for a portfolio. As the value of the portfolio drops, fewer units of it are held, and so there is less money to be lost from any further reduction in its unit value. In theory, any incompleteness in the market system caused by the absence of a meaningful market for the put option is insignificant because the put option can be replicated by using this *dynamic hedging strategy* on the underlying assets.

Before the days of dynamic hedging, traders who wished to hedge a position would usually put the hedge in place and leave it there until the position was liquidated. With dynamic hedging, the hedge was continuously monitored by indefatigable computers and adjusted to reflect changing market conditions. No human could track the market closely enough to make dynamic hedging work, but computers programmed for the task could easily manage even the largest institutional portfolio.

The problem with portfolio insurance is that the real world may not always satisfy the assumptions required by theory. The clients of Leland O'Brien Rubinstein Associates would learn this lesson the hard way in October 1987, as would those of Long-Term Capital Management many years later in a somewhat different context. The difficulty with portfolio insurance created for dynamic hedging is that the strategy requires that the stocks in the portfolio be continuously bought and sold at the prevailing market price. Of course, in the midst of a selling panic, there will be neither a prevailing market price nor the ability to buy or sell shares at will. As an insurance product, portfolio insurance has a fatal flaw—at the times when you need it the most, it cannot be used.

To make matters worse, portfolio insurance can destabilize the market because it involves increased selling when prices drop and increased buying when prices rise, the exact opposite of how the Walrasian auctioneer or any other mechanism designed to stabilize the market as it converges toward equilibrium would work. The successful marketing of portfolio insurance by Leland O'Brien Rubinstein Associates, which gave them a large client base and caused others to imitate their strategy, ensured that by October 1987 the strategy would exert a powerful influence over the market. Although their clients fared well during the bloodbath of the week before Black Monday—reducing their positions as the market fell to dampen the impact of the market's decline—their good fortune would not continue into the following week.

On Black Monday, the world witnessed just how destabilizing computer-based stock trading could be. Although the formal investigations launched in its wake did not attribute the collapse to any single factor, portfolio insurance loomed large in every explanation. Soon after the crash, incriminating stories with the air of urban legend about them began to circulate. One account of Black Monday blames the crash on a new analyst fresh from business school who was working for the pension fund of a major automaker. This young analyst misinterpreted the output of the portfolio insurance computer program and thought that the dollar amounts that had to be sold to insure the portfolio were actually share quantities, leading to the sale of nearly 50 times the stock indicated by the program. Although this story may well be apocryphal, the situation it describes is plausible and serves to illustrate the dangers that can arise when the use of destabilizing trading strategies becomes widespread.

Black Monday dealt financial innovation both a serious blow and an important reality check. The only regulatory change of any significance to come out of the crash was the institution of stock market circuit breakers, which as we saw earlier failed to work properly when they were eventually triggered 10 years later. In addition, exchanges instituted rules to keep computers on a "short leash" by curbing certain types of program trading after relatively small moves in the market, but it remains uncertain whether these *trading curbs* are anything other than a minor annoyance. While such rules may lend some comfort to those concerned with the possibility that computers—taking their cue from the murderous computer HAL in *2001: A Space Odyssey*—would usurp the market, they have likely served only to hamper the overall market efficiency.

As one would expect, the dynamic hedging approach to portfolio insurance fell into disfavor after Black Monday; however, the eventual development of active markets for options on a large variety of stock indexes provided a better way to achieve the same result. Just as the stock market recovered from the crash, going on to scale new heights, the basic ideas behind the financial innovations that contributed to the crash were so powerful that they continued to form the foundation upon which the new financial world would be built. While one could easily imagine socially conscious lawmakers calling for the abolition of options, derivative securities, portfolio insurance, and so on, an action of this kind would not only be unenforceable, its mere consideration would lead to turmoil in the financial markets. As we shall see in the next two chapters, options are the foundation on which the financial markets are built.

7

All the World's an Option

R
epercussions from the October 1987 crash were far-reaching
and the aftershocks continued into the 1990s. While many sec-
tors of the U.S. economy were only indirectly affected by the
crash, the financial world experienced a major setback. On Wall Street,
bonuses were slashed and jobs were eliminated. Even trendy restaurants
that had thrived on the business of free-spending investment bankers had
to shut their doors. (Traders, on the other hand, appear not to eat, they
simply refuel.)

Institutional investors, who had been stung either directly or indirectly
by portfolio insurance, stayed away from financial products that were even
remotely associated with options or derivative securities. Indeed, the very
word "derivative" had become almost unmentionable. When talk of derivative securities was unavoidable, they were sometimes referred to as the *D*-
word, an appellation formerly reserved for "Depression."

Derivatives were too valuable, however, to disappear entirely; indeed, after several years of retrenchment, they would reappear to dominate the financial markets in the mid-1990s. Nonetheless, traders and
fund managers were careful to avoid anything that remotely smacked of
portfolio insurance, limiting themselves to strategies unlikely to destabilize the market.

Ultimately, *risk management* drove the resurgence in derivatives and dynamic hedging. Financial institutions and industrial companies wanted to
concentrate their efforts on their core businesses, and then use derivative
securities to lay off any unwanted risks that they had acquired in the

process. For financial institutions, a sizeable market in *financial swaps* developed so that lenders could grant loans on the terms that borrowers desired and then "swap" away any risk that did not fit in with their overall portfolio of assets and liabilities. Among the earliest swaps were *interest rate swaps*, which enabled a lender who had granted a fixed-rate loan to swap it for a variable-rate loan and vice versa. Over time, markets for a wide range of swaps developed. Rivaling interest rate swaps in importance were *currency swaps*, which could limit exposure to foreign exchange markets, and *credit swaps*, which could limit exposure to the borrower's ability to repay a loan. Clever innovations, like *equity swaps*, could be used to create a private market for what were essentially the outlawed futures contracts on individual stocks. The power of swaps could be further enhanced through the prudent application of dynamic hedging strategies.

The use of derivatives to mold the risk exposure of a company grew to the point that it became a discipline in its own right—*financial engineering*. (Note: The term "financial engineering" can also be used pejoratively in the same sense as "creative accounting," that is, the use of legerdemain to disguise a firm's true condition by artificially inflating or smoothing its earnings, revenues, or other performance measures.) Derivatives served as the fundamental building blocks for the structures that financial engineers constructed. Every financial product, no matter how complex, was comprised of options.

Derivatives could not only be used to cast off risk, they could also be used to target it. The earliest hedge funds were among the first experts at risk targeting. They would hedge away undesired risks, such as any exposure to the general movements of the financial markets, and then magnify the risks where they wished to place their bets. Because options generally provide substantial leverage—the small amount of money used to purchase the option controls a much larger amount of the asset that underlies it—options and other derivative securities became extremely popular with hedge funds.

The use of derivatives was also promoted by accounting rules that allowed companies to keep some derivatives transactions off their balance sheets and relegate them to the footnotes of their financial statements. This less-than-wholly-respectable use of derivatives has kept them from achieving full first-class citizen status in some corners of the financial world.

Derivative securities, despite any lingering air of disrepute, are nonetheless omnipresent in the world of finance. Not only are more respectable securities—such as stocks and bonds—themselves fashioned from options; in the next chapter we will examine how options are integral to the market mechanism itself. Paradoxically, most options are inherently redundant securities, yet it is only because they are redundant that a value can be readily placed on them.

How Do You Value an Option?

Attempts to find an option valuation formula date back to the 1900 doctoral dissertation of Louis Bachelier, a student of the renowned French mathematician Henri Poincaré. Bachelier's thesis, "Theory of Speculation," pioneers a theory of randomness that Albert Einstein would later independently develop in his work on Brownian motion, the random movement of particles suspended in a fluid. Bachelier's work was forgotten until its rediscovery in the 1950s, just when Paul Samuelson's work on the efficient-market theory derived general conditions under which asset prices would follow a random walk, confirming the empirical results of statisticians. Because asset prices appeared to contain a random component that was relatively easy to quantify, the advanced mathematics used to handle this randomness would become an integral part of finance.

By the 1960s, a formula to value options had become the Holy Grail for the emerging field of financial economics. A leading practical statistician of the time, Professor Edward O. Thorp at MIT—whose book, *Beat the Dealer*, brought the card-counting methods for blackjack to the masses—was also determined to find a formula that could value options. Thorp's 1967 book about options, *Beat the Market*, co-authored with Sheen Kassouf, focused on statistical techniques for option valuation.

Professor Thorp failed to find an entirely satisfactory solution to the options pricing problem because he and his collaborator saw options largely from a statistical viewpoint. Like the economists who had worked on the problem before him, he ignored the market forces that acted on them to shape their value. Indeed, the value of an option is determined not by the mere shuffle of a card deck nor by the spin of a roulette wheel; it comes from the way in which related markets jointly converge to equilibrium. (In recent years, interest in purely statistical approaches to option valuation has experienced a comeback as one of the central thrusts of *econophysics*, the study of economic phenomena using the techniques of statistical physics.) The expertise required to put everything together in just the right way resided elsewhere on the MIT campus, in the minds of Robert Merton (a brilliant protégé of Paul Samuelson), Myron Scholes (a young finance professor with a Ph.D. from the University of Chicago), and Fischer Black (a consultant and friend of Scholes who would eventually teach at MIT on his way to Goldman, Sachs).

Before returning to MIT and the Holy Grail, it is worth looking at what is involved in placing a dollar value on options. Consider the example of a fortunate employee who receives a bonus that grants call options on 1,000 shares of her employer's stock. Assume that, as is common practice, these options can be exercised in five years to purchase the stock at its current market price of $50 per share, which becomes the *exercise price* for the options. (We will ignore the possibility that an external event, such as a merger, could allow for early exercise of the options.) Some companies, to impress upon their employees that their newly granted options have real value, provide them with a worksheet showing how much the options might be worth under hypothetical circumstances. Of course, this worksheet will likely include legal disclaimers not only stating that such circumstances might fail to materialize, but also that the options could end up being completely worthless if the stock price stays below the exercise price.

A typical options worksheet might project that the stock's price will double in five years, making each share worth $100 on the exercise date. At this price, each option has a cash value of $50 upon exercise because the shares can be bought using the options for $50 and then sold immediately to the market at $100, netting a gain of $50. Hence, by this reasoning, the entire package of 1,000 options is worth $50,000.

This example may be structured to make it easy for employees to understand, but it is plagued with basic errors that overstate the value of the options. The most striking problem with the example is that $50,000 received five years from now is worth significantly less than $50,000 received today. Even if we ignore the implicit cost of any abuse that the employee might have to endure at the hands of her employer for the five (long) years necessary to maintain the right to exercise the options, cash received in the future must still be discounted. The fundamental economic question that arises is how to compute the appropriate discount rate for this $50,000. Clearly, at a minimum, we should discount using the "risk-free" rate of interest, which is approximately the interest rate paid by the most-recently issued five-year U.S. Treasury Note.

In determining how to discount the future payoff of the option, we must also account for the stock's risk. Even if the projection that the value of the stock will double in five years is conservative, there is still a significant possibility that after five years the price of the stock would fall, say to $40 per share. This is bad news for the holder of the option because the option expires worthless; but the silver lining is that the optionholder, unlike the stockholder, does not lose $10 per share because she will choose not to purchase any stock with her options if a loss would result.

It would appear that when we begin to consider the risk associated with the stock that underlies the option, the value of the call option would depend on the ability of its holder to bear risk. In particular, it seems obvious that less risk-averse individuals would value the option more than those who were more risk-averse. First, less risk-averse individuals would place a lower discount rate on the ultimate payoff five years hence because they would require a smaller premium to compensate them for the risk that the stock would lose money. Furthermore, they would find a more volatile stock price to their advantage because of the one-sidedness of the option's payoff. On the downside, once the price falls below $50, the insurance aspect of the call option kicks in, so any optionholder, regardless of risk aversion, would not care whether the stock fell to $49, $40, $30, or all the way to $0. On the upside, a higher stock price is always better—if the stock rises to $120 instead of $100, the optionholder receives an extra $20 per share in five years.

If the value of an option, such as the call option in the above example, is jointly determined by the risk profiles of everyone in the market, then there would be little hope of coming up with any method to compute its value, much less an actual formula. But all hope is not lost, because there are situations where uncertainty is present but prices are set independently of how individuals value risk. We saw this in the two-season experimental market where the price in the second season was equal to the price in the first season plus the storage cost independent of how the market participants felt about risk. If prices in the second season got out of line with those in the first season, arbitrage would quickly bring them back together. Through the mechanism of arbitrage, the price in the second season was not free to move on its own; it was fully determined by two other prices: the price of the good in the first season and the price of storage. It turns out that options can be valued using a similar arbitrage argument in which the price of the option is set by prices in two related markets.

The value of an option is clearly tied to the value of its underlying stock; however, this relationship appears to depend on how far the stock price is from the exercise price of the option. For an *in-the-money* option, where the stock price is above the exercise price and so would generate a positive payoff if exercised immediately, changes in the stock price have a significant impact on the option value. In the extreme, options that are well in-the-money would tend to move dollar-for-dollar with their underlying stock. On the other hand, for an *out-of-the money* option, where the stock price is below the exercise price and so is not worth exercising immediately, there is much less linkage between the value of the option and the price of its underlying stock. Indeed, for options that are extremely out-of-the-money, only a large change in the price of the underlying stock would have any effect on the option. Finally, *at-the-money* options, which are at or near their exercise price, have absolute movements that are a bit more than half of those of their underlying stock, so that a $1 per share increase in the stock price might increase the price of a call option by $0.52 per share.

There is a trick that one can use to get a quick idea of how much the price of a call option will move relative to a $1 increase in the price of its underlying stock—a ratio known as *delta*. Consider the probability that when the option expires it is in-the-money, making it worth exercising. Notice that for a stock that is currently far in-the-money this probability will be close to 100 percent, for a stock way out-of-the-money it will be nearly 0 percent, and for a stock at-the-money it will be about 50 percent. This probability of ending up in-the-money turns out to be identical to delta for simple call options. (Incidentally, the delta for put options is just 100 percent minus this probability.) Hence, an option that is sufficiently in-the-money to have an 80 percent chance of still being in-the-money at expiration will move up 80 cents for every dollar its underlying stock moves up.

It should be clear that the relationship between the value of an option and the price of its underlying stock is not static because the probability that the option will expire in-the-money is always changing. When the option is in-the-money, its value is tightly linked to the stock; but when it is out-of-the-money, it is largely detached from it. Focusing on any single moment in time, however, the option can be viewed as representing some fraction of a share of stock. For that frozen moment in time, we can replicate the performance of the option through the purchase of a fractional share of stock. However, because this stock will cost more than the option, we will need to borrow money to replicate the leverage that the option provides. For example, a typical at-the-money option that can be replicated with one-half a share of stock might trade for 10 percent of the price of the stock. The equivalent amount of stock needed to replicate that option costs 50 percent of the price of a share. The option provides only 10 percent of that, so the other 40 percent must be borrowed to finance the fractional share purchase. Following this reasoning, one can replicate any option using two other assets: a fractional share of the underlying stock and a loan to finance its purchase. The value of the loan that the option implicitly gives its holder is determined by the prevailing interest rate and the time until the option expires. In particular, options are more valuable when interest rates are higher and when the time to expiration is longer.

We are now ready to rejoin Fischer Black, Myron Scholes, and Robert Merton at MIT. Their method for valuing options was equivalent to a dynamic trading strategy that continuously changes the amount of stock held and the amount of money borrowed in order to replicate the option. This equivalence does not come easily, however; it requires two very strong assumptions.

The first assumption is that changes in the price of the underlying asset follow what is essentially a random walk. Hence, based on Paul Samuelson's research, the market for the underlying asset is always perfectly efficient in the sense of reflecting all available information about the asset. This assumption reasonably characterizes how the prices of most assets behave most of the time.

The second assumption needed to value options requires an even greater degree of market efficiency. In order to implement the indicated dynamic hedging strategy, one must be able to buy and sell both the underlying asset and risk-free debt at their efficient-market prices at every moment in time.

The new kind of market perfection that Black, Scholes, and Merton needed to value options was perfect *liquidity*. Underlying the notion of perfect competition in markets is the assumption of a large number of buyers and sellers; something that laboratory market experiments indicated was not strictly required for the market to operate efficiently. One side effect of having so many buyers and sellers is that the market more readily accommodates the trades of any individual buyer or seller. This ease of transacting is equivalent to saying that the market is *liquid*; whereas, in an *illiquid* market, individuals might have to wait a long time in order to transact. The difficulty with this assumption, which turned into a major problem on Black Monday, is that markets take time to adjust to new information—sometimes minutes, sometimes hours, and sometimes (during a crisis) days. (In retrospect, *liquidity* is a misnomer because when a market *melts down* it becomes illiquid rather than liquid.)

The key assumptions of the Black-Scholes-Merton option valuation model may be unrealistic, but they are often a close enough approximation to reality to make the model an important and practical tool. Furthermore, having made these assumptions, they could then go on to do what statisticians and other economists could not—find an exact option valuation formula.

The Black-Scholes-Merton approach works because the replication argument holds regardless of the risk preferences of the individuals in the economy. In particular, a world in which everyone is risk-neutral will yield the same value for the option as our "real world," in which attitudes toward risk are both varied and unobservable. In this risk-neutral world, the mathematics of computing uncertain payoffs becomes unambiguous. Recall that, when we were in the grocery store hanging out by the peanut butter display, the possibility that a jar's value might depend on the flip of a coin was explored. For risk-neutral subjects, it is easy to value a jar that is worth $30 for heads and $10 for tails; the value is the mid-point of $20 as long as heads and tails are equally likely. Options can be valued in a similar manner; however, instead of two possible outcomes—heads and tails— there are considerably more possibilities.

Fortunately, the basic workings of options valuation can be understood by examining just three possibilities. In the employee stock option example given above, the company chose to present a rosy scenario for the future value of its shares. Suppose that in addition to fixing the flaws in the company's valuation method we add two more scenarios to provide a more balanced picture of the future possibilities. We will call these three scenarios *High*, *Average*, and *Low* to reflect the value of the stock when the option expires.

In our hypothetical world composed entirely of risk-neutral people, all securities will have the same expected rate of return because no one will need to be compensated for taking on risk. Hence, the expected rate of return for all assets will be the same as the risk-free rate of return. If we assume that over the five-year life of the option, the risk-free rate of return is 50 percent, which is about 8 percent per annum, then it follows that in the *Average* scenario, the company's stock will also rise 50 percent from $50 per share to $75 per share.

Constructing plausible *High* and *Low* scenarios for the stock requires that we know something about the variability of its return, in other words, its volatility. The risk-free asset is distinguished by having zero volatility; it pays the risk-free rate of return with absolute certainty. All other assets, including stocks, have positive volatilities. Suppose for the company in question that a reasonable *High* scenario is a 150 percent increase in the share price to $125 per share and that a reasonable *Low* scenario is a 50 percent decline to $25 per share. Finally, we will work on the assumption that the three scenarios have been chosen so that they are equally likely; that is, each has a probability of $\frac{1}{3}$.

The *Low* scenario is the easiest to handle because each option expires worthless. Indeed, it does not matter whether our guess of $25 for the price of the stock is accurate; the option has no value in any *Low* scenario where the stock price falls. In the *Average* scenario, the option will be exercised and generate a net return of $25: $75 minus the $50 exercise price. In the *High* scenario, things are even better. With the stock price up to $125 per share, the net return from exercising the option is $75.

Averaging the payoffs of $0, $25, and $75 for the three scenarios gives $33.33 as the value of the option in five years. To get its present value we must divide this by $\frac{2}{3}$ to take into account the 50 percent discount rate over the five-year period, which gives $22.22 per option. (Note that 50 percent more than $22.22 gets us back to $33.33.) This rough estimate produces a more reasonable value than the worksheet estimate of $50 per option.

Options valuation methods that use the Black-Scholes-Merton framework take this example and expand it to consider many more scenarios and use stock prices that are not just arbitrarily determined. The more complicated method of replicating the value of the option with the purchase of fractional shares of stock financed with debt does not need to be considered explicitly; however, the fact that such arbitrage exists allows us to operate with impunity in a risk-neutral world. The only major adjustment that we need to make in this hypothetical world is that rate of return for all assets is the same as the risk-free rate.

The Formula for Options

The more scenarios one considers, the more difficult and time-consuming it will be to compute the value of an option; however, this is true only as long as we consider only a finite number of scenarios. If we consider an infinite number of possibilities, things can become more manageable. Indeed, Fischer Black and Myron Scholes found that if we set up the infinite possibilities in just the right way, a general formula for valuing options falls right out.

Based on what we have seen thus far, in order to value an option we must know five things about it: the time until it expires, its exercise price, the risk-free rate of return, the price of its underlying stock, and the volatility of its underlying stock. The first two items are part of the specification of the option, so they are automatically known to us. The risk-free rate of return is only somewhat more difficult to ascertain. The yield on the Treasury security that most closely matches the life of the option provides an adequate approximation to the risk-free rate as noted earlier.

The final two items, stock price and volatility, are more difficult to determine because they are theoretical abstractions. The stock price would appear not to present any problems because all we have to do is obtain a real-time quote for the stock and we know its price. But the stock price that we need to know to value the option is the theoretical price at which the stock would be trading *right now*. In a rapidly moving market, even a quote a few seconds old might not be accurate enough to value the option, so that the problem of nonsynchronicity arises. (In some cases, a stock's options may trade more frequently than the stock itself, and so the option pricing mechanism can be inverted to estimate the current value of the stock given the prices of its options.) With this caveat duly noted and considered, the price at which a stock last traded is usually adequate for computing the value of an option on that stock.

A stock's price may not appear that abstract, but its volatility certainly is. Intuitively, a stock's volatility is quite real; the difference in volatility from stock to stock is something one can feel in one's gut. Some stocks seem barely to move, while others take their investors and traders on a terrifying roller-coaster ride. On a day-to-day basis, the movements of stocks and other assets depend on a combination of news and noise. Viewed over the longer term, individual stocks tend to "drift" higher on average, but a wide range of returns, including negative ones, is possible.

A historical graph of the rate of return received from owning stocks is approximately normally distributed. For example, the graph of the aggregate monthly rate of return for U.S. stocks in the postwar era (Figure 7.1) resembles the usual bell-shaped curve that describes a wide range of naturally occurring phenomena, such as men's or women's heights in a given population. However, these monthly returns, as well as those for most assets, are not quite normally distributed—their tails are "too fat"—so that extremely high or low returns occur more frequently than in a normal distribution.

Asset returns may not strictly be normally distributed, but the normal distribution is a close enough approximation for most casual analysis. The normal distribution has the advantage that we can characterize the infinity of possibilities that it represents by just two numbers: its mean value and its

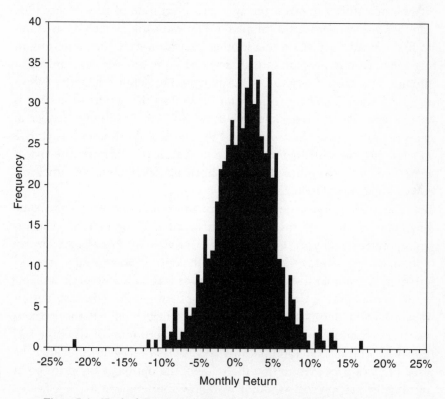

Figure 7.1 **Typical Frequency Distribution of Monthly Stock Return in the United States Since World War II**

standard deviation (the spread about the mean). For a stock, its mean return measures the natural tendency of the stock price to drift higher over
time and the standard deviation of the return is the amount that it will deviate from that upward drift on average. A typical stock might have a mean
annual return of 15 percent and a standard deviation of 30 percent. For the
normal distribution, approximately 95 percent of the time the result will
fall within two standard deviations of the mean, so the stock in question
would see a return of between -45 percent and +75 percent in 19 out of
20 years. In valuing the option, the mean return of 15 percent is no longer
relevant, because the valuation is done in the hypothetical risk-neutral
world where all mean returns are equal to the risk-free rate; however, the
volatility of that return remains critically important.

The Black-Scholes-Merton approach to option valuation assumes that
changes in stock prices are normally distributed and that the standard deviation of a stock's return is the appropriate measure of its volatility. One
can then use standard statistical methods for estimating standard deviations
to find the volatility of a stock or other asset from its historical returns. In
certain situations, procedures that are more complex may be required to
produce an accurate estimate of volatility and to adjust for the fat tails of
the distribution. The basic mathematics of valuing the option is the same as
in the three-scenario example, only now we have an infinite number of
possible stock prices that correspond to a normal distribution of returns.
(Technically, the distribution of stock prices on the exercise date that is
generated by these returns is not itself normally distributed, but rather follows a lognormal distribution.)

The mathematics required to derive an explicit formula for the value
of an option when returns are normally distributed comes from an analogous problem in physics. In addition to the five items that characterize an
option, we know one other thing about the option: how to value it at expiration. Recall that if the stock price exceeds the exercise price at expiration, a call option is worth the difference between the two; otherwise, it
is worthless. Conversely, put options are valuable only if the stock is
worth less than the exercise price. This characterization of what the option is worth at expiration, known as a *boundary condition*, can then be
used to work backward to find the value of the option at any prior point
in time. In the physical world, if we know the temperature of a heated
object—such as a pot on a stove—along its boundary, it is possible to
compute the temperature anywhere in the object at any later time by

computing how the heat diffuses through the object. Similarly, economists use a *diffusion process* based on the random walk of the stock's price
to compute the value of the option at any point in time before expiration. The only significant difference is that heat diffuses forward in time
from the heat source and option value diffuses backward in time from the
expiration date. By using a diffusion process that allowed them to average
the value of the option at each of the infinite points along the normal
distribution of stock prices, Black and Scholes derived a formula for valuing certain simple call options.

The Black–Scholes formula appeared at the just the right moment.
Within months of its publication in 1973, Hewlett-Packard introduced the
first programmable handheld calculator: its HP 65. Although it was designed with the computations of scientists and engineers in mind, the HP
65 turned out to be ideal for computing the value of options using the
Black–Scholes formula, which was sufficiently complex that a standard calculator without programming capabilities would have difficulty handling
it. Furthermore, the HP 65 was portable enough to be operated just about
anywhere, including the floor of the Chicago Board Options Exchange,
which also opened for business in 1973. The confluence of these three
events—the formula, the calculator, and the exchange—produced a boom
in options.

The Black–Scholes formula can be easily adapted to value some options and less easily to value others. In general, options that can be exercised only on their expiration date may be valued using an almost identical
formula. For example, the formulas for a put and call option are virtually
the same. What can complicate matters significantly is that most options,
like standard calls and puts, are exercisable at any time before their expiration date. These freely exercisable options are known as *American options*—
in contrast to the more restrictive *European options*—and they are too
complex to value precisely with a formula.

Any option with a value that can be affected by events occurring during its life usually cannot be valued using an exact formula. Instead, the
value of such an option must be approximated using numerical methods
or specially derived formulas. In addition to early exercise, a common
event that can affect the value of an option is a dividend payment, which
decreases the stock's price by approximately the amount of the dividend
while providing no offsetting benefit to the optionholder. Numerical
methods value options using *trees* that provide a discrete approximation of

everything that could happen between the acquisition and the expiration of the option. (The earlier example used a simple tree, a *trinomial tree* with a single node, to compute a rough approximation to the value of the option.) Each of the possibly millions of paths from the root (acquisition time) of the tree to the tip of one of its branches (expiration time) traces the evolution of the asset prices and the events that might affect the value of the option. While even the most elaborate tree cannot include every chain of events that might occur during the option's life, with proper design it can capture enough of them to value the option with reasonable accuracy. The trees generated for many derivative securities are sufficiently daunting that they will continue to tax even the most powerful computers for some time to come.

The assumptions required to value options, particularly those governing how asset prices change over time, are not always an accurate reflection of financial behavior. Because of the money at stake, research into ways to refine and extend the Black-Scholes model became a top priority on Wall Street. Much of this effort went into designing and testing better models of volatility, replacing the restrictive assumption of a normal distribution of returns with a more flexible specification that would allow volatility to change over time. These new models of volatility, which sometimes sport unattractive names such as GARCH, were better able to capture the fact that the occasional steep market plunge causes the tails of the returns distribution to be fatter than they would be with a normal distribution.

We face an even greater challenge if instead of taking volatility as an externally determined factor that appears to follow a given probability distribution, we try to build it into a general equilibrium model of the economy. Mordecai Kurz at Stanford University has made the development of such a model the central focus of his research program. By introducing the concept of *rational beliefs*, a less restrictive model of economic behavior than the rational expectation model allows for rational differences of opinion, Kurz and his collaborators look to extend general equilibrium models to explain volatility.

Although we cannot yet fully model volatility, there is much that we can do with it. Just as we could invert the option valuation procedure to find the stock price that corresponded to a particular option price, we can also invert it to compute the volatility associated with a given option price, which is known as the *implied volatility* of the option. Under ordinary circumstances, implied volatility is a more accurate estimate of the future volatility of an asset than anything that can be computed using historical data. The relationship between the volatility of options and their price has become so ingrained in financial markets that many options are quoted not in price, but in terms of their implied volatility. Speculators will often purchase an option if they think its true volatility is higher than its implied volatility and sell it if they think it is lower. Furthermore, just as stock speculation focuses on whether the price of a stock will rise or fall, professional option traders frequently bet on the future direction of an option's implied volatility.

Beginning in the 1980s, every major Wall Street investment firm hired large numbers of "rocket scientists"—some who had actually once been real rocket scientists, but mostly just Ph.D.s in mathematics and physics—to invent option-pricing models and apply them to the development of new financial products. The potential profitability of this enterprise was enormous; the ability to value options more accurately than your clients was a license to print money. Wall Street firms would compete on their ability to create complex new options that only the option's inventor knew how to value properly. Once relegated to the back pages of financial newspapers, options soon traded on several exchanges. Indeed, it seemed that everywhere one looked there were options waiting to be discovered.

The Universal Nature of Options

When Fischer Black and Myron Scholes first submitted the article with their formula to the *Journal of Political Economy*, it was rejected without the benefit of an outside referee's opinion. The *Journal* did not find the article worth considering because a technique for valuing a particular financial instrument was seen as too specialized for a journal with a reputation for publishing articles that made fundamental contributions to economics. Just as it had taken Vernon Smith considerable effort to get his first article on experimental markets accepted at the *Journal* more than 10 years earlier, Fischer Black and Myron Scholes went through their own publication ordeal. In order to make the article appeal to a broader audience, Black and Scholes made clear that options were not just an obscure financial instrument, but were in one way or another embedded in every security in the financial marketplace. The generalization of their results, along with the intervention of two of the journal's editors, led to the eventual publication of the article. Robert Merton's independent work on option valuation, which was published in a more specialized economics journal, similarly made the case that options were a fundamental part of finance.

The two most common types of securities, stocks and bonds, have options woven deeply into their fabric. As we noted earlier, stockholders have limited liability; if things go badly for the firm, they can just walk away, making those owed money by the firm its new owners. Viewed as an option, a share of stock is equivalent to a call option that never expires and that bears an exercise price of zero. Just as the holder of a call option should choose to let it expire worthless when the price of the underlying securities is below the exercise price, the stockholders of a company will abandon it when its liabilities exceed its assets.

For bonds, the options that they contain are less subtle. While the abandonment option embedded in stocks benefits the holder, the various options embedded in bonds benefit the issuer. This should come as no surprise once we recognize that the holder of the stock and the issuer of the bonds are the same entity: the owner of the company. Indeed, the abandonment option of the stock manifests itself in bonds as an option to default on the payment of the bond.

The option to default is just one of many options that most corporate bonds possess. The option to redeem the bond before its maturity at a specified *call price* is a standard feature of corporate bonds. A 10-year corporate bond will typically include a call provision that allows the issuer to redeem the bond according to a schedule of call prices at any time after the bond's fifth anniversary. Call provisions give the issuer the flexibility to refinance the company's debt if interest rates decline or to reduce the company's debt if a financial structure with less leverage is desirable. On the other hand, the *covenants* attached to a bond serve to limit the options available to the issuer. These covenants may limit the ability of the company to issue additional debt or take other actions that would impair its ability to repay its debt. In addition, the option to transfer the debt to a third party is usually restricted by the covenant.

While the owners of a company are free to embed whatever options they want into the bonds they issue, they must pay a price in the marketplace for the options they retain for themselves. The added flexibility that options give the issuer comes at the cost of the bondholder, and so competitive market forces drive up the interest rates on such bonds as compared with those with few or no options. Indeed, the bonds with the fewest options attached to them are those issued by the U.S. Treasury, which tend to provide the lowest dollar-denominated yields. With the exception of some callable bonds issued during a few years when interest rates were high, Treasury debt comes without options—even default is not a serious option.

Armed with fancy mathematical tools that could accommodate options, economists began to see options embedded in everything. At some universities, library closing times are a source of friction between students and the administration. Students may want libraries to be open around the clock, but the university administration, believing that the cost of keeping them open is not justified by the small number of students using them late at night and on weekends, are happy to see them close early. What the administration argument misses—and economics graduate students are eager to point out—is the *option demand* for the libraries. By keeping the libraries open late, a student could work on a project at all hours secure in the knowledge that if she needed to check a critical reference in the library it would be open. It did not matter that students rarely used the library at odd hours; the important thing (which registered neither on the clicker-toting library guards nor on the administrators who employed them) was the option that having the library open provided to students.

The options that exist beyond the financial world are known as *real options*. Real options are not limited to libraries, but extend in one way or another to almost every human activity. Companies may spend large amounts on research in order to expand their options. Although few corporate research efforts are seen all the way through to final products, even the products that do not make it to market provide valuable options for the company. Savvy research managers find themselves increasingly in the role of portfolio managers, where their portfolios consist of the patents and other technologies that they have either developed internally or have available to them through licensing agreements. The options created through research are valuable not only to their creator but also to its competitors; a patent not only grants options to its owner—it denies those options to everyone else.

Another source of real options concerns the timing of a decision. The ability to delay making a decision pending the arrival of new information can be a very valuable option. The entertainment industry has long appreciated the value of "buying time" to make a decision. Movie producers rarely purchase the screen rights to a book or a script without first optioning the material to determine whether they can assemble the director, cast, financing, and so forth. Only when a producer is relatively sure that the film can be made will he purchase the rights to it. Even when the screen rights are ultimately purchased, the producer retains the right to abandon production at any time—the rights to make a film generally do not obligate the producer either to complete it or bring it to market. Even though it is quite common for movie options not to be exercised—indeed, some material is repeatedly optioned before being produced or abandoned—these options are quite valuable and can command a sizeable fraction of the price of the screen rights. From an options point of view, procrastination is not as bad as some people might have you believe. What appears to be procrastination might just be the economically valuable activity of "keeping one's options open."

Options Rule on Wall Street

The greatest impact from the view that "all the world's an option" was felt on Wall Street. As we just saw, those who go to the financial markets for funding have a strong preference for embedded options that provide them with the most flexibility. On the other hand, many large institutional investors, such as pension funds, are legally restricted in the options that they can grant a borrower, especially the option to default. For example, pension funds can invest only a small fraction of their assets in debt that has not received an *investment grade* rating (from BBB– up through AAA, the highest rating) from a major ratings agency such as Standard & Poor's or Moody's. In addition, because the liabilities of pension funds, which take the form of the pensions they must ultimately pay out to employees, extend far into the future, they tend to place less value on debt that might be called prior to its maturity. Wall Street saw this mismatch between those who issue and those who purchase debt as presenting it with a major opportunity. By "slicing and dicing" debt securities, Wall Street could remove the options that were problematic for pension funds and sell them to investors and speculators who were more willing to bear the risk of an early call.

The U.S. market for mortgages on single-family homes became the frontier of slice-and-dice finance. Mortgages are debt instruments that contain a number of interesting options. The option of greatest financial interest is the prepayment option. Unlike corporate debt, which cannot be prepaid (called) for years after issuance, home mortgages can be prepaid at any time with little or no penalty. The ability to prepay provides the homeowner the option to move in order to take a new job or for any other reason without the continuing burden of the mortgage. More importantly, it allows the homeowner to refinance her mortgage in order to take advantage of a decline in interest rates or an increase in the value of the home covered by the mortgage.

Another way that options enter into home mortgages is that mortgages are secured loans with limited recourse. The house that is purchased with the mortgage effectively serves as the only security available to the lender. If the homeowner defaults on the mortgage by failing to make a payment on time, all the lender can do is take possession of the house (subject to the limitations of the state in which it is located) and place a black mark on the borrower's credit record. The lender will usually have a difficult time getting to the other assets of the borrower, providing the borrower with a potentially valuable option. If the value of the house falls below the balance of the mortgage, the homeowner can "walk away" from the home, leaving the lender with the loss that will generally be easier to write off than try to recoup. Of course, by declaring bankruptcy the borrower can sometimes escape the clutches of the mortgage lender completely.

Mortgage lending in the United States began as a community affair. As depicted in the Christmas cinema classic, *It's a Wonderful Life*, a local financial institution, the Bailey Building & Loan, would lend to homeowners using the money received from the deposits of the local citizens. This model of mortgage lending had two major limitations. First, the pool of money available for mortgages was limited by the propensity to save in the local community. Second, while mortgages were long-term commitments for the lender, the deposits that financed them were only short-term commitments for the depositors. Runs on these deposits, which were common during the Great Depression, would cause lenders—whose assets were tied up in the mortgages—to fail.

The two limitations facing the Bailey Building & Loan were eliminated by the creation of a nationwide mortgage market that issued *mortgage-backed securities*. The Federal National Mortgage Association (Fannie Mae), the Federal Home Loan Mortgage Corporation (Freddie Mac), and other government and private sources of mortgage finance create portfolios (or bundles) with large numbers of home mortgages and fund them by issuing debt that "passes through" the mortgage payments to the holders of this *passthrough debt*. (This process of turning mortgages into traded debt securities, which can also be applied to other types of debt, is known as *securitization*.) Local financial institutions could still originate mortgages by processing the applications and collecting the origination fees. When the mortgages closed, they would then sell them to be bundled with other mortgages from around the country.

The bundling of mortgages is financially advantageous because it diversifies away most of the "micro" risk associated with mortgage debt. Nonetheless, the bundle that is created still has a massive exposure to "macro" risk, especially the tendency of the prepayment option to be exercised whenever interest rates decline sufficiently. The exposure of these bundles to the options embedded in them, a property known as *optionality*, is enough to limit the appetite of pension funds for this kind of debt.

By the early 1980s, the more mathematically inclined and adventurous Wall Street professionals found that not only could the options contained within mortgages be valued, they could be sliced out of them by creating several *tranches* (the French word for "sections") of new securities that were backed by bundles of individual home mortgages. The top tranche is designed to have minimal exposure to prepayments, making it suitable for pension funds. The middle tranches have more exposure to prepayments; however, because this prepayment risk is related to interest rates, these tranches can be used to balance other risks in a diversified portfolio. The risk of default tends to be concentrated in the lowest tranches along with the prepayment risk left over from the middle tranches. At the very bottom is the *toxic waste* that is often difficult to sell to anyone because of the complexity of the options embedded in it. It is tempting for an investment banker eager to make a deal to hold the toxic waste in inventory until a buyer for it can be found. While mishaps related to retaining toxic waste were frequent before investment banks developed the information systems necessary to handle them—in one notable case, an investment banker literally hid the toxic waste in a desk drawer (at his next job, his desk drawers were nailed shut as a prank)—modern risk management practices hold investment bankers accountable for every risk to which they expose their firms.

Unfortunately, disasters in the frontier days of mortgage-backed securities were not always confined to a single financial institution. Some of the riskier tranches of mortgage-backed securities found their way back to the balance sheets of the same community lenders who used to hold the loans directly and this helped contribute to the Savings and Loan

(S&L) crisis of the late 1980s. The willingness of S&Ls to buy into toxic waste and other risky investments was itself an unintended side effect of an option in the form of the federal insurance provided to their depositors. The S&Ls were able to get deposits on favorable terms because the deposits were federally insured by the FSLIC (Federal Savings and Loan Insurance Corporation). The rising interest rates during the second half of the 1980s placed severe pressures on all financial institutions, but they especially stressed Savings & Loan institutions. As many S&Ls found themselves to be technically insolvent—that is, their liabilities exceeded their assets when valued at market prices (as opposed to the historical prices that the government let them get away with using in their accounting books)—the option to declare bankruptcy became quite valuable to them. They were in a position where they could raise their interest rates to attract (insured) deposits and then place the deposits in risky investments knowing that any further downside was limited. Although some S&Ls engaged in illegal activities as part of this speculative binge, most of the S&Ls that eventually went under violated no laws in the process; they simply exploited some unintended consequences of the deregulation of financial institutions.

By the middle of the 1990s, the securitization techniques developed for mortgages spread to other debt securities once the financial markets had time to recover. Even rock stars could make their name in the financial markets. *Bowie bonds* were structured around the anticipated future royalties from a catalog of songs written by musician and actor David Bowie. Similar *asset-backed securities* were created using almost any asset with reasonable prospects of generating future cash flows—first-run movies, accounting partnerships, auto loans and leases, credit cards, home improvement loans, and so on.

Some lenders discovered that the consequences of ignoring optionality could be most dire. In the United States, leases on automobiles and related vehicles typically give the lessee the option to purchase the vehicle when the lease expires. Even decades after the publication of the Black-Scholes formula, many finance companies did not take the value of this option into account when computing the lease terms. Given the high volatility of used car prices, this option could be quite valuable; even a lessee with no intention of keeping his or her vehicle may find it advantageous to purchase it at the end of the lease so he or she can sell it at a profit. The finance companies that failed to price this option into their leases ultimately found themselves submerged in an ocean of red ink.

Spreads and the Risk of Default

Wall Street reports the values of most taxable bonds, including asset-backed and corporate bonds, both in terms of their price and their *option-adjusted spread* (OAS). The OAS gives the difference in the interest rate between the bond after the embedded options have been stripped from it and the interest rate on an (option-free) U.S. Treasury security of comparable maturity. The quoted OAS may differ from broker to broker because of differences in modeling the future path of interest rates; however, most quotes are similar. (Many brokers and quote services provide software to their clients that lets them control how OAS is computed.)

For example, a corporate bond may have a yield of 9 percent if held to maturity, but if it is called prior to maturity it could yield as little as 6 percent—known as the yield to worst (YTW). The bond is more likely to be called early if interest rates decline, enabling the issuer to refinance the bond at a lower interest rate. The expected value of this bond's yield computed over all possible paths of future interest rates might come out to be 7.18 percent. If the comparable Treasury bond has a yield of 6.68 percent, then the OAS for the bond is 7.18 percent minus 6.68 percent or 0.50 percent. Spreads on bonds are usually quoted in hundredths of a percent, known as *basis points, b.p.* for short and pronounced "bip," so this bond would sport a spread of 50 b.p.

The difference between this bond's apparent yield of 9 percent and its true, option-adjusted yield of 7.18 percent shows the value of the call option that is embedded in it and makes the value of the bond particularly sensitive to changes in interest rates. This sensitivity to interest rates affects all bonds to some degree. The risk that comes from changes in the overall level of interest rates is known as *market risk*. Similarly, a stock has exposure to market risk to the extent that it is exposed to changes in overall stock prices as measured by a broad stock price index. Although the market risk of bonds and that of stocks overlap, they are distinct.

The option-adjusted spread adjusts only for options related to changes in interest rates. Another option, the option to default, accounts for much of the risk that the option-adjusted spread captures. The ability of the issuer to default introduces *credit risk* on top of the market risk already contained in the bond.

When they developed their option pricing model, Black, Scholes, and Merton were aware that their work could be applied to deriving a probability of default for a bond, also known as the bond's *expected default frequency* (EDF). For example, we find from historical data that AAA-rated bonds have an EDF of about 0.01 percent (1 b.p.) or one default per year for every 10,000 bonds.

The criteria for AAA ratings are so stringent that few corporate bonds have merited it in recent years. In modern times, only one corporation has defaulted on bonds within a year of bearing a triple-A rating. That company, Texaco, was driven into default not because of financial or operational problems, but because it unexpectedly received an extremely adverse ruling in an antitrust lawsuit brought against it by Pennzoil, a rival oil company, that drove it into bankruptcy.

Bonds with lower ratings will usually have higher EDFs. *High-yield bonds*, popularly known as *junk bonds*, are bonds that are considered so risky that they are unable to qualify for investment-grade ratings. Such bonds have high EDFs and so must have a higher interest rate to compensate for the increased credit risk.

Building on the insights of option pricing models one could estimate the default risk contained in a corporate bond using information about the issuer's stock—its market value and volatility—and data from its balance sheet to estimate the bond's EDF. Recall that it is the stockholders who hold the option to default on their company's debt, and so the value of this default option contributes to the value of the stock, at least if the financial markets are reasonably efficient. Over time, EDFs computed using option valuation theory—such as those provided by KMV Corporation, a San Francisco firm closely linked to the quantitative finance revolution—have been shown to enhance the predictive value of agency credit ratings.

Liquidity: The Ultimate Option

Estimating bond EDFs is just one of the many applications that the "everything is an option" viewpoint has spawned. The application of the option-based worldview to all of finance is complicated by the fact that the options embedded within a security are likely to interact with one another. In particular, if you take a bond and embed a single new option in it, the value of that option depends on all the options previously embedded in the bond. Hence, the value of each embedded option cannot be determined independently and then simply added together—a property known as *separability*. Options are inherently inseparable; the value of each depends on the context created by all the other options. What makes matters worse is that the interactions between these options are extremely challenging to model. For example, in a mortgage the prepayment option and the default option interact in numerous subtle ways. It is not enough to model the overall level of interest rates; we need to know the economic factors that influence them. Low interest rates that are a result of a decline in the price level (lower inflation) are very different from low interest rates brought about by a recession.

Embedded options and the interactions among them account for most of a bond's risk premium, but they do not account for it all. The remaining premium reflects the liquidity of the bond, which as we noted earlier was the ease with which it can be bought and sold. Bonds can be liquid to varying degrees; indeed, bonds from the same issuer may not enjoy the same liquidity. For example, not all Treasury securities provide equivalent liquidity. Treasury securities that have been recently issued, known as *on-the-run* bonds or notes, have a significantly lower yield than more seasoned issues, known as *off-the-run* bonds or notes.

Assets other than bonds also vary greatly in their liquidity. Furthermore, the liquidity of a given asset can change in response to market conditions. An asset that suddenly becomes unpopular can see its liquidity disappear completely. The premium attached to an illiquid security can be viewed as compensating the holder for the inconvenience that he or she may encounter when attempting to liquidate or rebalance a position in that security. The problems of Long-Term Capital Management, the hedge fund in which Robert Merton and Myron Scholes were partners, are rooted in a failure to appreciate the risk associated with the returns that it received for assuming *liquidity risk*.

A quick indication of an asset's liquidity is its bid/ask spread, the difference between the highest bid (to buy) and lowest offer (to sell) prices. For example, on the New York Stock Exchange, many of the actively traded companies, such as General Electric and IBM, often trade at a spread close to the smallest possible trading increment. Historically, this increment was $\frac{1}{8}$ of a dollar (12.5 cents); however, the switchover to decimal trading in 2001 dropped this increment to a single cent. The reduction of this increment was strongly resisted by members of the exchange, for whom a larger bid/ask means higher profits. As one would expect, securities that trade infrequently tend to have larger bid/ask spreads.

Liquidity tends to be more of a problem for bonds than for stocks. The *round lot* for shares of stock is 100 shares, so that a round lot of a stock selling for $20 per share would cost just $2,000. In contrast, the round lot for most corporate bonds has a *par value* (the value at maturity) of from $1,000,000 to $5,000,000. A typical bond offering of $200,000,000 will normally be allocated to a few dozen large institutional investors, such as insurance companies and pension funds, that intend to hold them until maturity to fund their outstanding liabilities to policy or pension holders. The typical stock, on the other hand, has many thousands of owners with relatively few of them committed to long-term holdings.

The investment bank that underwrites a bond offering will usually retain some bonds in order to make a secondary market in them. Even with the coming of electronic markets for bonds, few bonds are traded on exchanges, so the only way to trade bonds is to deal directly with the investment bank that underwrote the offering. The market power of the underwriter combined with the lack of liquidity for most corporate bonds allows it to maintain a large bid/ask spread. Usually, this spread is so embarrassingly large that the investment banks hide it from their customers by only providing the bid to potential sellers and the ask to potential buyers.

Like everything else, liquidity can manifest itself as an option. Call and put options, for example, come with a liquidity option already built into them. An American call option (exercisable at any time before its expiration) that gives the option to buy the stock at a price of $50 conveys that option regardless of the current liquidity of the stock (with the notable exception of formal trading halts imposed by exchanges or regulators). Similarly, an American put option includes a liquidity option that will facilitate its sale at a predetermined price. The options embedded in most securities, on the other hand, do not convey liquidity. Holders of stocks and bonds are stuck until they can find a willing buyer.

To the extent that liquidity exists for any given security, it exists not as an intrinsic property of that security, but rather it is as much a property of the market(s) in which the security trades. The general lack of liquidity in corporate bonds contributes a significant proportion of their spread relative to Treasury securities. For a large institutional investor planning to hold a corporate bond until redemption, its higher yield may be ample compensation for its lack of liquidity.

Our journey through the world of options has brought us back to the market mechanism itself, which is the source of all liquidity. Matching buyers and sellers together at mutually agreeable prices not only takes time, as we shall see in the next chapter, it also takes options. The dual requirements of time and options make it virtually impossible for this matching process to provide anything that approaches a perfectly liquid market. Indeed, sometimes ensuring even minimal liquidity can be quite a challenge.

8

The Invisible Hand Discovers Prices

The giant step that one must take to move from the abstract world of Adam Smith's invisible hand to the concrete world of markets—both in and out of the laboratory—is the specification of the dynamic process known as *price discovery*. Starting with Vernon Smith's oral double auctions, experiments have provided masses of raw data that demonstrate how the market uses the bids and offers of subjects to determine prices. Although experimental markets generally converge rapidly to the competitive price and quantity, the process by which the market equilibrates will necessarily involve trades away from equilibrium that temporarily impair efficiency. Hence, Milton Friedman's famous saying, "There is no such thing as a free lunch," ironically applies to his most beloved of institutions—the market. The tab for the feast of market efficiency is paid by the inefficiencies inherent in any process that discovers prices. Keeping open any possibility of finding a perfect market mechanism that can eliminate these inefficiencies requires a thorough understanding of price discovery.

Price discovery is complicated by a dilemma that every buyer and seller faces. Every time a buyer places a bid or a seller places an offer, he or she grants an option to the other participants in the market. For example, a buyer who bids $50 for a share of stock gives every seller an option to sell that stock to him for $50. Furthermore, the bidder provides free information to everyone else in the market—the stock is worth at least $50 to him. While the buyer may feel badly about giving away something valuable by the very act of bidding, unless he places a bid, he may not be able to purchase the item. Indeed, if buyers and sellers, recognizing the value of the options that they create for others in the market through their bids and offers, would all remain silent while waiting for someone else to move first, the market would fail completely. Absent bids and offers, trade is impossible.

This dilemma is not limited to the double oral auction, but extends to all trading situations. For example, face-to-face bargaining between a single buyer and a single seller has the problem that every action creates options and transfers information. Even the timing of an action conveys information. The last thing that a buyer or seller wants to see is that his initial bid or offer has been taken without hesitation. Unless the other party to the bargain is naïve or pressed for time, this is a clear indication that a better deal was possible. For this reason it never pays to take the first bid or offer; it is always better to let your bargaining adversary feel that he or she has driven a hard bargain rather than leave with the impression that he or she has been taken.

Most financial markets involve institutional arrangements that compound this dilemma. In these markets, the privilege of accepting an open bid or offer may not be granted to the public at large, but is only available to members of the exchange. The most that an outsider can expect is to be lucky enough to have his or her bid or offer *crossed* (directly matched up) with an identical order on the other side of the market. Some markets have provisions for crossing small orders before the members of the exchange can get to them in order to protect small investors; nonetheless, many exchanges have members who will gladly "scalp" both sides of a matching order. While experimental markets force buyers and sellers to name a limit price to prevent them from inadvertently trading at a loss, many brokers encourage the submission of *market orders*, which have no price limits, by charging extra for *limit orders*. A buyer or seller who submits a market order implicitly trusts his or her broker to execute the order at a price that is not only the best available, but is reasonable as well.

Many brokers, and discount brokers in particular, sell the *order flow* of their customers' market orders directly to market makers. In this way, they are able to capture some of the option value of the orders for themselves, which they may or may not pass on to their customers in the form of lower commissions. Of course, the value of the option embedded in an order, like a traditional option, will be higher for securities that are more volatile. It is easy to see why day traders can be a broker's most valuable customers. They not only generate a steady flow of commissions, but they also tend to favor volatile stocks, increasing the value of their order flow.

Exchanges may differ in how they process orders, but most of them are able to provide a bid price and an offer price for every security they list. The ideal situation for the members of the exchange is to maintain a healthy spread between these prices and limit the privilege of buying at the bid and selling at the offer to themselves. For example, a stock might be quoted at a bid of $40 and an offer of $41. Rather than match buyers and sellers *inside the spread*—for example, at the midpoint of $40.50—market makers would ideally like to pocket $1 on each pair of trades by buying at the bid of $40 and then turning around and selling at the offer of $41. While such profits can sometimes be excessive, at other times they are justified. By bidding $40 and offering $41, the market maker is in the position of offering two options to the market, so some of the profit made from maintaining the spread goes to offset the implicit cost of these options.

The static conditions of most experimental markets limit the option value of an order by restricting the volatility to that generated as the market approaches equilibrium. In contrast, naturally occurring markets are constantly buffeted by new information. A buyer who places a bid on a company's stock just when breaking news informs the market that it has lost its largest customer risks having the order executed before he has a chance to either cancel the order or resubmit it at a lower price.

Market makers live with the lingering concern that the market will take unfair advantage of the options that they provide to it. This concern is especially great among specialists on the New York Stock Exchange, who in return for maintaining the book of limit orders for a stock (which only they can see) and the exclusive right to participate in many of the trades on the exchange floor are required by the rules of the exchange to maintain an orderly market in the shares of the stock. This means that a specialist on the NYSE—unlike a typical market maker on other exchanges—must always be willing to buy or sell shares of the stock when it is open for trade. Under most circumstances, the cost of the options that the specialist must supply to the market is a small price in comparison with the power that comes with his unique position in the market.

Price Impact and Market Manipulations

The reluctance of any individual to bear the cost of price discovery in a market is an example of a more general economic situation known as the *free rider problem*, which arises whenever the costly actions of one individual benefit others without their having to pay for it. The free rider problem is most apparent for *public goods*, such as national defense and clean air, which create benefits for individuals in the economy collectively and where no mechanism exists to exclude individuals who do not pay (the free riders) from also receiving the benefit. In the United States, public television stations, which are partially funded with donations from their viewers, use their periodic fundraising campaigns to induce guilt among the free riders in their audiences in the hope that they will ante up their fair share of the station's expenses.

While most individual investors view commissions as the major cost of trading securities because they are so visible, the cost of commissions is often dwarfed by the *price impact* of a trade. Price impact, which is sometimes called *market impact*, is the amount by which a trade changes the price of a security. For example, if a stock is trading at $40 per share and filling a buy order for 10,000 shares is possible only by raising the price to $40.50, the price impact of the order is then $0.50 per share, or $5,000 on the entire order. If the buyer is lucky, the price will stick at the higher price he had to pay to acquire the stock, but more frequently the price will tend to return to its earlier level, leaving the buyer with an immediate (paper) loss for his purchase. Similarly, sales of stock have a price impact that reduces the proceeds that the seller receives.

Some of the largest trading costs come not from the trades that are completed, but from those that fail to execute. In an attempt to decrease price impact, a trader can place limit orders that are not matched during a rapidly rising or falling market. The implicit costs that result from failing to enter or exit a position according to plan are surely significant, but they are very difficult to measure.

Investment funds can be the victims of their own success because of the punishing execution costs they face when trading large quantities of stock. Mutual funds and hedge funds that start out with impressive track records can see their performance lag as their success expands their assets under management. Although some funds limit the assets they are willing to manage, the lure of high management fees usually makes expansion too tempting to resist. A fund with $10 million or even $100 million under management can move in and out of the market with limited price impact while holding a portfolio that targets specific stocks or industries. Although larger funds can reduce their price impact by holding more stocks in their portfolio, this will dilute any informational edge that the fund might have.

Once a fund gets sufficiently large, some of its holdings will grow to the point that they exceed the security's average daily trading volume. For the largest mutual fund families, holdings that exceed the average trading volume for an entire week are common. Clearly, positions of this size cannot be slipped in and out of the market. The only viable approach for liquidating a large position is to dribble shares out over an extended period; however, even this strategy is not foolproof. Rumors of further sales may depress the price of the shares in advance of them. In this case, the price impact will include not only the decline in price needed to sell the first installment of shares, but also what the market anticipates will be necessary to sell any remaining shares, even if they are never actually sold. Similarly, it is difficult for large funds to take positions in securities without driving the price up substantially. While some of this price rise works to the fund's advantage by increasing the value of the first shares it acquired, these benefits accrue only on paper given the difficulty of cashing in those profits without adversely affecting the market at some later date.

The trading disadvantage that large investors face runs contrary to the popular belief that big players have the ability to manipulate and control the market. Although anyone with sufficient capital can drive the market up or down in the short run simply by purchasing or selling a security, the real question is what happens next. If a buyer can run up the price of a stock in a way that attracts other buyers, the resulting price momentum could lead to a bubble that enables him to exit the stock at a higher price, creating an intentional version of the information mirage discussed earlier. On the other hand, in the more typical case where price momentum does not build, the buyer is stuck with shares whose sale will ultimately depress the market. In an efficient market, the possibility of a manufactured information mirage backfiring is enough to discourage rational individuals from trying to manipulate the market in this way.

The greatest scope for successful market manipulation is in a *speculative attack*. The idea behind a speculative attack is simple: If you drive the price of an overvalued security down far enough through relentless selling you may not have to worry about the price impact of buying it back. In particular, if you drive the issuer out of business, nothing needs to be bought back because the shares have become worthless. The concern that a speculative attack against a stock could drive down its price is part of the motivation for the uptick rule in the United States that limits short selling of stocks to times when they are moving upward. Speculative attacks need not drive their target out of business in order to be profitable; they can also be employed against overpriced assets. Currency markets—especially those that are supported by weak central banks—are popular targets for speculative attacks.

Successful speculative attacks, such as the one George Soros mounted against the British pound in September 1992 on behalf of his flagship hedge fund, the Quantum Fund, can be extraordinarily profitable. Because he was able to both outsmart and outmaneuver the Bank of England, Mr. Soros gained international notoriety. Years after this stunning coup, hedge funds remain at the head of the list of the usual suspects whenever exchange rates gyrate inexplicably.

The importance of price impact on the lives of the rich and famous reaches beyond the hedge-fund elite. The media appears fond of reporting on the value of the corporate stock held by technology titans such as Microsoft's Bill Gates and Oracle's Larry Ellison. It is common for these moguls to gain or lose billions of dollars in a single day from changes in the price of the stock they hold in their companies. Reports of these changes tend to exaggerate the true value of these holdings, as any attempt to dispose of them would have a price impact that would immediately decimate their value.

Sales of shares by corporate insiders are damaging not only because of their direct price impact, but because they are seen as reflecting a lack of confidence by those with the most intimate knowledge of a company. In a transparent effort to soften the blow of these sales, the press releases that follow their mandatory public disclosure frequently cite the need to diversify one's portfolio or to fund a charitable foundation. The only way for a major shareholder to liquidate his or her holdings without the consequent price impact is for the company to be acquired by a larger company for cash (or in the shares of the acquiring company, but only if they are sufficiently liquid). Of course, for most multibillionaires with substantial holdings in some of the world's largest companies, there is no one large enough to buy them out and so it is impossible to know the true value of their holdings from the market price of their shares.

Seeing how many of Wall Street's best and brightest eventually become victims of the market mechanism, it is natural to wonder whether computers, which have already demonstrated their dominance over humans at chess, might also fare better in the market. Researchers at the Santa Fe Institute, a renowned think tank that receives substantial support from financial institutions, were intrigued by the findings of double oral auction experiments. In the early 1990s, they held a tournament in which academics and finance professionals could submit computer programs that would act as *robot traders* in a computerized double oral auction market. The key difference between their markets and the typical laboratory experiments was that the traders were all computer programs. (In recent years, hybrid experiments with both human and robot traders are becoming popular.)

The most successful programs in the tournament were those that did little to aid in the price discovery process, but waited to pick up bargains, especially any left over at the end of a period. Recognizing the option cost of placing a bid or offer, the designers of these programs limited their ability to do much more than take bids and offers placed by other robot traders. These clever programs, however, depend on the existence of less clever ones for the profitability of their strategy. If enough of the programs are devious, then the market is overwhelmed by free riders, causing it to fail.

Another finding of the Santa Fe Institute market tournament was that the sequence of trades with robot traders was noticeably different from those observed in human market experiments. In particular, the convergence to equilibrium was much slower. Although computer programs are vastly better than humans at monitoring markets and making computations, the many subtleties of market behavior that are critical to the performance of human traders have thus far eluded computerized trading programs. The Gode and Sunder robot traders programmed to behave randomly described earlier also generated prices that clearly did not come from human traders; however, because they did not try to gain a strategic advantage, the structure of the double oral auction mechanism was enough to guide them to equilibrium.

Many auction sites on the Internet allow buyers to use a robot as a bidding agent, so that the buyer does not have to spend time sitting in front of a computer in order to participate in an auction that could run for days. Generally, the capabilities of these robots are limited to naïve behavior. A typical robot will scan an auction to see if a higher bid has arrived and then raise the bid within the parameters specified by the buyer. Of course, it is easy for two robot buyers to get into a price war; each bidding the other up until one drops out. Given that the profitability of auction sites is tied more to the sellers than the buyers, it is not surprising that auction sites would wish to promote tools that foster competition among buyers. As we shall see later, efforts to build intelligence into the market can extend beyond robotic capabilities for traders and into the market mechanism itself.

Toward Instantaneous Price Discovery

The double oral auction is such a messy affair because it is a *continuous market*, where trade is possible at any time when the market is open for business. The advantage of a continuous market is its immediacy. Advances in technology have made it possible for someone with news or information that will lose its value once it is incorporated into the market price to buy or sell a stock in seconds either over the phone or through the Internet. As we have seen in an experimental setting, the collective power of these actions can bring either stability or instability to the market. Nonetheless, immediacy is sufficiently valuable to some traders that they are willing to ignore the costs associated with it, both in terms of the options that they grant the market and the price impact of their trades.

While most securities trade in a continuous setting, there are other alternatives. For example, the New York Stock Exchange opens trade in each stock using a call market, in which the price of the stock is adjusted until a point is reached where the orders to buy at the open just match the orders to sell. In this call market, all trades occur at the same price and so no one is directly punished for participating in the price discovery process. In addition, traders do not have to worry that the other party to a trade is taking advantage of them—in a call market the other party is the entire market. Trade on the NYSE also closes with a call market, but far less price discovery occurs in the process of setting the closing price. Because the value of managed investment accounts, such as mutual funds, is computed using the closing price, institutional traders can be less finicky about that price. Funds can pass the cost of a poor execution on to their customers, who are required to place their orders for the day well in advance of the close.

If you observe the opening of the U.S. stock markets either on television or over the Internet, you will notice that the Dow Jones Industrial Average and the Nasdaq Composite average sometimes behave differently, especially on days when major news is moving the market. The Dow, which consists mostly of stocks that trade on the NYSE, will make any large opening move through a series of discrete jumps, a behavior sometimes known as the *trickle effect*. On the other hand, the Nasdaq Composite average, which consists solely of Nasdaq stocks, tends to open with a single large jump from the previous day's close, followed by several smaller adjustments. The reason for this difference in the opening behavior of the two stock indexes can be traced to the opening call for NYSE stocks. On a normal day, it takes a few minutes for all Dow stocks on the NYSE to open. In the midst of market turbulence, it can take much longer for the market to open, as it did in the 1987 crash on Terrible Tuesday or to a lesser extent after the first circuit breaker was tripped on Blue Monday in 1997. In contrast, Nasdaq is a network of market makers who begin non-binding negotiations before the open so that trade can commence immediately without the need for a market-clearing opening price.

Markets may be broadly divided into continuous and call markets, but within a category there can be major differences in the trading rules. In continuous markets, many of these differences concern the way that orders are crossed. For example, a broker may notice that he has received a buy order and a sell order for the same security at the same quantity and price. In certain circumstances, brokers can execute trades without forwarding orders to the exchange. For call markets, the differences can relate to the iterative process used to determine prices. In particular, call markets have various rules that govern how traders may or may not be able to adjust their orders before a final market-clearing price is reached.

The major conceptual difference between continuous and call markets is that in a continuous market, there can be many different transaction prices, while in a call market, there is only one. In theory, this can reduce the option value of orders (and the penalty for moving first) and increase efficiency in call markets. As long as the size of everyone's order is small relative to the overall market, the amount of one's bid or offer will not move the market. As a result, every buyer and seller has no incentive to place a bid price or any offer price that differs from the value he or she places on the item. Charles Polk, president of the electronic markets company Net Exchange, calls this property of call markets "truth without consequences." Another possible benefit of call markets is that the concentration of trading activity at the specific times when the auction is held increases the liquidity of the market. (Of course, in a pure call market, there is no liquidity at other times.)

Call markets have the theoretical potential to be perfect markets, converging instantly to the competitive equilibrium with minimal option cost or other transaction costs to traders, but so far their concrete implementations have yet to reach this potential. When these markets have been studied in the laboratory they take time to converge and, depending on the specifics of the market, can require longer to converge to equilibrium than comparable continuous markets. (The Vickery auction described below is a similar truth-revealing auction that also fails to perform in the laboratory as well as the theory indicates it should.) For sufficiently complex markets, such as the smart markets we will examine later, the ability to make all trades simultaneously may be required to help the market to work properly. For the indefinite future, financial markets are likely to consist of a combination of continuous and call markets regardless of the theoretical or experimental advantage of one type of auction over the other.

The largest call market by dollar volume is the version run by the U.S. Treasury to auction its new debt issues. Billions of dollars in Treasury securities are offered to the public several times each quarter using a two-stage process with two kinds of bids: noncompetitive and competitive. Noncompetitive bids, mostly from smaller investors, usually account for a small percentage of the debt being offered. In the first stage of the auction, these bids are deducted from the offering, leaving the securities to be offered on a competitive basis. The second stage is a one-sided call market. Dealers, who must be authorized by the Treasury in order to participate in these auctions, submit bids for a certain number of bonds at a specified yield. They generally submit multiple bids at different yields, indicating their willingness to purchase more Treasury securities at higher yields. The U.S. Treasury pools all the bids together and determines the lowest yield necessary to sell the entire offering. Securities are then issued at this yield to all noncompetitive bids and to all competitive bids made at or below the cutoff yield.

If the actions of buyers and sellers in a market are guided by an intelligent assessment of their possible consequences—even if these actions may not be aligned perfectly with some preconceived notion of rationality—then even the simplest market becomes a competitive arena governed by the interplay of complex individual strategies. Each market participant must evaluate the options that are available (in the form of bids and offers) as well as those that might become available in the future and then use this information to decide how and when to act, aware that every action creates options for others to exploit. In view of the vast complexity of even the most basic market, the tendency of most experimental markets to converge to equilibrium appears miraculous.

One-Sided Auction Markets

The possible interactions in a continuous double oral auction market are sufficiently complex that a complete analysis for these markets has yet to be derived. A more tractable auction mechanism is the traditional auction in which a single seller auctions items off to several competing buyers, such as the Treasury debt auctions discussed above. This type of auction has stood the twin tests of time and technology.

Just as the desire to find a bargain drove the proliferation of shopping channels in the early days of U.S. cable television, the explosion of the Internet saw the development of several auction sites, with the lion's share of the market going to eBay. These sites provided the infrastructure for a seller to offer an item for sale and for buyers to bid on that item. In return, the site received a share of the sale price, much like a traditional auction house. Unlike stock exchanges and auction houses, however, auction sites rarely provided the mechanism by which a transaction would clear—with the buyer getting the item he purchased and the seller receiving the proceeds from the sale. Instead, it was left for the parties to the transaction to work these details out on their own. If they desired, buyers and sellers could post feedback on each other to alert the market to fraud and other malfeasance, a topic that we will return to in the next chapter. Over time, Internet auctions have taken on the flavor of an electronic garage sale or flea market, providing enhanced liquidity for the world's tchotchkes and helping to create new classes of collectibles ranging from Beanie Babies to Pokémon. The more serious world of art and antiques has also participated in this boom courtesy of auctions conducted over the Internet by traditional auction houses, such as Sotheby's and Christie's.

The seller of an item that is suitable to be auctioned, whether over the Internet or in person, always wants to receive the highest possible price. While advertising and other means of promotion may be used to increase the pool of buyers, we choose to examine auctions starting from the point at which the set of potential buyers is determined. Each buyer can be viewed as coming to the market with a predetermined reservation price for the item, which is analogous to a redemption value assigned in a market experiment. Buyers will never pay more than their reservation price and will seek to pay as little as possible. Sellers have an *opportunity cost* for the item, which is analogous to the cost induced in an experiment, and will set the minimum sale price for the item at or above their opportunity cost. The opportunity cost reflects the value that the seller can receive for the item if she is unable to sell it at the auction, either by continuing to own it or by selling it through other means. We will proceed under the assumption that the seller's opportunity cost is easily met at auction and so is not a limiting factor.

To the seller in an auction, the best of all possible worlds would be to sell to the buyer who has the highest reservation price at, or very close to, that price. Of course, buyers do not have reservation prices stamped on their foreheads, so the price discovery process of the auction must be used to try to uncover the highest reservation price. The traditional auction mechanism is known as an *English auction*, which requires a minimum bid to open and in which buyers can then bid up the price until the auction is terminated with the highest bidder receiving the item up for auction. English auctions typically end either when a time limit is reached or when no new bids are received.

As an English auction proceeds, it eliminates buyers one-by-one as the reservation price of each is exceeded. If buyers drop out only when their reservations prices are exceeded, the auction will end when a single buyer, the one with the highest reservation price, is left. The seller is faced with the problem that the price must only exceed the second-highest reservation price in order to determine highest-valued buyer. For example, if two buyers remain and one has a reservation price of $75,000 and the other has a reservation price of $25,500 if the bidding proceeds in increments of $1,000, the item will likely sell for just $26,000. This outcome denies the seller of $49,000 in potential profits from the sale.

From the seller's viewpoint, a significant shortcoming of the English auction is that the price discovery process not only provides information to the seller, it provides information to all the buyers. While this information could lead buyers to either raise their reservation prices (an issue that will be addressed later in this chapter) or even ignore them amid the excitement of the auction, sellers cannot rely on this happening. Clearly, the greater the dispersion of reservation prices among buyers, the worse the English auction is for the seller and the better it is for the eventual buyer. On the other hand, when the reservation prices are tightly bunched at the top end, the seller suffers little from having the item sell at the second-highest reservation price rather than the highest one.

The most common alternative to the English auction is the *sealed-bid auction*. Sealed-bid auctions take many forms, but in the simplest version—known as a *first-price sealed-bid auction*—buyers submit private bids to the seller by a fixed deadline and the highest bidder receives the item at the price that he had bid. The advantage of this method is that no information is revealed to other buyers during the price discovery process. An offsetting disadvantage is that every buyer has an incentive to shade his bid, submitting a price below his reservation price. In practice, predicting how much each buyer will shade his bid is virtually impossible because it will depend on his perception of how much competition the other buyers pose and his willingness to risk losing the item. In theory, however, if we make certain restrictive assumptions on the redemption values and behavior of buyers, an equilibrium sale price for the auction can be estimated.

The first-price sealed-bid auction may be inefficient because the highest bidder may not have the highest reservation price. If it is easy for buyers to communicate after the auction, this inefficiency can be eliminated if the buyer with the highest reservation price can contact the winner of the auction and offer to buy the item; however, the seller receives no benefit from this side deal. Indeed, a buyer who knows his valuation is high but knows little about the other bidders, may refrain from bidding or submit an artificially low bid, preferring to deal directly with the winner of the auction rather than accept the outcome of the auction process. If this happens, some of the potential benefits that might have accrued to the seller are split between the winner of the auction and the ultimate buyer. Auctions, especially those conducted over the Internet, have rules that try to discourage side deals that circumvent the auction mechanism.

Vickery's Solution

Just as economists ignored experimental markets for much of the twentieth century, the closely related area of auction mechanism design was also an intellectual backwater until recently. William Vickery, a Canadian who taught at Columbia University and was known for roller-skating around Manhattan long before it became fashionable, was the first economist to perform a rigorous analysis of auctions. In October 1996, Professor Vickery was announced as a co-recipient of the Nobel Prize in Economics for his work on the economics of information; however, he never made the trip to Stockholm to collect the prize, dying tragically at the wheel of his automobile a few days after the announcement. It is difficult to overstate the importance of Vickery's work, which received little attention at the time it was published but has come to exert a profound influence on our understanding of markets.

Vickery's approach to auctions focused on the incentives of bidders to reveal information about themselves. In a world of perfect knowledge, auctions would be pointless; the seller would recognize the buyer with the highest value and the two of them would then bargain over the price with the seller being able to use her knowledge of the other buyers' value as leverage in bargaining. Vickery observed that auctions such as the one the Treasury used to issue its securities required very little information. Not only did buyers have private information, it was in their best interests to keep it private so that neither the seller nor the other buyers could exploit it. Hence, buyers had a powerful incentive to behave strategically in order to maintain the privacy of their information rather than reveal it to the world.

Vickery's conceptual breakthrough was that he could redesign the auction process so that buyers would have an incentive to reveal their reservation prices. This new auction was both ingeniously simple and strikingly elegant. In a first-price sealed-bid auction, the item is sold to the highest bidder at the highest price; in a Vickery auction (also known as a second-price auction), the item is sold to the highest bidder at the second-highest price. By incorporating this minor twist into the auction mechanism, Vickery creates a strong incentive for every bidder to submit his or her true reservation price independent of his attitude toward risk and his or her knowledge of other buyers' reservation prices. Generalizing Vickery's work, economic theorists later discovered that all desirable auction mechanisms could be designed in a way that would give buyers the incentive to reveal their reservation prices, a result known as the *revelation principle*.

The argument that buyers will reveal their reservation prices in a Vickery auction builds on the game-theoretic notion of Nash equilibrium introduced earlier. Each buyer begins his or her strategic line of thinking by considering what he or she would do if the other buyers were to submit bids equal to their reservation prices. The natural inclination to bid below one's reservation price would turn out to be counterproductive in this situation. Because the sale price is not based on one's own bid, but on the second-highest bid, lowering one's bid does not lower that price; it only increases the risk of losing the item to another bidder. Bidding above the reservation price is also counterproductive; it may increase one's chance of winning, but it only changes the outcome of the auction when the highest outstanding bid exceeds the buyer's reservation price. In this case, the (previously) high bid now becomes the second-highest bid, which is above the buyer's reservation price. The Nash equilibrium strategy for each buyer is then to bid his or her own reservation price since that is the best he or she can do given that all other buyers also bid their reservation prices.

Notice that the English and Vickery auctions both lead to the same overall predicted outcome: The highest-value buyer gets the item at the second-highest reservation price. Vernon Smith, James Cox, and others have tested this theoretical equivalence and their experiments tend to confirm it; however, there is a tendency toward higher prices with the English auction. Although the Vickery auction performs much like an English auction, it is rarely used outside of the laboratory.

Vickery's discovery also points out an inherent limitation of auction mechanisms. As long as the seller does not deceive buyers, there is no way both to get buyers to reveal their reservation prices and to sell the item at the highest reservation price. The trade-off for getting the truth out of buyers is to forgo selling at the best possible price. The conflict between the ability to learn private information and to fully exploit it is a fundamental property of economic interactions that we will explore further in the next chapter.

Edward Clarke and Theodore Groves extended Vickery's idea so that it would apply to public goods. Viewed in its most basic terms, the problem of whether government should provide its citizens with a public good, such as a park, comes down to determining whether the total benefit to those who would use the good exceeds its cost. Of course, the citizens—like the bidders in an auction—have no natural incentive to reveal their reservation price for the good, especially if the share of the cost levied on them depends on it. Clarke and Groves extended Vickery's logic to create a mechanism that would get individuals to reveal their true value for a public good by separating the amount of their assessment from that revelation.

By adding the revealed values together, the government could then determine the overall value of the public good and determine whether it exceeds the cost. In the case of public goods, the mechanism that gets individuals to reveal their reservation prices truthfully also has its downside; in general, the assessments that are collected from them will not match the cost, leaving the project either over or under its budget.

Deviant Auctions

Both the English auction and the Vickery auction are nearly perfect solutions to the problem of how to run an auction. The only way they deviate from the ideal of efficiency is in the case where only one of the bidders has a willingness to pay that is above the seller's reservation price. Then, the value of the second-highest buyer, which must be below the seller's reservation price, will not be high enough to allow the transaction to proceed. If the seller is somehow able to isolate this buyer before the auction begins, bargaining directly with that buyer is likely to provide the seller with a higher price. (Note that the Vickery auction does not provide a workable means of determining that buyer. If one-on-one bargaining is a possible outcome of the auction, then buyers will no longer have an incentive to reveal their reservation prices.)

Sellers are not always interested in assuring an efficient outcome. Clearly, sellers are happy if they can get buyers to overpay, even if that means that the wrong buyer purchases the item. Furthermore, there are cases where the sellers may want the buyer(s) to *underpay*. A striking example of where underpayment is standard operating procedure is in the initial public offering (IPO) of a company's stock. As we saw earlier, the U.S. Treasury uses a relatively sophisticated auction mechanism in an effort to get the best prices for its new debt issues, and one would think that investment banks would use a similar mechanism to offer stock to the public; but they rarely do.

Instead, the IPOs of most stocks are priced significantly below the perceived market price of the stock. This mispricing accrues to the benefit of the investment banks that underwrite the offering because they can assure that the offering is oversubscribed and use the allocation of the bargain shares to benefit themselves and to reward key clients. While the reason that the companies whose shares are offered tolerate this persistent underpricing has been a longstanding topic of debate among financial economists, there appears to be a simple explanation that has a basis in experimental economics.

Recall that in bubble experiments, positive price momentum was critical to the development of a bubble. When assets are underpriced in early periods, there is a natural tendency for their prices to rise, leading to a bubble. Investment banks who underwrite IPOs appear to use the artificially low offering price as a way to help manufacture a bubble in the stocks they bring to market. Owners are usually happy to go along because most IPOs involve only a small fraction of their company's shares. By providing a small number of shares at a discount now, the owners hope to sell even more shares at a premium later. Of course, this is just another form of market manipulation that should not work in an efficient market, where the price would simply rise immediately to its proper level and remain there pending additional news.

This is another behavioral quirk, known as the *winner's curse*, that sellers can try to cultivate so that buyers will be more likely to overpay for an item. Unlike other curses of modern life, such as may befall an athlete who appears on the cover of *Sports Illustrated*, the winner's curse is rooted not in superstition, but in cold, hard economics. The value of many items is uncertain at the time of their purchase. Although some uncertainty can be objectively quantified (for example, the value of an oil lease can be estimated through geological testing), much uncertainty has a substantial subjective element to it. When uncertainty is subjective, it is common for individuals to have markedly different assessments of the uncertain situation. Individuals with optimistic assessments will tend to place the highest values on an item, and so are more likely to be the winning bidder at an auction. If the true value of an item tends to be more in line with its average valuation, then the winner of the auction in his excessive optimism is likely to have overpaid for it. The winner's curse, also known as *buyer's remorse*, will then afflict him as he finds that the benefits from the item that he has won do not measure up to its inflated price.

The winner's curse is a well-known phenomenon to professional auction bidders, such as oil-drilling companies that must win the right to drill at auction before setting up a rig. They adapt to the curse by lowering their bids in an attempt to adjust for their optimism relative to other bidders. Nonetheless, there still exist situations in which even this adjustment is not enough. In particular, if bidders not only differ in their subjective assessments, but also have different information, the bidders with the worst information will tend to overpay for less valuable items and be outbid for the more valuable ones. There is a saying in poker: "If you don't know who the patsy is, then it's you."

Many bidding situations are designed to ensure that the winners will tend to be those with the least knowledge of an item's value.

Behavioral economists have long recognized that nonprofessional bidders, such as the typical university experimental subject, have difficulties taking the winner's curse into account when bidding. The key to avoiding the winner's curse is not to bid based on what one thinks the item is worth, but rather to bid based on the item's value in the situation where that bid is the winning bid. Because most student subjects have difficulty following this train of thought, the winner's curse demonstrates a limit to the rational decision-making process. While this type of irrationality is subtle, it is representative of a general problem that humans have in thinking through the consequences of the actions they take in various market settings.

The ability of a market to aggregate information requires a delicate balance between the information available to each side of it. When information is concentrated on one side of the market, it can become inhospitable to the uninformed, potentially reducing their efficiency to the point where they fail entirely. In particular, the seller of an item tends to know more about the item than its buyer. This *informational asymmetry* means that the buy-side and sell-side of the market are two fundamentally different markets. While this asymmetry is common in auction markets, it can afflict any type of market.

Finally, we should recognize that all items available for purchase in the marketplace, including financial securities, are only those that someone is willing to sell. Often, the most remunerative investments are never offered to the public, remaining instead under the control of private owners with superior knowledge of an asset's value and the actions required to enhance it. Frequently, a seller who chooses to sell an item has *adversely selected* that item because it was not valuable enough to retain for his or her own use. We will now see how *adverse selection* affects the market mechanism and then proceed to examine other types of informational asymmetries.

9

Sending Signals and Keeping Score

Alfred Marshall was able to craft a coherent quantitative framework for Adam Smith's free-market ideas by imposing a certain degree of uniformity on the market for each good. Although goods within a Marshallian market do not need to be identical, consumers must view them as freely interchangeable, making them *perfect substitutes* for one another. Without this interchangeability, markets will cease to be perfect, as Edward Chamberlin was quick to seize upon in his theory of monopolistic competition. He saw that that sellers' efforts to differentiate their products through advertising or other means would only increase their costs but not their profits, as other sellers in the market would compete them away. Just as Chamberlin's classroom exercise would eventually sprout the field of experimental economics, his introduction of product differentiation into Marshall's neoclassical framework would come to change how economists viewed goods.

Progress in economics, as in many disciplines, comes one dimension at a time. The new economic dimension introduced by Edward Chamberlin was quality. Unlike time, which is an objective part of the physical world that can be precisely quantified in seconds, minutes, hours, and so on, quality usually goes beyond objective measurement. For example, Coke and Pepsi are different cola beverages and the important differences are qualitative; simply assigning numbers to Coke and Pepsi on the basis of a chemical analysis fails to do them justice. Furthermore, the images and associations planted in the minds of consumers through extensive advertising appear nowhere in the physical manifestations of these products.

Introducing a quality dimension into the market system makes holes in the market inevitable. For markets to be complete with respect to quality, a separate market must exist for each possible quality of an item. When quality cannot be observed at the point of sale, problems arise. (Indeed, the quality of many products cannot be determined until long after their purchase, if at all.) In a world of perfect knowledge, one thing that a buyer should definitely know is the quality of the item purchased. While experiments have shown that the market mechanism can readily cope with the absence of certain types of information, the problem this kind of informational asymmetry poses is more serious.

Buyers and sellers who cannot achieve a meeting of the minds concerning the quality of the product being exchanged no longer conduct business in the same market. The goods sold by sellers are fundamentally not the same goods purchased by buyers because of this informational asymmetry.

Further complicating matters is the fact that sellers have a natural advantage over buyers when it comes to quality. Sellers may not only pick and choose which items to offer, they often can actively control the quality of the goods offered. The market mechanism is limited in its ability to compensate buyers for the disadvantageous position in which they find themselves relative to sellers. As we shall see, informational asymmetries may not only compromise the efficiency of the market mechanism, they can cause it to fail completely.

Lemons Squeeze the Market Mechanism

It takes only one field trip to a used car lot—or previously owned automobile emporium, if we wish to be more genteel—to understand how adverse selection on the quality dimension can affect a market. Except for specialty cars with long waiting lists that can delay delivery of a vehicle for years, the value of an automobile usually declines 10 percent to 20 percent the moment it is sold to its first owner, at which point it is no longer a new car. Much of this devaluation is based on the fear that any automobile that immediately comes back on the market after its original sale is a *lemon* with serious problems that the buyer quickly discovered. In anticipation of wariness by prospective buyers, many sellers of almost-new cars provide a cover story to go along with the sale—job transfer, divorce, day trading losses, and so forth. At best, a good story can make the sale of the automobile possible, but it will rarely erase much of the discount conferred by a suspicious market. (The enactment of *lemons laws*, that force car dealers to buy back their lemons, has only somewhat mitigated this problem given the difficulties of meeting the standards required to make a car a lemon in the eyes of the law.)

Lemons became part of the economic vocabulary in 1970 when Berkeley economist George Akerlof published a paper on the used-car phenomenon. Professor Akerlof examined the implications of the most fundamental problem of adverse selection in which the seller of an item knows its true value, but the buyer is left completely in the dark. In particular, he explored the situation where buyers have no recourse; if they receive a lower-quality item—the lemon—they are stuck with it. Akerlof then adapted the Marshallian picture of supply and demand to incorporate the possibility of lemons being brought to market.

As we saw earlier, the amount of an item supplied by sellers in a market tends to increase with its price. The existence of the lemons problem will exaggerate this tendency. At a low price, only a lemon will be offered for sale. Sellers with high-quality items will choose to withhold them from the market when prices are low. As prices rise, higher-quality items will join in with the lemons. Of course, an intelligent buyer will notice this phenomenon. Although buyers will normally have higher demand at lower prices, the fact that low prices disproportionately bring out the lemons will dampen demand. Similarly, the tendency for demand to drop at higher prices will be mitigated by the higher average quality of items available in the market.

The presence of lemons in a market can sometimes distort demand enough that a competitive equilibrium cannot be achieved. In particular, the demand curve may not slope downward so that it can intersect with the rising supply curve. Facing this type of demand, the market will fail because no price can bring supply and demand into equilibrium. Any attempt by sellers to coax buyers into the market with lower prices is futile because buyers see lower prices as indicating lower quality and so their demand drops.

The kind of *market failure* we see with lemons is aptly reflected in that famous saying of "Groucho" (no apparent relation to Karl) Marx: "I don't care to belong to any club that will have me as a member." Groucho could never enter into a "stable equilibrium relationship" with a club because its willingness to suffer the presence of someone like him indicates its lack of suitable standards. Analogously, the willingness of a seller to provide an item at a reasonable price may inform the buyer that it is a lemon.

The unreliability of the market mechanism in the presence of lemons comes from demanding too much of it. Normally, all that we ask of the market mechanism is to adjust the price of a good until the quantity supplied and demanded come into balance. When the possible delivery of lemons looms over the market, however, price also serves as a guide to quality. The effect of attempting to use one number—price— for two distinct purposes—setting both quantity and quality—is enough to throw a monkey wrench into the market mechanism. Indeed, what we are attempting to do is collapse many markets, one for each possible level of quality, into a single market. The absence of a complete set of markets along the quality dimension impairs efficiency to the point that the market can fail.

Akerlof's model vividly illustrates the potential problems that adverse selection can cause the market mechanism, but it is not intended as a literal account of economic reality. Indeed, the market mechanism does not react to the presence of lemons by breaking down; it looks for ways to solve the information problem. For example, Internet auction sites can attract sellers who not only dispense lemons, but also commit outright fraud. Reputable auction sites, which will suffer from any failures in the markets they manage, provide several mechanisms for dealing with these "bad apples." Although prices may be a limited conduit for information, there are richer channels of communication that can be used to supplement them. Indeed, it is standard practice for auction sites to have a feedback mechanism through which buyers can convey their experiences with specific sellers to the online buying public.

The incentive to *rip off* buyers is greatly reduced if the seller's reputation is damaged in the process. While a seller can readily assume a new identity, it is much more difficult to establish a reputation for fair dealing. Reputations are self-reinforcing because once a seller has managed to acquire a good reputation—allowing him to sell his goods at a premium price—the cost of losing that reputation is substantial enough that buyers can count on him to continue not to cheat them. The evolution of *brand names* and the premium that they fetch in the market is due largely to the fact that the cost to a seller of tarnishing a well-established brand is so high that under normal circumstances there is an enormous incentive not to take advantage of consumers.

The Theory of Market Signaling

One "industry" that has reputation as an essential part of its product is the higher-education industry. Colleges and universities not only provide their students with educations, they emboss them with a brand name that can convey a substantial competitive and monetary advantage in the job market. Soon after Akerlof's article on lemons appeared, a Harvard graduate student and Rhodes Scholar, A. Michael Spence, extended this work by considering how external indications of achievement, which he called *signals*, could be used instead of price as an indication of quality. Building on insights from his wife, Ann, who at the time worked in Harvard's undergraduate placement office, and extending the pioneering work of his Harvard mentors—Kenneth Arrow, Thomas Schelling, and Richard Zeckhauser—Spence developed a model of market signaling that was striking in both its simplicity and depth.

Professors during fleeting moments of self-doubt might wonder whether their pedagogical efforts really help their students. Such doubts cast an especially large shadow over business schools. In the 1970s, the intense competition for graduates by investment banks and consulting firms had reached the point that employers would aggressively court students early in their first year of graduate study. There were even instances of companies—happy just to know that their recruits had been accepted at a prestigious business school—encouraging students to skip their studies completely and come to work immediately at the same salary that they would receive with an MBA (Masters of Business Administration) degree two years later. This behavior was evidence that some employers used a business school education primarily as a screening device; for them, most of the value of the business school resided in the school's admissions office and not in its classrooms. In fact, some companies even believe that business school is counterproductive—indoctrinating students with values that could undermine their corporate culture—and so they train their employees at their own in-house facilities, often using moonlighting faculty from the very business schools that they would normally shun.

Michael Spence built on the inspiration provided by his spouse and mentors to construct a theoretical model of how signals, such as education, worked in the context of competitive markets. He first considered the extreme case of unproductive signals, in which the value of a worker's output to an employer was unaffected by his or her educational experience. Given that virtually all employers insisted on graduation before a permanent job would be offered, clearly there was more to education than the initial screening. If education itself was unproductive, why did the vast majority of employers insist that prospective hires waste their time going through the process?

Spence found a way out of this apparent contradiction by considering the possibility that the cost of education, as measured by the effort and anguish it required, was lower for more talented students than it was for less talented ones. In a simple variant of Spence's model, one might imagine two categories of jobs—professional and nonprofessional—and two categories of students—talented and ordinary. Suppose that professional jobs pay $75,000 in a perfectly competitive market and nonprofessional jobs pay $50,000 and that every month of graduate education costs a talented student $1,000 and an ordinary student $5,000. (All numbers used here are merely for illustration and they implicitly take into account that salaries are paid over a period of many years.) Finally, only talented students are capable of being productive professional workers; if one places an ordinary student in a professional job he or she will still only be worth the $50,000 associated with the nonprofessional job.

Now consider the case where we set a standard for professional jobs that requires one academic year (nine months) of graduate education. At the same time, we will require no additional education for nonprofessional jobs. For a talented student, the net compensation from a professional job will be $66,000, which is $75,000 minus the cost associated with nine months of education at $1,000 per month. This is more than the $50,000 paid by a nonprofessional job, and so all talented students will prefer to go to graduate school in order to qualify for professional jobs. Ordinary students, on the other hand, receive a net salary of only $30,000 for a professional job because their nine months of education cost them $45,000, substantially more than the $9,000 it costs talented students. For ordinary students the choice between the $50,000 for the nonprofessional job and the $30,000 that they can net from a professional job is obvious. Hence, requiring nine months of education for a professional job provides a hurdle that talented students can clear, but ordinary students cannot, keeping them out of the professional jobs to which they are not suited.

While this example presents an extremely oversimplified view of education and the labor market, it provides a sound theoretical basis for how market signaling might arise. Spence clearly shows how education, even when it does nothing to increase productivity, can be used as a signal that separates talented from ordinary students in the job market. While 9 months of education will effectively separate the two groups, in fact, the numbers work out so that any amount of education from 5 months to 25 months will also serve to separate them. If employers require more than 25 months of education, the groups no longer separate out because the talented students will prefer to take the nonprofessional jobs, as educational costs greater than $25,000 will more than offset the higher pay from a professional job.

In Spence's original signaling model, each level of education between 5 and 25 months serves as the basis for a *signaling equilibrium*, a variant of the Nash equilibrium that he applied to this problem. If employers happened to require two academic years of graduate education (18 months), they would be able to separate out the talented students from the ordinary and all would be fine. In practice, because education is costly, in a competitive market employers will try to attract employees by requiring less education. Such competition will cause the market to converge to a single competitive signaling equilibrium that generates the greatest net income for talented students, which nets them a bit less than $70,000 for a bit more than five months of education.

It is important to note that the effort of screening out the ordinary students, which costs each talented student at least $5,000, only makes economic sense if ordinary students are a significant proportion of the population and if their performance as professional workers is sufficiently detrimental to their employers. If the number of ordinary students is small or if they make reasonably good professional workers, then it will not pay to separate them out, and a *pooling equilibrium*—where talented and ordinary students are treated the same—is the expected outcome. In a pooling equilibrium, no one receives any education and everyone is given a professional job at a salary somewhat less than $75,000. (The discount to $75,000 depends on the exact ratio of ordinary to talented students in the population and their relative productivity.)

If there are too many ordinary students or if their presence in professional jobs is too damaging, then the pooling equilibrium unravels as the financial incentive for talented students to separate themselves out increases. In addition, separation is more likely to occur when the difference in the cost of acquiring the signal is large. In fact, if the cost advantage of the talented group is too small, the situation parallels the lemons problem and no equilibrium is possible.

The assumption that the acquisition of education does not make an individual more productive is not required in order to observe the signaling phenomenon; it only serves to emphasize that signaling may emerge even in the extreme case where the signal has no other purpose than to screen individuals. When the signal adds value to those receiving it, talented students will still likely need to obtain more than the efficient amount of education in order to distinguish them from ordinary students.

Taking the signaling model from labor markets to financial markets was an obvious next step. Joseph Stiglitz, in separate papers with Michael Rothschild and Andrew Weiss, examined risk screening in insurance and credit markets, respectively. Anyone who has ever purchased automobile insurance is likely to have noticed that the cost of insurance declines as the amount of the deductible rises. Consumers who choose a higher deductible are implicitly signaling to the insurance company that they are likely to be safer drivers because they are willing to pay more of the bill in case of an accident. In practice, this signal can be quite noisy, however, because the willingness to accept a high deductible can also be associated with a proclivity for risk-taking or with a lack of money to pay the premiums—two attributes that insurance companies would prefer to avoid. Similarly, screening in credit markets encounters difficulties because borrowers with no intention of repaying their debts are likely to ignore any restrictions attached to a loan.

Signaling behavior is not confined to students and consumers; corporations can also signal. Some of a company's major financial decisions—how much it borrows and what it pays out in dividends—can be used as a signal of its value to investors. Indeed, the tendency of stocks to overreact to a disappointing earnings announcement may be entirely rational when viewed from a signaling perspective. When the managers of a company lack the control necessary to coordinate their financial results with the expectations of the analysts who follow them, they may be signaling even deeper problems to the financial markets. It is not surprising then to find that disappointing earnings tend to reduce stock value by more than a direct analysis of expected future cash flows would indicate. Hence, the asymmetry of information between companies and their investors may add to the volatility of financial assets beyond what one would expect from the fundamentals.

Learning to Signal in the Laboratory

In order for a signal, such as education, to serve as an effective screening device, those receiving the signal must first learn how to interpret it. There are likely to be many potential signals in the marketplace, but only a small fraction of them are ever put to the test. Indeed, the market sometimes fails to recognize the most efficient signals, settling instead on inferior ones that come into use through historical accident.

The Law of Supply and Demand in its most basic form works because the market, under the guidance of the invisible hand, learns what price to charge for an item with relative ease. Determining not only which signal to use, but also how much of it to associate with a given level of quality, appears to be far more difficult for the invisible hand than mere price discovery. That individuals would somehow know the right signals to use a priori requires a degree of knowledge that it is unreasonable to assume that anyone would have. Indeed, the temporary inefficiency that comes while the market homes in on an equilibrium price can be trifling compared with the potential loss in market efficiency that could result from settling on a bad choice of signals.

The importance of human learning to signaling made it a natural area for experimental research. The author, in collaboration with Charles Plott, began a series of signaling and lemons experiments at Caltech in the early 1980s. In its youth, market experimentation was noted for the relative uniformity of its results. While many market experiments were viewed with considerable skepticism because so many of them were conducted using Caltech students, the ability to reproduce the basic results with other populations was reassuring. The outcome of a signaling experiment, however, appeared to depend on how quickly the subjects could learn to link the signal together with quality and price. The admissions process for Caltech students, which gave substantial weight to standardized tests of quantitative and reasoning ability, could be expected to give them an advantage in making the connections required for the market signaling to work.

As with previous experiments, the signaling experiments were designed to create as neutral a setting as possible. Education and jobs were far too personal to use in an experiment, especially with students as subjects.

Therefore, it was necessary to create an alternative signaling setting for these experiments. The burgeoning market for athletic shoes, the status footwear of the "Me Decade," provided the inspiration for the setting used in these experiments and subsequent ones that explored informational asymmetries.

Sellers in the market were divided into two "grades," those who sold "Regulars" and those who sold "Supers." The redemption values of buyers were arranged so that each buyer would receive more for a Super than for a Regular. (Supers are like the talented students who are more valuable than "Regular" students because they can excel in professional jobs. One can imagine that only Supers are suitable for road racing.) Sellers were not allowed to tell buyers whether they were selling Regulars or Supers; instead each seller could distinguish his product by adding "stripes" to it, drawing on the tendency for athletic shoe manufacturers to use stripes, swooshes, and so on to distinguish their products. Although stripes on shoes serve as a trademark rather than a true signal because the cost of applying the stripes or similar indicia is trivial, for experimental purposes, stripes provided a suitably neutral form of product differentiation.

The actual grade of a unit was revealed only after it was sold. Every item would come with a certain number of stripes, so that bids and offers would include both a price and a number of stripes. For a given seller, each stripe added to an item had the same cost; however, these stripes cost less for sellers of Supers than they do for sellers of Regulars. The relative costs of stripes were set so that stripes could effectively distinguish Supers from Regulars, just as education could be used to separate talented from ordinary students in Spence's model of educational signaling.

The results of the first signaling experiments were extremely varied. In experiments using Caltech subjects who had participated in previous market experiments, stripes rapidly emerged as a signal, with the more valuable Supers bearing more stripes than Regulars. In addition, competition tended to drive the number of stripes down to the minimum required for separation. With other pools of subjects, including less experienced Caltech subjects, separation occurred more slowly and the number of stripes stayed above the minimum level that would separate Supers from Regulars.

The signaling markets would sometimes converge to equilibrium so slowly that with less experienced subjects the market could remain far from equilibrium three hours into the experiment, which was the limit on how long subjects could be expected to participate. In an effort to speed up convergence, Supers and Regulars were circled with different colors of chalk at the end of each period in the later experiments. This straightforward institutional change had a dramatic effect on the market; subjects now quickly learned from the visual cues that units with more stripes tended to be Supers. It was striking to find that the color of chalk with which the experimenter's visible hand wrote on the blackboard could make such a difference in the workings of the market's invisible hand.

The fragility of experimental signaling markets appears typical of how markets behave when the informational burdens placed on buyers and sellers increase. In order for signaling to emerge, a critical mass of buyers need to "get it" and both the sellers and the market mechanism must help them along the way. If buyers fail to perceive the link between the signal and quality, the market tends to thrash about, as the frustrated efforts of the sellers of Supers to establish their product at a higher price and number of stripes than Regulars will prevent the market from stabilizing. Indeed, it was easy to increase this thrashing by increasing the cost of the stripes for sellers of Supers. This higher cost of stripes had the effect of reducing the combinations of stripes and prices that would separate the two grades. With fewer ways to signal their superiority, the market never figured out how to use stripes to separate Supers from Regulars even though the experiment was designed to make this separation theoretically possible.

The inability of markets to send out the correct signals presents a problem that is potentially as damaging to the market as bubbles. The efficient operation of markets depends on the ability of the participants to make the proper inferences from what they see in the market. Markets with features that tend to lead buyers and sellers astray will have more difficulty converging to equilibrium than those that help them create, transmit, and receive information.

The initial signaling experiments attracted the interest of the Federal Trade Commission (FTC). Under the leadership of Wendy Gramm, the wife of Texas Senator Phil Gramm and the future head of the Commodities Futures Trading Commission, the FTC's Bureau of Economics sponsored several sets of experiments to explore consumer protection issues. FTC economists Michael Lynch and Russell Porter joined Charles Plott and the author on a follow-up series of lemons experiments. These experiments were similar to the signaling experiments, except that only price—and not stripes—could be used to separate out the Supers from the Regulars. In addition, sellers were able to control whether each unit they produced was a Super or a Regular. Supers cost more to produce than

Regulars, but their premium value to buyers greatly exceeded the higher production cost. Sellers could make more money on a particular sale, however, by ripping off the buyer by selling the unit at a high price (to make him think it was a Super), but then delivering a Regular. Buyers usually only had to be ripped off a few times before the market for high-priced items disappeared and the lemons (Regulars) took over the market.

The ability of sellers not only to know the quality of the goods that they produced, but also to control it, added a new twist to these experiments, known to economists as *moral hazard*. While adverse selection, which is at the root of both lemons and signaling, is a passive phenomenon where bad sellers try to mix in with the good ones—moral hazard involves active deception on the part of the seller. Moral hazard brings us back to the subject of options, because the seller has the option of ripping off the buyer; the question is whether this option is even exercised.

In its role as a consumer watchdog, the mission of the FTC is to protect buyers from both moral hazard and adverse selection. While warranties and legal remedies may offer some protection to consumers, they can be both difficult to implement and costly to enforce. If something as easy as colored chalk in the signaling experiments could eliminate adverse selection, maybe there was an easy cure for certain consumer rip-offs, at least within the confines of the laboratory.

One remedy for rip-offs turned out to be quite simple—provide immediate and universal feedback to buyers. By requiring every seller to reveal the quality of a unit publicly to all buyers and sellers immediately after a sale was consummated, both rip-offs (Regulars at Super prices) and lemons (Regulars at any price) were quickly eliminated. As one might expect, any seller revealed to have sold a Regular at a Super price was instantly boycotted by buyers in favor of those with a reputation for selling only Supers. Sellers with poor reputations found it difficult to regain the trust of buyers. To avoid any "end period effects" in these experiments, they were usually terminated without prior notice to the subjects. In contrast to the experiments with public announcements, markets in which buyers who were ripped off had no way of informing other buyers of their misfortune were flooded with lemons (Regulars) and Supers were rarely produced because without the trust of buyers, sellers could not receive a premium price.

That Internet auctions would be forced by the market to establish mechanisms for providing feedback is not surprising given the findings of these experiments. Indeed, one has to question whether Internet auctions go far enough in providing their buyers with feedback, as it is frequently weeks or months before a seller with a bad reputation is driven from the market, as opposed to the instantaneous feedback of these experiments. Markets are not just about completing transactions, they are about learning. Over time, mechanisms that promote learning will tend to displace those that impede it. Furthermore, information that supplements market prices can help to fill the holes created by informational asymmetries.

Prices as Scorekeepers

Feedback is of such importance to the efficient functioning of markets that objective ways of "keeping score" are a natural part of a market's evolution. Thorstein Veblen, an itinerant Norwegian-American economist, was the first to zero in on the importance of keeping score in the economy. Wesley Mitchell, introduced in Chapter 4 as the father of business cycle research, referred to Veblen (with whom he served on the original faculty of the New School for Social Research in New York) as "a visitor from another world." Veblen was known for his eccentricities, such as washing his accumulated dirty dishes with a garden hose. Although Veblen had a hard time holding down a job and was generally ignored by his contemporaries in economics, the publication of his classic 1899 book, *The Theory of the Leisure Class*, was praised in literary circles for its biting portrayal of the emerging American upper-class. In that book, Veblen coined a phrase that lives on to this day, "conspicuous consumption," which is the consumption of goods purely to signal to others that their owner can afford them. Although in no way a follower of Karl Marx, Veblen viewed markets as inherently inefficient and proposed that the production and distribution of goods be professionally managed by engineers (his personal heroes) so that the economy would not be influenced by the whims of ordinary humans.

In the short run, history was kind to Veblen. The Roaring Twenties were times of conspicuous consumption in the United States beyond what could have been imagined in a country with puritanical roots, and the ensuing Depression caused others to join Veblen in his opposition of the market mechanism. In the long run, however, the failure of centrally planned economies along with the development of a mass culture that heartily embraced many of the proclivities that Veblen ridiculed, have served to limit Veblen's influence on contemporary economics. Nonetheless, the growing realization by economists that economic behavior can convey information—something that research on lemons and signaling brought to center stage—can be traced back to Veblen.

While the lemons problem illustrates what happens when we try to cram too much information into market prices, in general, market prices can provide us with a rich source of information and feedback. When information is openly available and markets are operating efficiently, market prices can be used to "reverse engineer" information about markets, a property known as *invertibility*. For example, suppose that a company is involved in a lawsuit whose ruling is due to be announced at 3:00 P.M. and where the outcome will have a large impact on its future earnings. As the announcement approaches, the market is evenly divided as to whether the company will win the case—that is, the price of the stock reflects a 50 percent probability of victory. If the only information available at 3:05 P.M. is a real-time feed of the company's stock price, then we can be reasonably certain that the ruling was favorable if the stock's price spiked up and was unfavorable if it spiked down. In the event that the stock price remains constant, it is reasonable to assume that the decision was delayed.

Derivative securities can yield extremely valuable market information, either directly or indirectly, through the reverse engineering of the information contained in their prices. The derivatives that tend to be the most useful are futures contracts, whose value is based on the market's assessment of the future price of a security or commodity. For example, the owner of a fleet of delivery vans concerned about the future price of fuel for his vans does not need to hire an economist to forecast these prices for him; he need only look up the price of gasoline futures in the newspaper. While these prices include neither taxes nor retail markups, they are an accurate estimate of the direction and magnitude of future changes in the price of gasoline. Even something as capricious as the future actions of the Federal Reserve can be inferred from the futures contracts on the federal funds rate. If the current rate is 6.00 percent and the rate for the futures contract directly after a Board meeting is 6.10 percent, then the probability of a 25-basis-point hike at the meeting is roughly 10 b.p. divided by 25 b.p. or 40 percent. It is not entirely coincidental that economic forecasting departments at almost every major financial institution were cut back or eliminated during the 1980s as the futures markets were expanding rapidly. (That most of these departments made consistently poor forecasts using the limited market feedback available to them did not help either.)

A prime example of the predictive value of market prices is the Iowa

Presidential Market. Since the first commercial mainframe computers arrived in the 1950s, political consultants have analyzed data collected by polling potential voters as a way of predicting the outcomes of elections. Although sophisticated statistical sampling techniques and the pollster's expert knowledge can help to assure that the sample being polled is roughly representative of the electorate as a whole, there is no economic incentive for the respondents to answer the poll truthfully. Indeed, voters for controversial candidates may be too embarrassed to state their true voting intentions to a pollster.

To overcome this problem with political polls, Robert Forsythe and some colleagues at the University of Iowa started an electronic market in the 1980s that sold "shares" in U.S. presidential candidates. Each share was a simple derivative security based on the outcome of the election. The shares provided a binary (0 or 1) payoff: a share in the winner (of the popular vote) paid $1 and a share in the loser(s) paid $0. At any time before the election, the price of a share in a candidate approximates the market's estimate that the candidate will win; for example, shares trading at $0.56 indicate a 56 percent probability of victory. The predictive capacity of this market has been impressive, only failing to pick the winner of the popular vote in the extremely close and controversial Bush–Gore election of 2000.

The Art of Indexing

Prices make the best scorekeepers when they are focused on a single event, such as a Federal Reserve interest rate decision or a presidential election. Difficulties begin to surface when we try to aggregate prices over several goods or securities simultaneously. In the U.S. stock market, indexes have long been constructed to represent "the market" as a whole. The oldest of these indexes still in common use is the Dow Jones Industrial Average. As with all stock indexes, the stocks that make up the Dow have changed considerably over time; indeed, with the addition of retailers (Wal-Mart and Home Depot), financials (American Express and J. P. Morgan Chase), and a software firm (Microsoft), the Dow is no longer truly an "industrial" average.

How we determine a representative index for asset prices is not merely a matter of convenience. According to the asset pricing models derived from modern portfolio theory, holding the entire basket of productive assets in the proper proportion makes for an efficient portfolio in which all security-specific risk is eliminated. Under the efficient-market theory, investors should use this basket as the basis for their asset holdings, tweaking it to take into account their individual risk aversion and the specifics of their financial situation. The original motivation behind stock index investment funds was to give investors a way to own such a basket and benefit from its lower trading costs, reduced taxable capital gains, and—most of all—its diversification.

In practice, all stock indexes have biases—for example, the Standard & Poor's 500 Stock Index is biased toward larger companies—so they do not accurately represent the market as a whole. Even the use of broader indexes, such as the Wilshire 5000 and Russell 3000, does not provide perfect diversification because the market basket advocated by Capital Asset Pricing Model and related efficient-market theories includes all assets in the global economy, not just those for which stock is traded in the United States. Indeed, investment managers and consultants who take efficient-market theory seriously advocate holding foreign stocks and real estate in addition to the more standard investments in stocks and bonds. Moreover, by holding stakes in privately held companies, investors can avoid the problem of adverse selection discussed earlier.

Price indexes are another type of index with enormous economic significance. In the United States, a significant amount of economic activity is tied directly to the Consumer Price Index (CPI), which is reported monthly by the Bureau of Labor Statistics (BLS). Social Security payments, income tax schedules, wages set by union contracts, interest on certain U.S. Treasury bonds, and much more are computed using formulas that include adjustments to reflect the current level of prices as measured by the CPI.

The CPI is computed under the assumption that all consumers buy the same basket of goods, including shelter, food, medical care, entertainment, and so on, each month. This approach has two major flaws. First, consumers do not all purchase the same basket of goods. Although the Bureau of Labor Statistics publishes several price indexes to account for some of this variation, these supplemental indexes are largely ignored. Because it is theoretically impossible to create a standard basket of goods, the government's choice of a bundle appears arbitrary.

Even if a truly representative basket existed, the contents of the basket would change from month to month in response to the changes in prices, as illustrated by the Marshallian demand curve. Furthermore, the quality of the goods in the market basket is also subject to monthly changes. The BLS has begun to use statistical methods to adjust the market basket each month to account for changing prices and qualities. Aside from the usual limitations associated with statistical adjustments, the BLS has had difficulty making these adjustments correctly. In September 2000, a significant error was discovered in how the quality of housing was adjusted, leading to a retroactive increase in the CPI to correct an error; however, investors in inflation-indexed U.S. Treasury securities were never compensated for this error.

The difficulty of constructing a perfect consumer price index has its roots in a deeper economic problem—the construction of an objective measure of economic well-being. The neoclassical attempt to solve this problem was to create the concept of *utility*. Consumers, when contemplating which goods to purchase, implicitly assigned a score to the utility or satisfaction to be obtained when the goods were ultimately consumed. The neoclassicists thought that utility was something very real—much like the ether that physicists believed filled the empty spaces of the universe—and that in time scientific advances would enable us to measure it. The unit of measurement for utility is given a number of different names. The standard appellation is *utils*, but the author prefers the term introduced to him by Stanford professor Roger Noll—*jollies* (singular: *jolly*).

The preference for one bundle of goods over another could be explained by noting that the first bundle provided 150.717 jollies, while the second one yielded only 122.534 jollies. It might appear that using jollies to measure utility does not give any more information than assigning them a monetary value. Indeed, if the bundles of goods being compared are a small portion of a consumer's expenditures, dollars and utility can be used almost interchangeably as utility measures. The problem comes when we wish to compare the entire bundle of activities in which a consumer engages; balancing the utility of the products that he or she consumes with the *disutility* of the time that he or she must spend working to earn the money to purchase them. In this case, the consumer has no money to begin with (he or she has not earned it yet) and we must resort to utility as a yardstick of economic welfare.

The ability of an individual to associate a numerical measure of utility with the things that he or she consumes implies a certain degree of rationality as long as his or her actions are consistent with the numbers. Numerical utility allows us to associate the basic properties of numbers with the consumer's actions. For example, given any two numbers, x and y, one (and only one) of three relationships between the two numbers can hold: x is greater than y, x is less than y, or x is equal to y. In terms of individual preference, this means that either one bundle is preferred to another or the consumer is *indifferent* between the two. (Just as economists use "rational" in a nonstandard way, "indifference" simply means having no preference without regard to whether one actually "cares" about the choice at hand.)

A more important property of numerical utility is that it facilitates the extension of the notion of preference from two items to any number of items. This is done using the property of transitivity, which was mentioned earlier in the context of individual rationality. Transitivity is the property of numbers that makes it so that when x is greater than y and y is greater than z, then x must also be greater than z. For example, 1,000 is greater than 100, which in turn is greater than 10, clearly making 1,000 greater than 10. In terms of preference, this means that if a consumer prefers pizza to pasta and prefers pasta to peanut butter, then he prefers pizza to peanut butter. When it is possible to associate an appropriate number of jollies to consumption patterns, then transitivity of preferences is automatic. Economists see transitivity as an important requirement for rationality, both for individuals and for society as a whole.

The major limitation of utility is that it focuses on what individuals receive rather than on the process by which they receive it. Psychological studies of economic decision making provide strong experimental evidence that the process by which a decision is reached frequently influences the choices of individuals. In financial decision making, the research of Richard Thaler has shown the importance of *mental accounting*, which has investors behave differently depending on whether the money at risk is their own money or "house money," the accumulated appreciation of their holdings. In such cases, while it is still possible to model individual decision making, it is not possible to collapse individual preferences into a single number, such as utility. In a similar vein, even if the individual preferences can be neatly quantified, their preferences considered in aggregate may not be.

The Limits to Aggregation

The possibility that utility might be observable fired the imaginations of British economists at the end of the nineteenth century. With the industrial age well under way and the emergence of engineering as a serious discipline in the physical realm, the possibility of social engineering based on the new science of economics seemed close at hand. With utility as a way to score the happiness of individuals, adding those scores together will then determine the utility of society as a whole. The goal of humanity—a never-ending source of philosophical debate—became apparent: the maximization of *social utility*.

Although any attempt to measure utility objectively has long been abandoned, the *utilitarian* philosophy had a revolutionary impact on both politics and economics. Utilitarianism was important not because of the details involved in measuring and aggregating utility, but because it placed the individual desires of humans above all else, beyond deity and state. In the secular philosophy of the British Empire, Plato's Republic had served as the paradigm for the perfect society, with an abstract notion of virtue— rather than the preferences of individuals—guiding the actions of the state. In contrast, the utilitarians, beginning at the end of the eighteenth century with Jeremy Bentham—a noted eccentric who arranged to have his body dissected by his friends and then stuffed for public display upon his death—saw human pleasure as the highest virtue.

In its purest form, utilitarianism is strong on efficiency and weak on fairness. The mathematics of maximizing social utility are such that any allocation that generates the most social utility must also satisfy a property known as *Pareto optimality*, after the Italian economist Vilfredo Pareto, who succeeded Leon Walras as the intellectual leader of the Lausanne School in Switzerland. An allocation of goods in an economy is Pareto optimal if there is no other way to allocate goods that will make someone better off without making someone else worse off. In a zero-sum game, such as the division of $10 between two people, all the allocations are Pareto optimal—any gain by one person must come at the expense of another. Under the right conditions, such as those found in many laboratory experiments, the allocations generated by the market mechanism are Pareto optimal; however, just because an allocation of goods is Pareto optimal does not make it socially worthwhile. In particular, many Pareto-optimal allocations are highly inequitable, concentrating wealth in the hands of a few. The Fascist politics of Pareto himself have served to help cast an unflattering light on his concept of optimality.

Any efforts to balance efficiency with equity are likely to be frustrated. Karl Marx had a utopian vision of a world in which labor would be extracted "from each according to his ability" and goods allocated "to each according to his need." The real-world application of these principles is fraught with moral hazard as each individual in the economy has powerful incentives to understate ability and overstate need.

While market-based economies are not so radical as to coerce their most able to work the hardest in service of society as a whole, the use of an income tax both to finance the government and redistribute income carries with it a sizeable efficiency cost. These problems parallel those that arise in educational signaling. An individual's true productivity, which parallels Marx's concept of "ability," is not readily observable. Instead, one's income, especially that generated by one's own labor, is observable, serving as a signal of productivity. An individual's income, however, depends not only on productivity, but also on the amount and intensity of effort exerted. By placing a tax on income, the government creates moral hazard, it gives everyone who is taxed an incentive to reduce his or her effort. In a world of perfect information, the government could observe an individual's productivity and levy a tax on it directly, uncoupling the tax from an individual's effort and eliminating moral hazard and the incentive to shirk.

Not surprisingly, William Vickery, the father of auction theory, was among the first to understand the moral hazard involved in income taxation, writing about it in the 1940s. By the 1970s, James Mirrlees at Oxford derived a formal theory of optimal income taxation that required sophisticated mathematics comparable to that used by Black, Scholes, and Merton to price options. The most striking of Mirrlees' results was that under a wide range of assumptions, the optimal income tax appeared to be a flat tax with a marginal rate around 20 percent and a "negative income tax" feature in which those at the bottom of the income scale actually received money from the government rather than paying it in. At the time that Mirrlees' work was published, most developed countries had income tax schedules that were confiscatory at even moderately high income levels, damaging efficiency out of proportion to any gains in equity. As knowledge of Mirrlees' work spread, developed countries began to experiment with lower marginal tax rates, with the United States adopting a nearly flat tax schedule under President Ronald Reagan. This schedule remained in place until President George Bush broke his infamous pledge: "Read my lips, no new taxes." Although President Bush—as well as President Clinton after him—moved away from a relatively flat income tax, Professors Vickery and Mirrlees jointly received the 1996 Nobel Prize in Economics for their work on taxation, which inspired much of the research into informational asymmetries, including lemons and signaling.

The general problem of how to allocate goods within an economy, striking the proper balance between efficiency and equity, involves aggregating the preferences of individuals in the economy. Any solution to this problem involves not only the measurement of individual utility, but also the construction of a weighting scheme to balance one individual's utility against another's. In the late 1940s, Kenneth Arrow was searching for a topic for his doctoral dissertation at Columbia University, and found the problem of aggregating individual preferences into social preferences. This problem had its roots in a paradox discovered by the Marquis de Condorcet, one of the leading philosophers of the French Enlightenment.

The *Condorcet paradox* can be illustrated with a simple example involving three individuals—Amy, Barb, and Cathy—who must choose among three alternatives—x, y, and z. Suppose that Amy prefers x to y, y to z, and x to z; Barb prefers y to x, y to z, and z to x; and Cathy prefers x to y, z to y, and z to x. Notice that everyone's preferences are transitive. Now, consider aggregating the preferences of the three individuals in the only obvious way, using majority rule. Between x and y, Amy and Cathy form a majority, and so x is preferred to y. Between y and z, Amy and Barb form a majority, and so y is preferred to z. Finally, between x and z, Barb and Cathy form a majority, and so z is preferred to x. Although all the individual choices are transitive, the social choice determined by majority rule is not: x should be preferred to z, but instead z is preferred to x. Because transitivity is critical to any notion of rationality, the Condorcet paradox calls into question the rationality of social preferences that try to be consistent with individual preferences.

Arrow's world-shaking contribution to economics, political science, and philosophy was to show that Condorcet's paradox could be generalized beyond voting to any social choice mechanism, including markets. The only way that Arrow found to ensure the rationality of social choice was to dodge the aggregation problem by appointing one individual as a dictator, whose preferences would be imposed on all of society. Such a dictator would have to rule strictly according to his own personal preferences; a benevolent dictator who desired the best for his subjects would himself fall victim to Arrow's impossibility result in his efforts to consider the preferences of his subjects in a consistent manner.

The use of formal mechanisms to allocate goods in an economy does not appear promising. Arrow's negative findings were further reinforced by those of Oxford economist Amartya Sen, who was awarded the 1998 Nobel Prize in Economics for work on social choice mechanisms. Professor Sen showed that under very general circumstances any political mechanism that allowed individuals any input into the affairs of others could not avoid being inefficient.

Bad news about social choice mechanisms also came from the laboratory. Charles Plott, who was pioneering the application of experimental methods to problems of social choice while he was running his first market experiments, teamed up with University of Southern California law professor Michael Levine (who went on to become a major figure in the U.S. airline industry) to examine how agenda, the order in which decisions are made, influences choice. Professor Levine belonged to a flying club that had to decide which makes and models of airplanes to purchase for its members' use and began thinking about the possibility that the order in which votes were taken (the agenda) could influence the selection of airplanes by the club. For example, in a situation where the Condorcet paradox given above is applicable, if one can limit the agenda to voting on one pair of alternatives at a time, then the order in which the votes are taken will determine the outcome. If Amy controls the agenda and wants to have her first choice, x, prevail, she should arrange for the first vote to be between y and z because the winner of that vote (y) will then lose to x. Following a somewhat more complex line of reasoning, Professors Plott and Levine developed a series of laboratory experiments to show that the flying club's choice of aircraft could be reliably manipulated by controlling the agenda used to choose among all possible aircraft.

The work of Kenneth Arrow and those who followed him may have precluded the construction of an ideal social choice mechanism based on individual preferences as envisioned by the utilitarians, but the world has managed somehow to muddle along using a variety of flawed measures. For example, the economic welfare of any group of people can be roughly measured by their total income suitably adjusted to account for how equally or unequally that income is distributed. The money that people receive in the form of income serves not only as an economic yardstick, but also as the ultimate lubricant for the gears of commerce. Given the special role of money in economics, the next chapter is dedicated entirely to it.

10

It All Comes
Down to Money

I n the perfect economic world, there would be no money. Money is an artifice designed to patch up the market's largest holes. If these holes did not exist, then neither would money. As we saw earlier, the assumption that every market has effectively unbounded liquidity leads to difficulties that can culminate in a Black Monday. Given that overall liquidity in a market system may be limited, it makes sense to choose a single market to serve as the liquidity reservoir on which other markets can draw. The name we give to the good whose market provides this liquidity is *money*. Earlier, we euphemistically referred to derivative securities as helper securities because they helped to fill the holes in the market system. Modern money can be viewed as the ultimate helper or derivative security that requires only faith to support its value.

The path of human progress is reflected in the changing nature of money. From its humble origins as large and unwieldy stone disks, the substance of money has evolved from gold to paper to plastic and (ultimately) to electrons. While most people think of money in concrete terms—coins and bills that facilitate their everyday economic transactions—money at its essence is the purest of abstractions. Money is the supreme form of economic liquidity—the universal medium of payment for goods and services. In advanced economies, money is protean, assuming numerous forms that blur the distinction between it and other assets. Indeed, sufficiently liquid assets, such as U.S. Treasury Bills, serve as money for many financial transactions. In the world of high finance, money only rarely takes on a physical form; the largest financial transactions are simply electronic transfers from one account to another that are divorced from the conventional image of "money changing hands."

The liquidity that money provides comes with a cost. Money pays less interest than comparable debt securities; indeed, traditional forms of money—cash and simple checking accounts—pay no interest at all. Demand deposits at banks, which are nearly as liquid as currency because they can be withdrawn at any time, pay less interest than deposits with limits or penalties attached to their withdrawal. Any financial asset that is risky enough to garner a premium rate of return is likely to be too risky to serve as money. The demand for money, like anything else, is influenced by its "price," the interest forgone by holding money rather than tying the funds up in a less liquid investment.

The supply of money is a bit more complicated than its demand. The amount of money that is available is determined by a country's financial system. Generally, the controlling authority of this system is a central bank, such as the Federal Reserve Bank in the United States or the European Central Bank in Europe. Both direct intervention in the financial markets, known in the U.S. as open market operations, and indirect intervention in the form of regulations that govern financial institutions can influence the supply of money in the economy.

Money—in whatever forms it takes—works only because of the trust that its users place in it. Viewed at face value, a hundred-dollar bill or a hundred-pound note is just a piece of paper with fancy engravings and embedded doodads designed to make it difficult to counterfeit. Unlike earlier forms of money that were backed by gold or other precious metals, present-day currency is *fiat money*—it does not convert into anything, making it beyond redemption. Some tax protesters have refused to pay taxes claiming that the fiat money in which they are paid is not real money for tax purposes, but rather "greenies"—not to be confused with the affectionate nickname given Alan Greenspan by some Fed watchers—that have no value and so are exempt from taxation. The courts have not taken kindly to such arguments and give the protestors the choice of parting with the greenies owed to the government or going to jail.

Although it might seem preferable to have money backed by something real, like gold, the value of fiat money is easier to control. The problem with "real money" is the possibility that its precious backing could suddenly become less precious without warning or reason. For example, the 1849 California gold rush reduced the value of gold-backed money by increasing the supply of gold. Alternatively, fiat money requires a faith in government and central banks that may not always be warranted.

The establishment of the faith that people currently place in money has taken a long time to develop, with several notable crises of confidence in the past century alone periodically testing that faith. The most spectacular monetary crisis occurred in Germany during the 1920s. At the time, the Weimar Republic was heavily burdened with the debt incurred from the massive cost of World War I, including the reparation payments owed to the Allies. Out of financial desperation, the Weimar authorities undermined the value of the currency by printing more money. The resulting *hyperinflation*, in which the value of the mark plummeted by the minute— so that prices in restaurants would rise while diners ate and workers were paid twice a day—served as an object lesson in the dangers of shattering the faith that stands behind money. To both Germany and the world the cost of this lesson was most horrific, as the collapse of the Weimar Republic brought about by the hyperinflation set the stage for the rise to power of Hitler and the Nazis.

Soon after the German hyperinflation, the United States experienced its own monetary crisis. Building on the inventions of Thomas Alva Edison, Orville and Wilbur Wright, Alexander Graham Bell, and many others, the United States had catapulted itself from a backwater agrarian economy recovering from a painful Civil War to a modern paragon of technological innovation. Many Americans viewed the coming of the "modern age" with suspicion, especially the majority of the population that continued to live outside the new metropolises. When the Great Depression began, the fact that banks did not have all their depositors' money on hand, but rather had lent it out to earn interest, fed this suspicion. The unhappy result was a series of runs on banks in which depositors would besiege banks in an effort to withdraw their money while they still could.

President Franklin Delano Roosevelt declared a "bank holiday" soon after his inauguration in March 1933 to buy the time necessary to shore up the banking system and enact the reforms that would restore the lost faith in the banking system. Eventually, faith in the financial system was restored, even though it required weakening the link between dollar-denominated currency and the gold that had traditionally backed it. This intervention in the financial markets established the precedent that would resurface in the form of stock-market circuit breakers.

Money, Expectations, and Illusion

In a theoretical world of perfect markets, money is perfectly redundant. General equilibrium theory, created in the neoclassical mold by Leon Walras and then worked out fully by Kenneth Arrow and Gerard Debreu, has no place for money. In the neoclassical framework, supply and demand in each market is determined only by the *relative* prices of goods; hence, all economic transactions can be done using barter. Anyone stuck with an item that is useless to him can ultimately barter it away for something useful. The absolute determination of prices that money provides is an arbitrary convenience that has no effect on the allocation of goods. Typically, one can designate a single good—such as gold or silver—to be what Walras called a *numeraire*—the standard against which all other prices are denominated.

Just because an economic construct, such as money, is theoretically redundant, does not mean that we would be better off without it. Recall that options were redundant and this redundancy was required to value them. However, the redundancy of options relied on an unrealistic assumption, perfect liquidity, that no market could be expected to meet it. As a result, the absence of options in the market would not only be noticed, it could be destabilizing.

In its own way, money is more redundant than any option. Nonetheless, in a world where liquidity is valued, the convenience and relatively low cost of money more than offsets its redundancy. In the neoclassical model with money appended to it, the relative prices of goods remain the determinant of supply and demand. If the quantity of money were instantaneously doubled—with every "old" dollar becoming two "new" dollars—then, in theory at least, the response would be for all prices to double. This would maintain the original competitive equilibrium quantities, but with every price at exactly double its former level.

The neoclassicists had an excellent reason to strongly embrace this *quantity theory of money*. Viewed mechanistically, changing the amount of money in circulation is equivalent to restating the units in which prices are measured. Any reasonable theory of the physical world must be independent of the units of measurement—a car travels at the same speed regardless of whether it is measured in miles per hour, feet per second, or kilometers per minute—and so the economic world should also operate without regard to monetary units. The only problem with this analogy is that the economy is not purely mechanistic; its behavior depends on the perceptions and expectations of its producers and consumers.

The most dramatic illustration of the possible link between money and economic activity is the *Phillips curve*—an outgrowth of Keynesian economics. The British economist A. W. Phillips observed that unemployment and inflation in the United Kingdom were inversely correlated; when inflation was high unemployment was low and vice versa. When properly plotted on a two-dimensional graph, unemployment and inflation rates appeared to fit so nicely along a curve that most Keynesian economists embraced this curve and named it after Phillips.

A straightforward explanation for the inverse relationship between unemployment and inflation given by the Phillips curve is money illusion. Consumers are fooled by the extra money they receive into thinking that they are richer, so they increase their spending, which stimulates output and employment. In the 1960s, the Phillips curve was all the rage, with only Milton Friedman and his followers, known as *monetarists*, waving the flag for the quantity theory of money and standing in opposition to the popular Keynesians.

Monetarists opposed using monetary policy to stimulate the economy, believing that the Federal Reserve should target the level of the money supply so that it would rise at the same rate as the overall growth rate of the economy. In this way, the supply of money and the amount of goods in the economy would stay in balance. Although the prices of individual goods would fluctuate to reflect changes in supply and demand, the overall level of prices would stay the same, making the inflation rate equal to zero. If money is to exist merely as a convenience, it will be the most convenient if its users do not need to track changes in its value from one moment to the next.

By the 1970s, Wall Street focused on a single number for clues about future inflation, the weekly money supply figures released by the Federal Reserve. Large increases in this number, which were viewed as a signal of future inflation, would spook financial markets. Soon, the thinking of Milton Friedman and the monetarists took hold at the Fed and it started to use the policy tools at its disposal to keep the growth of the money supply in check. These efforts were eventually abandoned as advances in technology began to raise questions as to what money was anyway.

A major financial advance of the 1970s, which was a response to accelerating inflation and regulatory limits on interest payments, was the development of interest-bearing savings and money market accounts that came with check-writing privileges. From a legal point of view these "checks," which were known by names such as *negotiable orders of withdrawal* (NOW), were not really checks; nonetheless, merchants treated them like any other check. Several competing measures—the monetary base, M1, M2, and M3—could now represent the abstraction of money in economists' policy models, with each measure including some forms of money and excluding others. With inflation eventually coming under control, the various M's, none of which worked particularly well, have been largely forgotten while the concept of money grows fuzzier all the time.

Then two events derailed the Phillips curve and brought Milton Friedman's Chicago School to the forefront of the economics profession. First, the persistent inflation of the 1970s pushed many economies off the Phillips curve. As inflation persisted, it no longer came as a surprise and so unemployment no longer fell in response to it. Inflation that had been a benign element of a growing economy turned into the dreaded *stagflation*—inflation in a stagnating economy. Second, Robert Lucas updated monetary theory to incorporate the ideas of information and learning that were used in the signaling models and created the theory of *rational expectations*.

In a rational expectations equilibrium, consumers may be dazzled by the bounty that inflation initially bestows upon them; however, they immediately realize that because inflation raises prices throughout the economy, they are not really any richer. The breakthrough that Lucas made was to extend the notion of rationality beyond the ability to choose among known alternatives to an ability to think through the "global" consequences of an event such as an increase in inflation. Lucas was not the first economist to believe that individuals could spin economic theories in their heads: Recall that Marshall believed that in a world of perfect knowledge everyone could solve the equations of supply and demand in their heads so that they would all know what prices should be. Furthermore, the assumption that agents in an economy could reason through the consequences of inflation is similar to that made by Keynes in his beauty contest analogy for the stock market. For Lucas, economic rationality extended beyond "consistent greed" to an understanding of the inner workings of the economy.

The triumph of rational expectations over the Phillips curve does not mean that the theory of rational expectations is not without its shortcomings. A joke that has circulated among economists for years involves an economics professor walking down a street with one of his graduate students when they see a hundred-dollar bill on the sidewalk. The graduate student, who is farther from the bill, says to his professor, "Why don't you pick that bill up?" The professor—clearly of the Chicago persuasion—replies, "Haven't you learned anything I've taught you? If it were real, someone else would certainly have picked it up by now."

Although this is a joke that only an economist could love, it does point out a serious limitation of rational expectations that formed the basis for a most enlightening article by Sanford Grossman and Joseph Stiglitz. They proved that under general conditions it would be difficult to get anyone to pick up the "money left on the streets" of a world composed solely of economically rational individuals. In addition, they showed that our ability to reverse engineer information about the state of the world from market prices is compromised when reliable information is either concentrated among a few, privileged individuals or is costly to obtain. The problem is that information is often a public good and so it is entirely rational for individuals to try to "free ride" off of the information-gathering efforts of others. Of course, if everyone thinks this way—assuming that market prices accurately reflect all available information—then everyone will be wrong because no one expended the effort to gather the information in the first place. Notice that this free rider problem closely parallels that facing the price discovery process of the market mechanism itself.

The Phillips Curve may have been buried deeply in the graveyard of economic theory; however, the possibility that money illusion exists in some form lives on in a theory developed by Franco Modigliani and Richard Cohn. This theory was one of many that was inspired by the stagflation that battered both stock and bond markets in the 1970s. Modigliani and Cohn noticed that there was a strong tendency for profits reported by corporations to lag inflation at times when inflation was increasing. While companies and their investors could readily deal with changes in relative prices, which do not affect common financial measures such as price/earnings ratios and dividend yields, Modigliani and Cohn found that inflation could significantly depress the earnings that companies reported in a subtle way that did not affect their true, inflation-adjusted earnings.

As inflation increases, firms must pay higher interest rates on the money they borrow to compensate the lenders for the reduced future value of principal and interest payments. For example, if inflation increases from 2 percent per annum to 5 percent per annum, then interest on a firm's debt that was at 6 percent before the increase would have to go up to 9 percent in order to insulate the lender from the effects of inflation. In economic terms, the increase in the *nominal interest rate* from 6 percent to 9 percent was necessary to keep the *real interest rate* at 4 percent. (Actually, to compensate for any taxes on interest income, the interest rate would have to go up by even more to generate the same real after-tax return to the lender.)

The accounting procedures for deducting the cost of interest on a company's outstanding debt do not take into account that the value of money used to repay the debt may be worth less than the money that was originally borrowed. The failure to make this adjustment leads to an illusion that profits decline (relative to other prices) when inflation increases. Hence, some of the relative decline in corporate profits observed in the 1970s, which dragged stock prices down with them, was just an accounting illusion.

Interest in the Modigliani-Cohn theory was rekindled in the late 1990s as a steady decline in inflation from the peaks attained several years earlier coincided with the longest bull market in American history. In addition, while any assumption that required individuals to be afflicted with any form of illusion was a radical departure in the heyday of rational expectations, the rise of behavioral finance positioned research on money illusion closer to the mainstream of financial thought. Just as increases in inflation will artificially depress reported corporate profits, decreases will artificially enhance them. These illusory increases cannot go on forever because low inflation alone is not enough to keep them going; inflation must spiral downward indefinitely. Once inflation stabilizes or turns back up, the eventual increase in the cost of debt will eat into reported profits.

The author, in collaboration with Evan Schulman, who developed some of the first computerized trading systems and auction markets, found new statistical evidence to support the theory of money illusion. As discussed earlier, it may be difficult to determine in the laboratory whether stock prices are too high or too low; however, this is not the only way that money illusion will manifest itself. A less ambiguous symptom of money illusion is statistical evidence that shows that the stock market and the bond market are more likely to move in the same direction—with higher yields on bonds (lower bond prices) driving down stock prices and vice versa—when inflation is high. Although money illusion is not the only possible explanation for this phenomenon, when money illusion is present, one would expect it to have a greater impact when prices (and nominal interest rates) are high than when they are low. This result is significant for many investment managers because it indicates that the diversification one normally gains from holding stocks and bonds together in a portfolio may be greatly reduced during inflationary times.

Money illusion is also a fruitful area for experimental study because it is relatively easy to take a laboratory exchange environment, run it until it converges, and then uniformly shift all the parameters at the beginning of a period to see how the market responds. Ernest Fehr at the University of Zurich and Jean-Robert Tyran at the University of St. Gallen in Switzerland have done exactly that in a small-scale experiment that employs four subjects, and their preliminary experiments show that money illusion is easily induced in this controlled setting.

The Emergence of Money

The greatest money illusion might just be money itself. Over time, the evolution of money can be viewed as a steady path from the material to the virtual. Convenience has certainly been a primary driver of this change. Originally, large hunks of base metals were replaced by the smaller hunks of precious metal that ultimately became coins. Then, you could leave the precious metal with a bank and carry around paper that was essentially a receipt for the precious metal. Finally, with the advent of fiat money, the link to the physical world was broken and so the journey into the information world could begin.

The economic force that hastens the movement away from physical forms of money is the higher cost of processing it. Already, it is common for dollar-denominated travelers checks to be worth more than paper dollars outside of the United States. This is because the physical dollars must ultimately be shipped back to the United States for redemption in the local currency, while travelers checks can be settled at a much lower cost electronically.

It is reasonable to expect that technology will facilitate the conversion of virtually all money to electronic form. Computer visionaries see a day in the near future where coins and currency become obsolete. In these visions, an all-purpose handheld computer-based communications device along the lines of contemporary palm-sized computers will instantly transfer money to pay for purchases on an electromagnetic beam "zapped" from the device to the merchant at the point of sale.

The generally recognized cyberprophet of the future world of virtual money is none other than F. A. Hayek. In 1978, he argued against the issuance of money by central banks, proposing instead that money itself could be the product of the spontaneous order brought about by the market system. Embedded within all the complexity of a market economy, no one has to consciously create money; rather, money just emerges, making it what scientists who study complex systems call an *emergent property* of the system.

The emergence of money has recently become the focus of economic experimentation. John Duffy and Jack Ochs at the University of Pittsburgh have created trading environments in the laboratory and have found circumstances under which one good emerges as money—the way traders can hold balances for transactions in future periods. (This is like the carry-over that occurred in the original Miller, Plott, and Smith speculation experiments except that the good carried over—money—may have no consumption value.) The learning that is required of subjects in these experiments is similar to that required in the signaling experiments described in the previous chapter, and so the good that emerges as money is not always the most efficient. Even though the results of this line of research are still quite preliminary, it is encouraging to see that money can emerge spontaneously in a controlled environment.

Future Money

Physical money cannot vanish until several major technological issues are addressed. A number of advances in *cryptography*, the science of secret codes, may be able to resolve several concerns about the security and privacy of electronic transactions. Still, the early days of electronic commerce have uncovered many instances where transactions over the Internet have been neither secure nor private. While cryptography has focused on codes that are theoretically unbreakable, they also need to develop codes that are foolproof. An important lesson comes from the entertainment world, where the regional encryption method for Digital Video (or Versatile) Discs (DVDs), known as the Content Scrambling System (CSS), was compromised soon after it was introduced by the careless actions of a single DVD producer.

An even more serious challenge is the public acceptance of electronic money. A 1997–1998 trial of a rudimentary form of electronic cash, the smart card, in New York City's affluent Upper West Side conducted by a consortium of some of the world's largest banks and credit card issuers was a resounding failure. The 100,000 consumers and 600 merchants enrolled in the 14-month trial shunned the system; electronic cash was used for just over $1 million in transactions, or $10 per card. In a press release issued at the end of the trial, the consortium noted that the trial "provided important learnings [*sic*] about the benefits and challenges involved with smart cards in a concentrated urban environment." It appears likely that more learning will be necessary before a system of electronic money will be found that comes close to reaching universal acceptance.

In its ultimate electronic form, money will effectively disappear completely, becoming "transparent" to its users. In a world of transparent currencies, everyone could transact in a familiar currency and the translation from one currency to another would take place automatically, without the costly intervention of middlemen. In effect, the market mechanism itself could serve as a "universal translator" allowing everyone to "speak" in his own currency while being able to transact with everyone else in the world market. The costs associated with maintaining not just a single redundant form of money—but an entire universe of them—would be almost entirely eliminated and the overall liquidity of the marketplace would be vastly enhanced.

The basic function of money, to serve as a link between transactions separated over time and space, does not require any physical manifestation—it can be embodied in the networks of computers that constitute the financial system. In theory, using computers to provide liquidity rather than a harder form of currency should generate substantial cost savings—the convenience of real money comes with a significant price tag attached to it.

A global financial monetary system based on virtual money is not without its dangers. With the liquidity of the economy built right into the financial network, when the network fails, so does the economy. In September 1998, the world got its first peek at how such a failure might appear. The final part of this book begins by looking at the future of financial disasters and considering how the connections within the market mechanism might be designed to prevent them.

PART III

GRIDLOCK AND THE ROAD TO SMART MARKETS

11

The Market Is
Tied Up in Knots

As long as there have been markets, industrious individuals have
sought to profit from networking them together. In turn, these
networked markets provide many advantages to the economy. Intuitively, as a market system becomes better connected—a trend spurred
on by improvements in information technology—it should also become
more efficient. However, as the markets become more tightly linked, the
risk of *financial contagion*—where troubles in one market spread to another
like an infectious disease—is increased. Furthermore, entirely new kinds of
problems arise that cannot be traced to any individual market, but rather to
the linkages among them.

To see how things might go awry within a market network, consider
a network of another type: the network of streets and highways that are
at the core of the transportation system in developed economies. Although early roads were prone to structural problems that advances in
civil engineering would overcome, excess traffic was rarely a consideration. The high cost of vehicles kept traffic light on all but the most traveled roads.

The mass production of automobiles in the 1920s introduced a new
phenomenon to the civilized world: the traffic jam. Accidents or excess
traffic could cause the agonizing slowdowns that have come to be identified with modern life. Still, the modern traffic jam was merciful in that it

would usually resolve itself. When the obstruction was cleared or traffic thinned out of its own accord, vehicular flow would return to normal.

Beginning in the 1970s, midtown Manhattan in New York City regularly experienced traffic jams that were not so easily resolved. Unlike other older cities with roads that were formerly cow paths, midtown streets form a manmade rectangular grid with Broadway on the diagonal. The capacity of this grid has not grown over time because most buildings are set so close to the street that any significant street widening would be prohibitively expensive. Notwithstanding parking fees so high that they leave many visitors to the city in a state of shock, automobile traffic into Manhattan grew steadily in the postwar years as the workforce expanded and moved to the suburbs, often without convenient access to mass transit. As a result, Manhattan's traffic network would increasingly find itself in a state of *gridlock*.

In gridlock, there are so many cars in the traffic grid that cars become trapped in major intersections. These cars block the progress of other cars, so the problem spreads to neighboring intersections. Unlike the traffic jams of yesteryear, gridlock may not simply resolve itself; police intervention can be required to back enough cars out of the grid so that the normal flow of traffic can be restored. Over time, many people have come to use the terms "traffic jam" and "gridlock" interchangeably; however, true gridlock involves traffic that has come to a halt not just at a few points, but where the stoppage has spread through the grid.

Traffic engineers fought gridlock in a number of ways. The most obvious of these measures is the "Don't Block the Box" law that imposes a hefty fine on any car that becomes stuck in midtown intersections, many of which are marked with a white box. Drivers must ensure that there is space for their vehicles on the other side of an intersection before they proceed through it. In addition, limits on turns at key intersections help to keep traffic flowing, especially when uniformed personnel are assigned to monitor those intersections at peak travel times. Finally, the City announces "gridlock alerts" to discourage drivers from taking their vehicles into areas expected to have heavy traffic, such as near the United Nations when a head of state visits or around Fifth Avenue when holiday shoppers descend on it.

What all these anti-gridlock measures have in common is that they are designed to restrict the options of drivers, either by limiting their behavior once they are in the grid or keeping them from entering it in the first place. Any inconvenience imposed on an individual driver by the inability to travel freely is a small cost relative to that of gridlock, which impedes all travel. Similarly, within a network of markets the maintenance of free trade throughout the system may also require a transfer of options from individual traders to the market mechanism.

As it stood at the end of the twentieth century, the global financial market system was more like a collection of cow paths than the traffic grid of a modern city. Almost every link between markets was provided not as a spontaneous action of the market system, but rather through the deliberate efforts of arbitrageurs and speculators. Nonetheless, our current financial system can still provide insight into the pitfalls that a sophisticated market network might face.

Long-Term Gridlock

It is difficult to imagine a scenario in which financial markets could become so entangled that government intervention would be necessary to back traders' positions out of the system like automobiles caught in gridlock. Nonetheless, in September 1998, the Federal Reserve Bank of New York under the watchful eye of Fed Chairman Alan Greenspan oversaw the unwinding of what might well be the first major instance of financial gridlock.

The financial vehicle blocking global financial traffic in September 1998 was Long-Term Capital Management (LTCM), a hedge fund operating out of Greenwich, Connecticut, putting it just out of reach of the New York State tax collector. LTCM opened for business in 1994, operating as a hedge fund that really hedged. Piloted by John Meriwether and the brain trust that he brought with him from Salomon Brothers, LTCM methodically searched the financial markets for arbitrage opportunities. Each time an opportunity was spotted, LTCM established a sizeable, expertly hedged position in two or more related securities that would generate a profit when their prices returned to equilibrium.

In the early days of the fund, LTCM focused on U.S. Treasury and other fixed-income securities, the specialty of Meriwether's team at Salomon before they became entangled in a Treasury securities bidding scandal that effectively drove them out of Salomon Brothers. As we noted earlier, some Treasury securities attract a premium price (and a correspondingly lower yield) because the market for them is more liquid—that is, they have a lower bid/ask spread and a deep market (lots of bids and offers near the going price). This premium has tended to be the greatest for the 30-year Treasury bond, which often has a significantly higher price (and lower yield) than the bond with the next longest maturity, a "seasoned" 30-year bond issued within the past year. (To simplify matters, we will refer to these bonds as 29-year bonds, even though they can have maturities as long as 29 years and 9 months.) Much of this premium comes from a "boundary effect" that arises because the 30-year bond has the longest available maturity, making it the bond of choice to hedge annuity and pension fund obligations that extend into the distant future. Because the premium on the 30-year bond is not permanent—it will begin to vanish as soon as a new 30-year bond appears on the horizon—money can be made by buying the 29-year bond and selling an equal amount of the 30-year bond.

LTCM's business strategy was brilliant in its simplicity. By exploiting its superior brainpower and state-of-the-art information systems, LTCM would work to be the first to uncover apparent mispricing in the market and establish positions that would profit from prices coming back into line. This type of trading that exploits transient mispricing that the market mechanism should ultimately correct is known as *convergence trading* when the prices must converge by a predetermined date and *relative value trading* when convergence in a reasonable amount of time is not assured. Because they often found only slightly mispriced securities, LTCM used as much margin as its brokers would provide to leverage its position up so that it could make a significant return on its capital. The price impact of LTCM's trades was likely to squeeze out some of the mispricing immediately and the discovery of the mispricing by other traders would eventually bring the market back into approximate equilibrium. At this point, LTCM could unwind the position and realize its profits. The "Long-Term" in Long-Term Capital Management's name implied that it was willing to stick with its positions as long as necessary for markets to equilibrate and make its trades profitable. (It also signaled to investors that they should be prepared to entrust LTCM with their money for the long term.)

The critical problem that LTCM faced was the incentive for other Wall Street players to free ride off its advantage in the marketplace. While emulation of its strategies by its financial rivals was desirable after LTCM had established its position—providing LTCM with the opportunity to exit gracefully—they had to establish their positions under a veil of absolute secrecy. Unfortunately for LTCM, the only brokers large enough to handle the volume of LTCM's trades had their own proprietary trading groups that directly competed with LTCM. Although securities law requires a "Chinese Wall" that keeps the information that brokers receive from leaking to the rest of their firm, LTCM undoubtedly knew from experience of its street-smart partners the ease with which such information could penetrate walls.

Even with security at the "I could tell you, but then I'd have to kill you" level of paranoia, LTCM's strategies were subject to "widespread emulation" as the Bank of International Settlements later termed it in their report. While LTCM may have prided itself in its ability to figure out its trades to a fraction of a basis point using some of the most sophisticated mathematics in the financial world, any trader who received a fresh MBA would likely have learned the same basic techniques from the teachers, classmates, or students of LTCM's brain trust.

While LTCM may have worked hard to conceal its strategies, it proudly trumpeted its track record, which was among the best of hedge funds that exploited asset mispricing. Given the pool of talent that was running the firm, it did not take a rocket scientist to figure out roughly what LTCM was doing to get such impressive results.

By 1997 LTCM and the growing rank of traders who emulated it had exhausted the easy money to be made through arbitrage; one could no longer expect to find hundred-dollar bills lying on the sidewalk. Recognizing the increasing scarcity of arbitrage opportunities and wishing to capitalize on the few that remained for their own accounts, the partners of LTCM not only closed their fund to new investors, they returned a sizeable amount of their investors' money. Meanwhile, the proprietary trading operation that John Meriwether and his LTCM partners had left behind at Salomon Brothers—now part of Salomon Smith Barney and preparing to become part of Citigroup when the pending merger of Citicorp and Travelers Group (parent of Salomon Smith Barney) closed—could no longer trade profitably and so it was disbanded. As it turned out, the investors whose stakes in LTCM were downsized and the holders of Citigroup shares would be the lucky ones.

With opportunities for risk-free arbitrage becoming increasingly rare—just as the efficient market theory predicts—LTCM began plunging into the unfamiliar waters of *risk arbitrage*, in which the profits from arbitrage are realized only if the outcome of an uncertain financial event, such as a corporate takeover, is correctly predicted. The stock price of a company targeted for acquisition usually trades at a discount to the price payable on completion of the takeover. This discount is not competed away because should the takeover fail, which is possible for a variety of reasons, the stock price of the target is likely to plummet unless a substitute buyer is quickly found. As one would expect, this discount tends to be larger the greater the chance that the takeover will fail. When the acquisition is made using shares of the acquirer's stock, this discount will take the form of an apparent arbitrage opportunity that can be exploited by buying the stock of the target and selling the stock of the acquirer in the proper proportions, usually those specified in the takeover agreement.

The move to riskier strategies certainly contributed to LTCM's downfall, but there was a more fundamental reason why they had failed to manage their risks properly. LTCM started by employing arbitrage strategies in which all market risk was hedged. The overall position that they took was neither long nor short interest rates, making them appear completely free from risk. But they were not. On the contrary, their aggregate position contained massive amounts of liquidity risk. Because LTCM's positions did not include sufficient options—such as those contained in puts and calls— that would guarantee them a way out, they ended up taking a long position on the future liquidity of the market. In essence, they were betting that the financial grid would be freely navigable if and when they needed to exit their positions.

In the summer of 1998, holding a long position in liquidity turned out to be most uncomfortable. Russia shocked the financial markets by effectively defaulting on its debt in August. As concern grew that other issuers of risky debt might follow Russia's lead, the premium that the market demanded for assuming credit risk, as measured by their yield spread relative to "risk-free" Treasury securities, shot up to levels that had never been seen, much less imagined. In fact, the published yields tended to understate the seriousness of the problem because many high-risk bonds had stopped trading altogether.

Under normal circumstances, the value attached to high-risk bond portfolios, such as those held by mutual funds, is only an estimate provided by a bond-pricing service. Many risky bonds do not trade every day, and may not even trade every month, and so statistical methods must be used to estimate the value of the bonds that do not trade from the market prices of those that do—a procedure known as *matrix pricing*. With Russia undermining confidence in the market, bond prices had entered the realm of total fantasy. Saddled with losses that had reduced the estimated value of its assets from $4.8 billion on December 31, 1997 to $2.3 billion on August 31, 1998, the paralysis facing the market in September raised the possibility that LTCM would fail.

LTCM's practice of dividing its positions among several brokers contributed to its difficulties, although LTCM did try to maintain positions that offset as much risk as possible at each broker without giving away too much information. Consider the hypothetical case where LTCM has a long position of $100 million in bonds at Bear, Stearns and an offsetting short position of $100 million of the same bonds at Merrill, Lynch. (In practice, it is doubtful that LTCM would have such perfectly offsetting positions at two different brokers; however, it was common for them to have offsetting positions in very similar bonds.)

The problem with spreading an arbitrage position around Wall Street is that in an illiquid market each broker will tend to value the position on terms that are the most favorable to it. In our hypothetical example, Bear, Stearns might value the long part of the position at $95 million and Merrill, Lynch might value the short part at $105 million in the absence of a liquid market for the bonds. Instantly, LTCM is $10 million in the hole, and that $10 million must come from somewhere to keep it square with its brokers. To make matters worse, as LTCM's troubles became known, liquidity further dried up as Wall Street (and the world) worried about the impact of a forced liquidation of LTCM's holdings. Overnight, the capital required to maintain this hypothetical position could increase by another $10 million if Bear, Stearns were to drop its (long) value to $90 million and Merrill, Lynch were to raise its (short) value to $110 million. Even holding these offsetting positions within the same brokerage house could lead to the same problems if their holdings resided in independent subsidiaries of the firm, as they often would.

LTCM became caught in a gridlock of valuations in which bankruptcy loomed. It was on the verge of no longer having the capital required to cover its positions and it was unable to liquidate enough positions to raise it. On paper, LTCM still had a positive value at the prices provided by pricing services. But those prices were purely hypothetical, sometimes only representing the market price for a single ($1 million) unit—not the tens or hundreds of them that LTCM might hold. The market simply could not handle a "fire sale" liquidation of LTCM's positions and those that could be liquidated quickly would likely generate such a large loss that the fund would rapidly be driven into the red. If LTCM had been a small hedge fund, its inability to post the capital as the value of its positions were marked down would have driven it into bankruptcy and it would have been liquidated under the relatively friendly laws of its offshore domicile. (LTCM's hedge fund operations were incorporated in the Cayman Islands, one of several Caribbean locations popular with hedge funds.)

The shortcomings of LTCM's theoretical models may have gotten it into trouble, but they also helped it avoid bankruptcy. LTCM possessed a rare advantage that went beyond anything contained in its trading models—the financial community viewed it as potentially "too big to fail." Central bankers had become gravely concerned that the failure of LTCM could set off a chain reaction of defaults, starting with the brokers and banks that lent to it. Such a failure would spread immediately because of the special role that these financial institutions played in the world's economy. Furthermore, none of these transactions was backed by government insurance, relying instead on the common belief that no government could afford a widespread financial collapse.

Much as police intervention is required for the orderly disentanglement of traffic gridlock, the intervention by the government and/or LTCM's brokers appeared necessary to extricate LTCM and its positions from the global financial system. The Federal Reserve hosted a meeting of LTCM's major creditors, which included all the major Wall Street investment banks, at its Wall Street fortress. There, these creditors (with the notable exception of Bear, Stearns, which felt that it already had enough exposure to LTCM) quickly worked out a rescue deal that gave the rescuers 90 percent ownership of the firm in exchange for an infusion of capital sufficient to get LTCM through its troubles. (An alternative "rescue plan" that would have handed LTCM over lock, stock, and barrel to a private group of investors that included some of its creditors was rejected by LTCM as too draconian.)

LTCM's creditors were able to liquidate the firm without incident over the next two years. The principals of LTCM were kept on at substantially reduced pay to help untangle the mess that they had created. Nonetheless, the terms of the liquidation drove many of LTCM's management team into personal bankruptcy because they could no longer support the enormous personal debt they had assumed in order to finance their ownership shares in LTCM.

The final terms of the LTCM bailout were set on Monday, September 28, 1998. On the next day, the Federal Reserve Board, which had not taken any action whatsoever on interest rates during the preceding year and a half—a period of time that included the Asian financial market meltdown that culminated in Blue Monday—made the first of three rapid-fire cuts in the federal funds rate. These cuts, which totaled 75 basis points, were designed to "inject liquidity" into the financial system. This action can be viewed as the Fed's attempt to aid in clearing the financial grid of the load that LTCM had placed upon it.

Although the Federal Reserve Bank served as a facilitator for the transaction, the bailout of LTCM was a strictly private matter, and so the details of the 60,000+ positions that had to be unwound in its liquidation were not made public. The formal report on LTCM submitted to the U.S. Congress by Robert Rubin (Treasury Secretary), Alan Greenspan (Fed Chairman), Arthur Levitt (SEC Chairman), and Brooksley Born (CFTC Chairperson) in April 1999 does not supply many specifics concerning the LTCM affair. (The Harvard Business School case on this matter is more specific, yet leaves much to the imagination.) Still, the impression that some form of financial gridlock existed and that some form of rescue was necessary to remedy it comes through quite clearly even if the term "gridlock" never appears in any report. The wisdom of having privileged, private parties (hedge funds, trading desks, etc.) perform the function of cross-market equilibration is never questioned at all.

Arbitrage Has Its Limits

The irony of the LTCM fiasco is that its demise was hastened by the conceptual shortcomings of the arbitrage-based theories of LTCM's two intellectual giants, Myron Scholes and Robert Merton, whose ideas permeate present-day financial markets. As we saw, the analytic revolution that they—along with Fischer Black and others—helped to bring about provides the framework for slicing and dicing financial instruments. Furthermore, their theories assume that any financial position can be reconfigured at will. For their financial models to work as they imagined, liquid markets must exist for even the most obscure financial security.

Both the rise of LTCM and its fall can be ascribed to flaws in the market mechanism. Their early success came from exploiting those flaws, which allowed the prices of related bonds to drift out of synchronization, creating arbitrage opportunities for them. Because the market mechanism failed to provide a bridge between securities with similar characteristics,

LTCM built that bridge itself, extracting a toll from other traders in the process. As market forces eventually closed the price gaps, the bridge they constructed became unnecessary, freeing up the capital and leaving LTCM free to invest its time and capital discovering new gaps in the market. Their downfall came when the same market mechanism that was responsible for the gaps began to work against them rather than with them. As the gaps widened, the bridges that LTCM built needed to be lengthened, that is, their capital requirements increased. These bridges ultimately collapsed when it became clear that their positions could not be maintained without outside infusions of capital that came with the condition that they relinquish control of their assets.

The fall of LTCM helped fuel an ongoing shift in financial economics away from nearly complete faith in efficient-market theories and toward a greater openness to behavioral theories. More than a year before LTCM's collapse Andrei Shleifer at Harvard and Robert Vishny at Chicago published an article, "The Limits of Arbitrage," in the *Journal of Finance* that presented a theoretical argument that arbitrage, such as that pursued by LTCM and other hedge funds, could not be counted on to bring markets into equilibrium. In a world where noise traders were plentiful and capital was limited, the efforts of arbitrageurs to profit from bringing rationality to the market could easily be thwarted by random market fluctuations that moved against them. The details of the Shleifer-Vishny model bear only passing resemblance to the situation faced by LTCM—indeed, the principals of LTCM were aware of the model but unconcerned by it—still its general message was clearly on target. The times when the greatest arbitrage profits are possible (because markets are farthest away from equilibrium) are also the times when arbitrageurs may find it the most difficult to obtain the capital required to exploit these opportunities.

The model built by Shleifer and Vishny demonstrated that arbitrage was limited because under the adverse market conditions that would give rise to arbitrage opportunities investors would fire their money managers, depriving them of the capital required to profit from bringing the market back into equilibrium. LTCM did not have this problem and explicitly structured the contracts it had with investors to guarantee that LTCM had their funds for the long term. In fact, had LTCM resided in the financial world assumed by the Shleifer-Vishny model, life would have been much easier for them. Shleifer and Vishny, following the lead of similar prior models, assume a world of infinite liquidity in which arbitrageurs can purchase and sell any asset at its going market price except for capital, which they must get from their investors.

The partners at LTCM, like many great hedge-fund managers before and after them, would have been happy to conclude that their losses were so great that given the reduced prospect of future profits they faced, it was best to liquidate their positions, close their fund, and start a new one with a clean slate. This tendency for hedge-fund managers to abandon their investors before their investors abandon them is usually the result of a standard hedge-fund contract provision establishing a "high-water mark" that forces managers to recoup any losses before they can share in their investors' gains. But LTCM, like a car in gridlock, could not get out—they were trapped and so were their investors, who unlike those in the Shleifer-Vishny model were contractually bound to keep their funds in LTCM. The markets failed to provide LTCM with any meaningful liquidity, much less infinite liquidity.

The Shleifer-Vishny model was just the latest of a string of behavioral finance models that challenged the efficient-market assumption that the actions of arbitrageurs could be relied upon to bring markets into equilibrium. In fact, John Maynard Keynes himself said to a friend contemplating taking a plunge in the market, "Markets can remain irrational longer than you can remain solvent." Without arbitrage to equilibrate markets, irrationality and inefficiency might reign supreme and financial valuation methods that were based on the efficient operation of the market system could not be trusted.

The limitations on arbitrage may help to explain why a growing cadre of researchers have been finding anomalies in real-world financial data that cast doubt on the efficiency of markets. Because capital is costly and can be easily drained from the market in times of crisis, it may be foolish to rely solely on individual players in the market for its efficient operation. The clear alternative to relying on hedge funds, day traders, and other speculative forces whose capital is limited to bridge the efficiency gaps between markets is to construct a market mechanism that is intelligent enough to prevent such gaps from forming in the first place. Furthermore, by providing formal links between markets, so that trade in multiple securities can be executed in a truly simultaneous manner, the potential for gridlock in markets may be substantially reduced. In order to see how such intelligence might be added to the market mechanism, it is first necessary to look a little deeper at how the global financial marketplace works.

Markets as Matchmakers

Financial markets face a task of immense proportions. They must provide individuals and businesses with the capital required to fund their operations while simultaneously offering suitable investment vehicles with desirable combinations of risk and reward. Capital can be raised by issuing debt, equity, or a hybrid of both. Legal restrictions on how capital can be raised abound. For example, constitutional guarantees of personal liberty prevent people from issuing equity in themselves, but they can issue equity or debt that is structured around assets they own or services they can provide. It is rare that a single investment will satisfy a given investor, and so the investor must construct a portfolio that consists of both the investment opportunities available and financial instruments derived from those investments.

The link between the sources and uses of capital usually requires the services of financial intermediaries to convert the debt and equity instruments used to raise capital into a form more suitable for investors. Using the slice-and-dice approach to finance, risks can be pooled together and reconstituted into forms that satisfy investor requirements.

Disintermediation, the reduction or elimination of the role of financial intermediaries, is a long-term trend that continues to influence the course of financial markets. When a new product is first introduced, the service and convenience that intermediaries provide can cover their costs; however, market forces ultimately lead their customers to find ways to eliminate them from the financial food chain. Financial intermediaries have managed to dodge extinction because technology continues to pare their costs and the constant march of financial innovation always creates new niches in which intermediaries can thrive.

Not every financial function is ripe for disintermediation. In particular, some premier financial institutions impart a valuable "spin" to the flow of information in financial markets and can facilitate a transaction by their mere presence. Many serious investors take note of the lead underwriter for an initial public offering of securities. Because a new company may have no reputation in the marketplace when it goes public, the reputation of the underwriter serves as a signal of the company's prospects. The top investment banks may go to great lengths to advertise the superior returns of their offerings relative to those underwritten by competitors.

Most investment banking and brokerage activities take the form of financial matchmaking. Trade in listed securities is the lowest form of matchmaking. Such trades can be easily executed by discount brokerages who serve merely as a front-end to the exchange mechanisms of the markets, most of which are highly automated. Intense competition for these transactions limits their potential for profit to those firms that are able to gain a competitive advantage through marketing, customer service, and operational efficiency.

Full-service brokers justify charging higher fees, at either the account or individual transaction level, by injecting meaningful human interaction and intelligence into the transaction process. This human interaction brings not only greeting cards and the occasional cheery voice, but also a variety of advice both from the broker and his firm's research department. Investors who question the value of these additional services are not likely to patronize full-service brokers.

High-margin financial matchmaking is targeted at corporations. Many corporate transactions are so complex that they can be structured in many different ways. For example, a multinational corporation may wish to hedge its interest rate and currency risk in every country where it does business. An investment bank can help the corporation to develop the appropriate hedging strategy; the actual trades that implement the strategy are merely incidental. In this kind of relationship, the input that the customer provides the investment banker is not a set of trades, but rather a set of financial goals. The hedging program that the investment bank designs for the client creates the transactions that are most likely to achieve those goals.

Individuals and institutions purchase stock not only to become passive recipients of a firm's cash flows; investors with enough voting shares in a company can take an active role in its decisions. Transactions large enough to involve either a partial or complete transfer of corporate control usually require the services of a professional financial matchmaker. While one could, in theory, acquire control of a company through the direct purchase of more than 50 percent of its shares, a company consists of more than its outstanding shares of stock. Increasingly, the corporate assets assume the form of people and ideas rather than industrial facilities. Hostile or inept transfers of control can greatly reduce the value of both human and intellectual capital. Whenever mergers and acquisitions are involved, the human touch may be essential to a successful transfer of control.

Given the broad range of Wall Street's matchmaking functions, it is reasonable to expect that some of them will always elude the grasp of automation. However, as the woes of LTCM illustrate, the human talent for making matches does not always bring with it a corresponding talent for unmaking them. Leaving it to LTCM and its brokers to take over where the market's matchmaking capability left off created a web of positions that were the raw material of gridlock. Of course, in a world where the market mechanism had the power and intelligence to extricate LTCM instantly, it is likely that LTCM's strategies would have been not only redundant but also unprofitable. Moreover, any market system smart enough to supplant the mightiest of hedge funds would have to be designed with gridlock prevention woven into its very fabric.

Smart Enough to Weave a Basket

Given the range of intelligence involved in financial matchmaking, it is natural to wonder just how much of this process can be automated—in other words, just how smart can markets get? Clearly, those matchmaking functions that rely on human intelligence rather than purely mechanical reasoning will not be incorporated into the market mechanism any time soon. Given the challenge of creating a robot trader that can exercise anything like human discretion, the creation of a full-scale robotic market that can replace existing financial markets is unlikely for some time.

When the field of artificial intelligence was young, it would have appeared easy to program a market mechanism with intelligence. The dominant position of researchers in artificial intelligence as late as the 1980s was that constructing a computerized "inference engine" and providing it with a concrete goal along with the rules that must be followed to reach that goal would be sufficient to endow the computer with something akin to human intelligence. For example, a computer program for playing chess that is given the goal of winning the game along with the rules of chess can then use formal logic to infer the optimal move at each juncture of the game.

Unfortunately, this "brute force" approach to artificial intelligence has met with only mixed success in part because of a phenomenon known as *combinatorial explosion*. In chess, for example, the number of moves possible from any position of pieces on the board grows almost exponentially the more moves one looks ahead. Because the number of moves that one must examine to "solve" the game of chess exceeds the number of atoms in the universe, the exhaustive logical approach to chess has been rejected in favor of approaches that are more intuitive. These new methods, including those used by IBM's victorious Deep Blue computer, use rules that can exploit human insights into chess and "learn" from experience as a way to focus the computer's immense power on a more reasonable set of possibilities.

The matchmaking mechanism of the market can be as complex as the game of chess, and just as susceptible to combinatorial explosion. Although markets are not driven by an explicit goal, they behave as if they had been programmed to maximize total surplus. In a single market at a given point in time, just following the rules of the double auction appears to be enough to satisfy that goal, as supported by the existing body of evidence. Problems arise, however, as the dimensions of our market expand to numerous markets at many points in time. In order to keep combinatorial explosion at bay, one must somehow limit the scope of the market.

A key area where automated intelligence can aid financial markets is in the satisfaction of contingencies. A contingency makes the execution of an order dependent on the state of the market. While we will explore contingent orders in more detail shortly, for the moment we will focus on a specific type of contingency: the basket order. Making the purchase of any security in a basket contingent on the purchase of all the other securities in the basket is a simple form of intelligent matchmaking.

Many financial assets possess an economic property known as *complementarity*. A classic example of goods that are *complements* is the combination of peanut butter, jelly, and bread. All three goods taken together create a peanut butter and jelly sandwich, a culinary delight favored by many young Americans. Omitting one or more of the ingredients makes for less palatable fare. In financial markets, the omission of a security from a carefully planned risk-hedging transaction can have larger financial consequences than the sticky dryness of an unjellied sandwich. For a hedge to work, every one of its pieces must be in place. Indeed, it is preferable to have none of a hedged transaction executed than only selected parts of it.

Taking complementarity into account, it may be desirable to order a basket of securities rather than its individual constituents. Increasingly, one can purchase an entire basket of securities designed so that it trades like an ordinary share of stock. In particular, basket shares based on popular stock indexes that include the S&P 500 (SPDRs), Dow Jones Industrial Average (DIAMONDS), and Nasdaq 100 (known as "The Qs" or "Cubes" for its ticker symbol, QQQ) consistently rank among the most active shares. These baskets, which are known as *exchange-traded funds* (ETFs), rely on arbitrageurs to keep the value of the units in line with the value of the stock that underlies them.

While individual holders of stock index shares cannot cash out their market basket shares, authorized institutional investors can both buy and sell *Creation Units*, which are usually equivalent to 50,000 shares in the trust, giving them a multimillion-dollar value. The basket of stocks used to construct a Creation Unit does not have to match the index perfectly; the managers of the trust can determine what constitutes a sufficiently close match. Although arbitrage by the institutions that assemble and cash in Creation Units does not keep the price of individual shares exactly at their asset value, it prevents the larger deviations found in some portfolio investment vehicles. In the next chapter, we will see that even in a world with perfect arbitrage that is built into the market mechanism, one cannot expect individual shares and Creation Units to be priced the same.

An older form of investment fund, the closed-end mutual fund, which also trades like stock, does not have the conversion feature of ETFs. These funds are well known to financial economists for the tendency of their units to trade substantially away from their asset value. Because shares in closed-end funds cannot be readily "cashed out" into the assets that underlie them, arbitrage has difficulty keeping their price in line with their asset value.

Currently, ETFs provide the tightest link between a stock index basket and the price of its components during trading hours. Stock index futures, which as noted earlier are settled in cash on their delivery date, have greater scope to deviate because there is no mechanism for instantaneous conversion between the index and its components.

Stock index baskets marketed as traditional (open-end) mutual funds are similar to ETFs. The difference is that they trade only once a day—orders must be placed well before the market closes and the daily price of shares is published after the close. Although this means that the shares in the fund are bought and sold before their price is known, that price is computed using the closing prices of the fund's holdings and so closely tracks the index.

Most stock index funds, like exchange-traded funds, do not hold the stocks that constitute the index in the exact proportion to their weights in the index. Clever management of positions in the smaller and less liquid components of the index along with judicious use of stock index futures can lower trading costs without causing significant *tracking error*, that is, movements away from the index value. In some cases, investment managers are able to offer "enhanced" returns that slightly outperform the target index using a variety of strategies that expose the fund to small, calculated risks.

In the current financial architecture, systems that can create and maintain a portfolio that perfectly matches any but the smallest stock index by purchasing the individual stocks directly are only beginning to be developed on the periphery of the securities markets. Even if we ignore changes in the components of the index, dividend reinvestment, and other technicalities—both large and small investors encounter major problems when they attempt to replicate broad market indexes exactly. For large investors, the illiquidity of the smaller companies in the index can make it difficult to establish a position in the index at will. For small investors, acquiring each stock in the proper proportion will be impractical because of the small and irregular size of each transaction.

One system designed specifically for customized basket trading is FOLIO *Investing*, the first product from a company (FOLIOfn) founded by a former SEC commissioner, Steven Wallman. FOLIO *Investing* manages trading in smaller baskets (originally, 50 stocks or less), which it calls "folios," by providing a front-end to the financial markets that enables its clients to submit orders for folios. The folio system takes care of fractional-share ownership and other messy details, just like a mutual fund. Folios, however, are not designed to be mutual funds or ETFs because they convey the ownership in the underlying shares of stock to their buyer. These shares can be transferred into and out of the FOLIO *Investing* system by any investor, providing folios with a grounding in external prices that is more fluid than the Creation Unit mechanism employed by ETFs.

Intelligent market mechanisms take the folio idea to the next step not only by making direct ownership of stock baskets a viable alternative to ETFs, stock index futures, and mutual funds but by seamlessly linking these baskets to their underlying components. Using a smart market, a single order can be placed for the entire index at a specified limit price. If an order that matches the entire basket were not available, the smart market mechanism would then try to assemble the index portfolio from its constituents at or below the limit price. If the basket could be purchased directly or assembled from its pieces, the trade would go through; otherwise, the order would remain in the system until it expires. Maintaining the link between baskets and their components is a major technical challenge, but as we shall see in the next chapter, it can be done.

Before we examine the development of a market mechanism sufficiently intelligent to assemble and disassemble baskets of stocks on the fly, it is worth thinking about the possibilities that lie beyond the mere "passive" bundling of stocks. There is no reason that an intelligent market mechanism would need to limit itself to predetermined baskets of stocks, such as those belonging to a given index. For example, you might want to own an entire index except for one stock that is objectionable on ethical grounds; you could purchase the index basket and then sell off the shares in that stock. (Here the sale is a true sale of shares that are removed from the basket and not merely a short sale taken against a position in the index.) When you want to liquidate the portfolio, you can decide whether to sell the shares individually or temporarily purchase back the missing shares in order to complete the basket for sale as a single unit.

While establishing a position in a stock index requires that the entire basket of stocks in the index be purchased nearly simultaneously, maintaining the basket so that it continues to track the index requires additional intelligence. What distinguishes a stock index from a mere basket of stocks is that it changes over time to reflect market conditions. If only because of the regular occurrence of mergers and delistings, no stock index can be entirely static. In addition, most indexes have a theme—the Dow Jones Industrial Average is for blue chips, the S&P 500 is for large companies, and so on—and so companies that no longer fit the theme are displaced by other companies that do. Both the design and ongoing maintenance of an index in an evolving economy require human intelligence, especially if that index is to survive in a world where many financial institutions and the companies that serve them desire the prestige, name recognition, and royalties associated with establishing a successful index.

12

Making Markets Intelligent

The simple double oral auction that was first run in a controlled setting by Vernon Smith provides a useful baseline when thinking about market intelligence; it is a dumb market that nonetheless turns in an admirable performance. Any order submitted to the order book is allowed just one contingency—the limit price for that transaction. When an order is entered into the order book, it creates a temporary option that others in the market are free to exploit until the order is taken or canceled. By providing the trader with a contingency and the market with a potentially valuable option, the process of price discovery is free to proceed. While this process is ongoing, all the bid prices on the order book remain lower than all the offer prices. Moreover, after a few repetitions of the market, bids and offers converge so that most trades are made at the competitive equilibrium price.

Ideally, in going from a single market to a network of markets we would like the superior performance of the double auction to carry over to every auction in the network. A mechanism that links markets together but fails to maintain the proper relation between bids and offers may have difficulty converging to equilibrium at all. Unreliable linkages return us to the world of Chamberlin's original market experiment, where the matching of buyers and sellers is governed more by accident than design, with any forgone opportunities driving down the efficiency of the market. Properly designed linkages, which are the focus of this chapter, not only preserve the smooth efficiency of the double auction, but enhance liquidity by broadening the scope of each market to include the entire network.

Any successful linkage of markets must entail modifications in the contingencies that traders can place on their orders and the options that they grant to the market mechanism. In particular, additional options granted to the market mechanism are like the traffic restrictions that are imposed to prevent gridlock. As we noted earlier, a driver entering midtown Manhattan forgoes some of the options she would have in less-congested areas; she can no longer breeze through every intersection.

A market mechanism that is indiscriminate in the contingencies that it allows can invite gridlock. The best illustration of this phenomenon is the classic "Alphonse and Gaston" problem. Alphonse, a comic-strip character created by Frederick B. Opper, was known for saying "after you, my dear Gaston," to which his companion would reply, "after you, my dear Alphonse." Because both Alphonse and Gaston were too polite to proceed first, ultimately neither of them could move. By analogy, if we make one order contingent on the execution of another order, which in turn is contingent on the execution of the first, neither order will ever be executed. Computer scientists refer to this kind of gridlock, which can bedevil information systems in numerous ways, as a *deadly embrace*.

Fortunately, it is possible to endow the market mechanism with sufficient intelligence to avoid the clutches of a deadly embrace. In particular, a market system that assembles and disassembles baskets of securities on the fly can be designed so that it retains the virtues of our baseline mechanism—the double oral auction—while performing the cross-market equilibration functions previously left in the hands of arbitrageurs. If we let traders specify a limit price for an entire basket of securities, which is a more powerful contingency than a limit price on a single security, then the option that each order gives the market will need to be more comprehensive.

It is heartening to know that the virtues of the market mechanism can be extended to encompass baskets of securities, but that is where the good news ends. By introducing a simple contingency into the market—the *all-or-none* contingency—some of the desirable properties of the market mechanism will no longer obtain. This result does not preclude the construction of highly intelligent market mechanisms, only that such mechanisms will be more complex than Adam Smith or Alfred Marshall could have imagined. In particular, these mechanisms are no longer able to aggregate all the information about each good into a unique price.

It would be easy at this point in the book to merely state that smart markets are great, that they will save the world, and leave it at that. At the calculated risk of bogging the reader down with specifics, this chapter and the one that follows it provide several examples of how some basic smart market mechanisms work. The reason for providing all this detail is simple: Smart markets may well be great, but they are potentially dangerous, and these examples highlight where some of those dangers lie. The failure of a single market is unfortunate, but the collapse of an entire network of them is a catastrophe.

Adding Baskets to the Market

The bundling of goods into baskets goes on all the time, but historically it has received little attention from economists. On the rare occasions that bundling is mentioned, it is usually in the context of monopoly. A common way that monopolists are thought to take advantage of their market power is by selling goods only in bundles so that buyers cannot buy the goods they want without also purchasing some less valuable goods bundled in with them.

The market mechanism that we will examine contains no such restriction; it allows free trade in baskets as well as each of their components. Furthermore, this mechanism also has the intelligence to link these markets together so that it can assemble and disassemble baskets as needed to satisfy the market.

The fundamental properties of an intelligent mechanism for basket trading can be seen in a simple market network with two securities, A and B, and one basket, AB. Each AB unit contains one unit of A and one unit of B. The two components and the basket trade in markets with distinct order books, and we can view the bids and offers on each of them at all times. To simplify matters, the examples in this chapter omit the identities of traders. While trader anonymity is a major unresolved issue in many financial markets, the mechanics of a smart market are essentially the same whether identities are published or concealed.

We will now consider how orders might appear on these three order books. In the following example, A trades near 30, B trades near 70, and AB trades near 100. Currently, there is a single bid and a single offer outstanding for each component as well as for the basket as shown in the following set of order books:

	A		B		AB
Bid	*Offer*	*Bid*	*Offer*	*Bid*	*Offer*
29.90		69.90		99.50	
	30.10		70.10		100.50

The markets for A and B have a bid/offer spread of 0.20 (which is 30.10 - 29.90 for A and 70.10 - 69.90 for B) while the market for the basket AB, which is less liquid, has a bid/offer spread of 1.00 (which is 100.50 - 99.50). A trader considering a purchase of the AB basket could go to the AB market directly and pay the current offer price of 100.50, or he could shop around and buy A and B separately in their own markets for a total price of 100.20 (which is 30.10 + 70.10).

Now consider what happens if we explicitly link the market for the basket AB with the markets for its components. If the market for basket AB is provided with the intelligence to assemble the basket on its own from A and B, it can construct a *virtual offer* for the basket at a price of 100.20. Similarly, using the bid of 29.90 for A and 69.90 for B, the AB market can construct a *virtual bid* for the basket at a price of 99.80. Adding the virtual bids and offers to the market for AB and using italics to differentiate them from ordinary orders, the three order books become:

	A		B		AB
Bid	*Offer*	*Bid*	*Offer*	*Bid*	*Offer*
				99.50	
29.90		69.90		*99.80*	
	30.10		70.10		*100.20*
					100.50

Our ability to construct virtual bids and offers does not end here. The order books for A and B reflect only the direct bids and offers for these components. In addition to direct purchase, each component may be obtained by purchasing the basket AB and immediately selling the superfluous component. For example, a purchase of A is equivalent to a purchase of AB at the offer of 100.50 coupled with a sale of B at the bid of 69.90.

Obtaining A in this manner yields a net price of 30.60. Similarly, B can be obtained by purchasing AB at 100.50 and selling A at 29.90, for a net price of 70.60. Hence, we can add two virtual offers to the order book at price of 30.60 for A and 70.60 for B. While neither of these offers beats the existing offers, each will become a best offer when the existing best offers are either filled or canceled. The new state of the order books, again with virtual orders in italics, is as follows:

A		B		AB	
Bid	*Offer*	*Bid*	*Offer*	*Bid*	*Offer*
				99.50	
29.90		69.90		*99.80*	
	30.10		70.10		*100.20*
	30.60		*70.60*		100.50

Finally, notice that we can sell either A or B by first buying the other component needed to complete the basket and then selling the entire basket. For example, we can sell A by buying B at the offer of 70.10 and then selling AB at the bid of 99.50, which nets a virtual bid of 29.40. In the same manner, B can be sold for 69.40. Adding these virtual bids to the order books gives the following configuration:

A		B		AB	
Bid	*Offer*	*Bid*	*Offer*	*Bid*	*Offer*
29.40		*69.40*		99.50	
29.90		69.90		*99.80*	
	30.10		*70.10*		*100.20*
	30.60		*70.60*		100.50

By considering all possible combinations, the original set of three bids and three offers has now doubled to six bids and six offers, generating better prices in the AB market and a deeper market for both components. Of course, the acceptance of any of the bids or offers will not only lead to the removal of that order, but will also eliminate the virtual orders that were constructed using it. For example, if someone buys AB at the virtual offer of 100.20, the offer of A at 30.10 and the offer of B at 70.10 are filled in the process, so the order books become:

A		B		AB	
Bid	*Offer*	*Bid*	*Offer*	*Bid*	*Offer*
29.40		69.40		99.50	
29.90		69.90		99.80	
	30.60		70.60		100.50

With the direct offers for *A* and *B* removed by this basket purchase, the only remaining way to purchase either *A* or *B* is to buy the basket and sell the other component simultaneously.

The creation and removal of virtual orders must be done with care to ensure that all virtual orders are supported by real orders. If one accidentally combines virtual orders into a new virtual order, it is possible that the same real order will be used twice. This problem is easy to avoid in this smart market; however, as we shall see later in this chapter, it can lead to complications for other intelligent market mechanisms.

Self-Arbitraging Markets

Directly linking the markets for *A* and *B* with that for *AB* automatically provides an important added element of efficiency that was not present in the separate markets: Profitable (risk-free) arbitrage between the markets is now precluded. Because the order book for *AB* contains every way to construct the basket from *A* and *B* in the form of virtual orders, as long as the best bid for *AB* is less than the best offer, we are assured that no immediate arbitrage opportunities have been overlooked. Such a market system is known as *arbitrage-free*.

This basic method for creating an arbitrage-free market system can be readily expanded to any number of components, which can then be assembled into any desired basket that contains one unit of each component. Although combinatorial explosion, the tendency for the virtual orders to grow exponentially with the number of markets, is a theoretical possibility here, in practice, it is unlikely to arise. Even though the number of virtual orders grows faster than the number of markets, most of them will be far from the best bid and offer in a given market. While a virtual order book system could have billions of virtual orders on it at any given time, it is only necessary to compute and post the top several bids and offers, which will be a small subset of the total order book.

To participants in this market system, the enhanced marketplace looks like a traditional market; every component and every basket contains a valid set of bids and offers. Although we used italics to indicate virtual orders in the example given above, this information does not need to be made available to the public. From the point of view of an individual buyer or seller, how an order was constructed is irrelevant. Even in traditional markets, most trades are not done in isolation, but are driven by portfolio or hedging strategies that are not disclosed to the individual markets.

The construction of this arbitrage-free market system relied implicitly on the assumption that virtual orders were created instantaneously from real orders and that all orders reside in the same place on separate order books. In practice, it may be desirable to have each of the order books maintained separately, possibly even in different physical locations that are connected by high-speed communications lines. Even when it is possible to keep the order books within a single computer system, order throughput and security are much greater when the order books can be managed in parallel. If the time it takes the order books to communicate with each other is less-than-instantaneous, they can get out of synch, opening the door for arbitrage by traders.

The practical impossibility of traders being able to instantaneously interact with any order books that they desire is a result of the natural *friction* of the market system. Fischer Black has argued that in the absence of any friction, traders would place every imaginable order to give them priority within the market system and then selectively cancel their orders as information becomes available. Traders who attempted such a strategy in any real-world financial market would end up making many unintentional trades. Just as friction in the physical world is necessary to keep objects in their places, some friction in the market system is not only unavoidable, it is essential. Only when friction reaches the point that orders cannot be processed in a timely manner, as occurred in a major way on Black Monday, is efficiency likely to be threatened.

Fortunately, there is a way that we can keep our decentralized market system arbitrage-free. While the details are messy, the idea behind preventing arbitrage is straightforward: Virtual orders generated by the market mechanism are always given priority over orders from traders. Before the market system allows a trader to take a bid or offer that is on its books, it looks around the network to make sure that it cannot construct a "virtual match" to that order. These inquiries do not need to be made continuously, only when someone wants to remove an order by either taking or canceling it.

One way of viewing this *self-arbitraging* market mechanism is that it removes the possibility that any arbitrage opportunities are created for traders by *front running* them—that is, executing trades ahead of them. While front running is unethical, if not illegal, for market makers and brokers to engage in for their own benefit, it can be an efficient thing for a market mechanism to do. Hence, anyone who finds an arbitrage opportunity and then attempts to profit from it will simply alert the market system to its existence. The system will then harvest the opportunity for itself. Furthermore, any order that might inadvertently create an arbitrage opportunity for someone else will also cause the market to spring into action.

Returning to the example of the markets for A, B, and AB, we can see how this might work. Again, we will start with the three markets before any virtual orders have been added to them:

A		B		AB	
Bid	*Offer*	*Bid*	*Offer*	*Bid*	*Offer*
30.90		69.90		99.50	
	31.10		70.10		100.50

The lines between the three order books indicate that they reside in separate locations. The bid and offer prices are the same as in the earlier example except that the prices for A are higher than before. The bid at 30.90 is shown in bold to indicate that it has just been received by the order book for A.

The receipt of an order automatically triggers a search to all linked markets for a virtual match to it. As before, when the market updated simultaneously, a virtual offer of 30.60 is available by buying the basket AB at the offer of 100.50 and selling the superfluous B at the bid of 69.90. Adding this virtual offer to the market gives the following:

A		B		AB	
Bid	*Offer*	*Bid*	*Offer*	*Bid*	*Offer*
30.90		69.90		99.50	
	30.60				
	31.10		70.10		100.50

The addition of this virtual offer creates a temporarily unsettling situation in which the best bid for *A* (30.90) exceeds the best offer (30.60), which is a clear indication that profitable arbitrage is possible. This situation is easily resolved by crossing the bid for *A* at 30.90 with the bid for *B* at 69.90 and the offer for *AB* at 100.50 leaving:

A		B		AB	
Bid	*Offer*	*Bid*	*Offer*	*Bid*	*Offer*
	31.10		70.10	99.50	

Although the market was able to execute this arbitrage transaction, traders in the market could not. Entry of any leg of an arbitrage transaction automatically triggers the market to look for the deal itself, locking traders out of the markets for a moment until all opportunities for arbitrage have been exhausted. The additional liquidity that a self-arbitraging market system provides through the proliferation of virtual orders is beneficial because it replaces the less efficient operation of outside arbitrageurs.

A pleasant problem that remains is what to do with the 0.30 in arbitrage profits generated by this transaction. The use of private arbitrage to help equilibrate markets did not pose this kind of problem because arbitrageurs would just pocket all the profits, net of what the government recaptured through taxes and its brokers pocketed in commissions. A self-arbitraging market system, which could be either privately or publicly operated, would have to consider how to allocate its arbitrage "profits" between providing favorable fills to its traders and funding its operation. Just as traders punish brokers who fill their orders poorly by taking their business elsewhere, a market system that ruthlessly seizes every arbitrage opportunity may see its profits diminished by the loss of future business.

There is good reason to believe that a self-arbitraging market may not be unduly profitable. When the equilibration of the market is left to arbitrageurs, a serious contradiction arises. At the same time that arbitrageurs make markets more efficient, they reduce the profitability of arbitrage. Perfect efficiency is impossible because that would give arbitrageurs no profits, so they would leave the market and take its efficiency with them. Hence, the market for arbitrage itself must then come into equilibrium, and it can only do so at a level where arbitrageurs can expect to profit, hence making markets inefficient. While human arbitrageurs may not be satisfied to stay in a market once they have profited from bringing it into equilibrium, a self-arbitraging market can weather long periods of market calm by living off its past profits or, as a last resort, by using a funding mechanism that does not impair the market's functions. (Shutting down the market mechanism for periodic fund drives does not constitute an acceptable funding mechanism.)

The benefits of a self-arbitraging market system only come from increasing the implicit option cost of every order. Because orders that are submitted to the system are sporadically frozen while the system seeks out virtual matches, the option that is granted to the market system by placing an order is greater than in a traditional market system where each market is separate. In effect, the option provided by an order is not restricted to the market in which the order is placed, but extends to every market in the network.

There are two sound reasons to believe that the higher option cost of each order will not hurt the market. First, the additional liquidity from linking markets together provides a benefit to all traders that should greatly outweigh the added option costs. While the communications traffic between markets may delay some orders, more orders are likely to be filled than would be possible with separate markets. Second, it is doubtful that traders will notice any difference during periods of normal trading activity. Currently, securities markets move so rapidly that having bids and offers disappear before one can act on them is a common, if frustrating, occurrence. (This frustration is particularly acute when the order that vanished was in the process of being canceled.) Masked by the flurry of market activity, the self-arbitraging activities of the market system would be hard to detect.

The most important feature of a self-arbitraging market system is that all of its markets, both for baskets and their components, satisfy the same basic properties as a double auction considered in isolation. In particular, despite the presence of virtual orders on the book, the best bid price in every market is less than the best offer price, a property that we will call the *Fundamental Invariant for Auction Markets*. A self-arbitraging market system enforces this invariant by executing the appropriate (profit-generating) trades whenever an order enters the system whose entry into an order book would violate it. Just as the Marshallian (supply and demand) market behaves as if its goal were to maximize the total surplus of buyers and sellers, every arbitrage-free auction market behaves as if its goal were to satisfy the Fundamental Invariant.

Recombinant Securities Markets

A self-arbitraging market mechanism is not limited to a single basket with two components; it extends not only to arbitrarily large baskets, but also to networks of multiple baskets with overlapping components. A complex network of markets requires more individual markets for its operation, including intermediate markets for subbaskets of components that several baskets may share. These internally generated intermediate markets, which can be established and eliminated as they are needed, still have well-defined buy and sell sides even though all their orders are virtual ones. As long as the Fundamental Invariant is maintained throughout the market system, which includes these intermediate markets, traders will be unable to risklessly arbitrage the market at any moment in time.

Stock baskets are not the only securities that can be readily broken down into their constituent pieces. U.S. Treasury securities that cannot be called before they mature can be decomposed into several individual coupons and a single return of principal at maturity. The STRIPS program of the U.S. Treasury provides the electronic bookkeeping to enable its authorized brokers and dealers to decompose and reconstitute Treasury securities on demand. Turning this electronic bookkeeping system into a smart market system creates more political issues than it does technological ones. Although trade in Treasury securities is in the process of becoming automated, the existing market is dominated by the major dealers registered with the Treasury. Determining who would run a smart market for Treasury securities directly linked to the Treasury's computers and how the profits would be divided up is a difficult problem to resolve.

The ease with which many bonds can be rearranged makes them ideal securities for smart markets. One can even imagine taking the toxic waste from asset-backed securities and recycling it back into the plethora of casinos that have blossomed on the American landscape. Given the pervasive role of technology in the gaming industry, it will make little difference to gamblers whether the numbers and fruit-like objects that appear on their slot machines, state lotteries, and Internet displays come from a microprocessor-based random number generator or are the leftovers from the kitchens of Wall Street's financial engineers. Day trading activity that is redirected to financial sludge custom-engineered to provide excitement could isolate the primary financial markets from speculative activities that are more likely to destabilize them. Furthermore, the isolation of the toxic elements of securities by the market mechanism is likely to substantially boost the overall liquidity of financial markets by enabling investors to buy securities that are better targeted to their risk profiles. Although Keynes's views on the evils of speculation in retrospect were clearly more alarmist than rational, the arrangement described above puts an interesting twist on his pronouncement that "when the capital development of a country becomes a by-product of the activities of a casino, the job is likely to be ill-done."

Before proceeding, it is important to note that the self-arbitraging markets introduced earlier, which are limited to creating and taking apart baskets on the fly, perform only the most rudimentary arbitrage. This kind of arbitrage is easy for the market mechanism to carry out because it requires no capital, just the options that traders implicitly grant the market in their orders. The market cannot perform arbitrage based on the eventual convergence in value of securities at a predetermined future point in time, such as was LTCM's specialty, without using capital. One might want to let the market mechanism retain the capital necessary to exploit more sophisticated arbitrage opportunities within some predetermined limits—even casinos require significant capital to fund their operations.

More problematic, however, is arbitrage that relies on economic models laden with assumptions that only approximate the reality of the market. For example, while the Black-Scholes-Merton approach to option value provides a way to dynamically replicate an option using the underlying equity and risk-free debt, this replication is not only cumbersome, but it involves assumptions that are never strictly satisfied. Any market mechanism that blindly relies on textbook economic theory certainly cannot be considered intelligent.

All or Nothing at All

As we noted earlier when we were conjuring up the ghosts of Alphonse and Gaston from the comic-strip graveyard, some contingencies are mutually exclusive. Any attempt to satisfy them simultaneously takes us down the road to gridlock. Even if we exercise care and avoid the possibility of mutually inconsistent contingencies, the addition of a seemingly minor contingency can drastically alter the nature of the market mechanism.

Until now, we have considered only single-unit trades for baskets and their components. Just as buyers might want to create a basket of several securities, they might also want to create a multiunit bundle of an item, which itself could either be a single component or a basket. To keep matters simple, we will focus on trade in multiple units of a single security without any further consideration of how that security could be bundled or decomposed.

Normally, a trader who places an order for multiple units of stock—say, 500 shares at $50/share—may have to be satisfied with a partial fill of the order because exchanges will treat the order as if it were five separate orders for the standard trading unit of 100 shares. There are many times, however, when it is desirable for an order to be executed in its entirety or not at all. This restriction on an order is known as an *all-or-none (AON) contingency*. Basket orders employ a type of AON contingency: All components in a basket have to be purchased or sold together or else the order will not execute.

Consider a market system in which the following two orders have been submitted:

Bid: 50.00 for 100 shares AON
Offer: 49.50 for 200 shares AON

The AON at the end of each order specifies that the quantities are all-or-none, so the offer of 49.50 for 200 shares can only be satisfied by selling all 200 shares at once.

One way to look at this situation is to consider the orders for each quantity of shares as a separate market and then link the markets together as we did above to construct baskets. With these two orders, trades of 100 or 200 shares are possible, and the order books at these two quantities appear as follows:

	100		200	
Bid	*Offer*		*Bid*	*Offer*
50.00				49.50

Although the offer is lower than the bid, we cannot cross the two orders because they are for different quantities.

Now consider what happens if we bundle the bid for 100 at 50.00 and the offer of 200 at 49.50. The bid covers 100 of the 200 shares and $5,000 of the $9,900 total sale price (200 times $49.50), so the net order that is created is an offer of 100 at 49. The updated set of order books that includes this (italicized) virtual offer appears as follows:

	100		200
Bid	Offer	Bid	Offer
50.00	*49.00*		49.50

Now, it is tempting to cross the real bid for 100 at 50.00 with the virtual offer for 100 at 49.00; however, we cannot do this because we would use the same bid (100 at 50.00) twice—once (directly) on the bid side and once (through the virtual offer) on the offer side. While we can still impose rules on this market that make it self-arbitraging, we can no longer accomplish this while maintaining the Fundamental Invariant for Auction Markets. In essence, the all-or-none contingency precludes the Fundamental Invariant, and so this auction does not share a basic property of the standard double auction.

This result is especially striking when we consider that this problem did not arise when constructing baskets of different securities, yet it readily surfaces when the "baskets" are units of the same security. The reason for this difference is that baskets constructed from single units of a fixed set of securities have an orderly hierarchical structure, formally known as a *lattice*, that limits how one basket can be transformed into another. (A lattice is just a network in which it is impossible to create a knot—all possible bundles can be neatly ordered. Family trees in which there is no inbreeding are an example of a lattice.) When the units that make up a bundle can cross to the other side of the market, we then have the ability to "tie the market into a knot." The bid and offer sides of the market are no longer independent of each other and so the violation of the Fundamental Invariant follows.

Breaking the Law of a Single Price

The ease with which the Fundamental Invariant can be violated illustrates the fragility of neoclassical economics in a world of intelligent markets. An even deeper economic principle that fails in the face of contingencies is the Law of a Single Price. The Marshallian view of markets requires that the entire market for an item come into balance at a single price. The virtue of the market mechanism, its efficiency, depends on the unique price for each good guiding the actions of buyers and sellers. Efficiency is no longer guaranteed when every tradable quantity of a good can have a different price.

That the market for single 100-share units of stock and larger blocks of the same stock might be fundamentally different markets trading at different prices may be news to some economic theorists but it is not news to the financial markets. There, the execution of small orders for stock—1,000 shares or less—is almost entirely automated, while large orders often receive human attention to facilitate their execution with as little price impact as possible.

The inherent difficulty of managing all-or-none contingencies within a system that hopes to maintain the fiction of a single price does not appear to be lost on the rule-making committees of financial exchanges. To the extent that all-or-none orders are permitted, they tend to be segregated from other orders and are certainly not processed using an intelligent trading mechanism such as the one described above. Nasdaq's efforts to incorporate all-or-none orders into its Small Order Execution System (SOES) were a complete fiasco. These orders never appeared on the order books that Nasdaq market makers display to traders, making them an excellent vehicle for stealth trading. Furthermore, loopholes in the way that all-or-none orders were handled by SOES led to their exploitation by clever traders who become known as *SOES bandits*, and so Nasdaq stopped accepting them on January 20, 1997.

Most of the time, the price difference for trades of different sizes is likely to be small enough that "a single price" is a reasonable approximation to the reality of the market. There is some anecdotal evidence that for actively traded stocks the share price of a single unit (100 shares) is generally within $\$^1/_8$ (12.5 cents) of a small block (10,000 shares). When shares on the New York Stock Exchange were traded in eighths of a dollar, trade in small blocks generally went smoothly; in order for smaller trades to interfere, they would have to trade at least $\$^1/_8$ better than the block price. However, when U.S. stocks began trading in one-cent multiples in 2001, block trading became more difficult as smaller quantities at neighboring cents started to interfere with them. The loss of market efficiency that market professionals ascribed to this penny-ante trading was partially due to the activities of arbitrageurs performing an assembly process that a self-arbitraging market system would be better equipped to perform.

Although the Law of a Single Price may not characterize many financial markets—especially illiquid ones—this does not prevent the financial community from behaving as if the law held universally. Although many securities now trade around the clock somewhere in the world, an official *closing price* for most securities is recognized for legal purposes. Closing prices are printed in newspapers and are widely available on the Internet. Each exchange has its own procedure for determining the closing price, which is not necessarily the price of the last trade, in order to assure that this price is truly representative of conditions at the close rather than the result of a single, anomalous trade. In turn, these prices are used to compute the asset value of mutual funds and other investment pools.

Under normal circumstances, using closing prices to get asset values is both meaningful and accurate. However, in volatile or illiquid markets, the closing price may not be indicative of what the next trade will be. To deal with this possibility, it is standard practice for mutual funds to reserve the right to use an independent estimate of asset value instead of closing prices. Because the exercise of this right is so unsettling to investors, mutual funds rarely resort to it. However, the potential for being victimized by arbitrageurs makes it imperative that a fund be able to value itself as close to its "fair value" as possible, even when this diverges from the closing price.

It is worth noting that the violation of the Law of the Single Price given here is much different from a more obvious apparent violation of the Law that one can see every day. Consumer goods, like peanut butter, have lower unit prices when purchased in larger containers. A half-pound jar bought at a convenience store might sell for as much as $10 a pound, while a 50-pound tub bought at a warehouse store could reduce the unit price to $1 per pound. Larger quantities sell at a discount for sound economic reasons, not because they constitute a different market. For consumer items, both packaging and transaction costs are higher per unit for smaller quantities. In addition, sellers of large quantities tend to locate where rents and land values are low. Finally, in order to cover their fixed costs of operation, retailers try to charge higher prices to their customers with less elastic demand, who are willing to pay a premium (per unit) price for a smaller size.

These quantity discounts are driven by costs and so are fundamentally different from the violation of the Law of a Single Price that can occur in an intelligent market with all-or-none contingencies. The most obvious difference is that with discounting in consumer markets, larger quantities always mean lower prices. With all-or-none contingencies, the presence of buyers for large blocks can make the price higher for larger quantities.

In many cases, convenience is the driver behind all-or-none contingencies. For large traders and investors, many positions are not worth the bother of tracking and managing unless they can be obtained in a size that represents a significant fraction of the assets under management. For this reason, many investment managers completely ignore small capitalization stocks; they can never purchase enough to amass holdings that would produce a noticeable effect on their performance.

Market participants may recognize that different quantities of the same item can be different markets, but neoclassical economic theory does not. The ability to associate one—and only one—price with every good or service in an economy is the most basic and important consequence of this theory. The efficiency of competitive markets depends on the ability to compress all the information held by buyers and sellers down to a single price. The presence of information asymmetries—lemons, signals, and so forth—can impede this process, but even those adjustments to the theory rely on prices being independent from quantities.

Viewed in a positive light, we can see that the market mechanism remains an intelligent and efficient way to allocate resources in situations that had not even been contemplated by its staunchest advocates. If markets can work where the determination of prices is either poorly defined or even impossible, then an intelligent market might even be used under circumstances long believed to require regulatory intervention. While the addition of contingencies to a market can undermine a traditional market mechanism—introducing what economists call *nonconvexities*—a smart market mechanism can uncover the efficient allocation without having to resort to uniform prices. Next, using a popular board game as our point of reference, we will see how smart markets can do things that markets have never done before.

13

The Smart Auction Block

T he reconsideration of capitalism brought about by the 1929 Crash and the Great Depression that followed was not confined to the intellectual contributions of John Maynard Keynes, F. A. Hayek, Edward Chamberlin, and other academics. Simultaneously, on the popular culture front, Charles B. Darrow developed a board game that was an instant success and has become the way most Americans are introduced to high finance: *Monopoly*. Although the Monopoly game's origins are still in dispute, it is known that a more politicized predecessor of the game, The Landlord's Game by Elizabeth (Lizzie) J. Magie, had achieved cult status in the 1920s. Ms. Magie's game was popular at Ivy League economics departments, including Harvard's, where Chamberlin was hatching his theory of monopolistic competition for his doctoral dissertation.

The Monopoly game features two important concepts that had been largely overlooked by the prevailing economic theory: location and synergy. Twenty-eight of the 40 squares on the Monopoly board represent real estate, railroad, or utility properties that become the exclusive possession of the player who holds it, giving that player a local monopoly. At this level, the game resembles monopolistic competition, except that the rents that accrue to players are set by the rules of the game and, unlike the prices of Chamberlin's monopolistic competitors, are immune to competition from other landlords.

The Monopoly game takes a major step beyond product differentiation by making collections of related properties much more valuable collectively than individually. In particular, ownership of all the real estate in a color group enables their owner to develop the properties and reap the higher rents charged for houses and, ultimately, hotels. The timely exploitation of these synergies is a critical element of any winning strategy. (As in real life, luck also plays an important role.)

This natural combination of location and synergy is not something that the neoclassical theory can easily process with its analytic machinery. Indeed, in this chapter, we will demonstrate why traditional market institutions will tend to inhibit the coordination that is necessary for firms to exploit synergies and share these benefits with their customers. In particular, the value of many innovative products depends on how widely they are used. These *network economies*, as they are known, often require coordinated action in the markets to reach critical mass, so that each user receives value from others using the same product.

A classic example of network economies comes out of the 1980s battle between VHS and Betamax videocassette recorders (VCRs) and tapes. Even though the Betamax format was technologically superior by objective performance measures (lines of resolution, etc.), the incompatible VHS format came to dominate the market. Any deficiencies in VHS were more than counterbalanced by the aggressive marketing efforts of the consortium that backed the format. The Sony Corporation, which licensed Betamax, stood virtually alone against the rest of the electronics industry, and ended up losing the battle as a result. As the popularity of videotape rentals increased, it became apparent that the inventory and display costs of carrying two formats in video stores were sufficiently high that only one format could survive. Additional pressure was placed on the market by the widespread practice of tape swapping; one could only exchange tapes without rerecording if both users had the same format.

Bandwidth for Sale

Clearly, any communications technology has substantial network economies because you only communicate with other users on (or linked to) your network. Hence, network economies are not limited to concrete objects such as videotapes; they literally extend into the ether—or the electromagnetic spectrum to be more precise. Wireless communication in any form—radio, television, cellular telephone, and so on—is possible because we can use electronic equipment to encode our message into electromagnetic waves, which are then transmitted at the speed of light to one or more recipients, who can then use the appropriate equipment to decode the message. Millions of messages can be sent and received simultaneously if we allocate a specific segment of the electromagnetic spectrum to each message. These segments are identified by their (central) *frequency* and how wide they are, that is, their *bandwidth*. One can think of the electromagnetic spectrum as an extremely long line that can be divided into countless pieces—some very large, like those required to transmit high-definition television signals, and some very small, like those needed to carry a single cellular telephone call.

A signal uses the electromagnetic spectrum for only as far as it propagates. (Many signals are capable of traveling into outer space, but they are so weakened by their journey that it takes a sensitive extraterrestrial receiver to pick them up.) Although signal propagation depends on many factors, the two most important are the signal's frequency and the power with which it is transmitted. Signals having frequencies or physical locations too close together will *interfere* with each other, making them more difficult to receive, and so proper management of the electromagnetic spectrum focuses on how to deal with this interference.

The electromagnetic spectrum is "owned" by the national governments of the world, with international law governing any signals that travel across national boundaries. National governments grant licenses through the appropriate regulatory agency—the Federal Communication Commission (FCC) in the United States—to allow companies and individuals the use of specific bandwidth in specific locations. The rationale behind this arrangement is that without rules to allocate the spectrum, the resulting interference would greatly reduce its value to everyone.

Until the 1990s, the spectrum allocation process was entirely political. Government bureaucrats, who selected those worthy of a license, allocated all but the most trivial bits of spectrum. Except for nominal fees, the U.S. Treasury never got a penny for the licenses. Thus, being granted a broadcast license was like winning a lottery in which political influence, rather than dumb luck, determined the outcome. Those with the right connections, like Texas broadcaster turned U.S. president Lyndon Baines Johnson, got rich and the rest of us could just sit back and watch the show.

Economists have long recognized that there is no reason to give the electromagnetic spectrum away when you could lease it out at a substantial profit. Although regulators found it politically untenable to auction off existing licenses when they came up for renewal, new services, notably in the area of wireless telecommunications, seemed ripe for the auction block. Auctions of the frequency spectrum would not only raise money for the government, they would be more likely than a political or random process to get the licenses into the hands of those who could create the most value with them, making their allocation of the spectrum more efficient.

Location, Location, Location . . . and Synergy, Too

The issues that arise when auctioning off the electromagnetic spectrum are easily illustrated by a hypothetical example that turns the United States into a series of properties arranged like those on a Monopoly board. To keep things simple, we will shrink the board from 40 spaces down to 8 spaces and ignore the niceties of the game like the "No Parking" space and the kitschy playing pieces. Also, even though a license has several dimensions (bandwidth, propagation limits, etc.), we will limit our analysis to the choice of physical location, as represented by a region of the country. Each of the eight spaces represents one region: NorthEast, SouthWest, and so forth. The four major telecommunications companies are located at the four corners of the board. The NorthEast Company (NECO) provides local telephone service in the NorthEast and so on around the board. The other four spaces have their own regional carriers and there are also many independent telecom companies, but they are too small to compete with the four major industry players in new markets and so we can safely ignore them.

Consider a new frequency that the government is considering making available for wireless communications. Figure 13.1 shows the value of a license for the new frequency to each of the four major companies in each of the eight regions. Although these values are arranged like a game board to make it easy for us to analyze this situation, neither the companies nor the auctioneer has the advantage of seeing all this information laid out before it. Each company knows only its own values and the auctioneer knows none of them. Notice that the values on the game board follow a simple pattern. The value is highest in a company's home region—for example, the NorthEast is worth 80 to NECO—and then declines by 20 for each space that one moves away from home, so the North and East are worth only 60 to NECO.

As noted in the middle of the board, each license is worthless unless an adjacent license is also held. Hence, NECO must acquire either the North

NorthWest		North		NorthEast	
Owner	Value	Owner	Value	Owner	Value
NECO	40	NECO	60	NECO	80
SECO	0	SECO	0	SECO	15
SWCO	20	SWCO	0	SWCO	0
NWCO	30	NWCO	10	NWCO	0

West		Owner must also own an adjacent property or the property is worthless		East	
Owner	Value			Owner	Value
NECO	20			NECO	60
SECO	0			SECO	35
SWCO	40			SWCO	0
NWCO	10			NWCO	0

SouthWest		South		SouthEast	
Owner	Value	Owner	Value	Owner	Value
NECO	0	NECO	20	NECO	40
SECO	15	SECO	35	SECO	55
SWCO	60	SWCO	40	SWCO	20
NWCO	0	NWCO	0	NWCO	0

Figure 13.1 **Hypothetical Values for Electromagnetic
Spectrum in Eight Adjacent Regions**

or East licenses to cash in on the 80 provided by the NorthEast license. This requirement reflects a basic synergy—the value of any region's wireless service depends on the ability to connect with neighboring regions. This synergy is typical of most telecommunications networks (though usually not as extreme as indicated here). While this example does not faithfully represent the economics of real-world wireless services, it captures a salient feature of them.

Unlike a board game with its protracted sequence of moves, the allocation of frequency spectrum is ideally a one-shot affair, with the regulator assigning licenses to companies and then leaving the deployment process to them. Until 1994 such allocations were driven by politics rather than money. A typical political solution would be to allocate each region's frequencies according to the prevailing politics, so that NECO would get the NorthEast, etc., with the in-between regions going to the smaller regional companies located there. This apparently fair division of frequencies that might pass muster in hearings conducted by Congress has the unfortunate consequence that lacking the critical mass to operate and a Solomon to set things straight, each license is worthless. Although this way of viewing things is a vast oversimplification, it helps to show why the United States has historically been slow to adopt new telecommunications technologies.

Before settling upon a market solution, the FCC tried using lotteries to allocate spectrum. Lotteries are the traditional way that the government assigns oil and mineral rights on public lands. Telecommunications and resource rights are quite different, however. Synergy plays a much smaller role in natural resource development and, anyway, most winners of the lottery were eager to flip their rights to a big oil company that could afford the cost of extracting the resources. Telecommunications lotteries were quickly abandoned because with many companies likely to enter the lottery, the resulting allocation would likely come out as a patchwork that would take considerable effort to consolidate into meaningful collections of licenses.

The solution to the FCC's problem was to auction off the frequencies. By using prices to determine ownership, not only did it seem likely that each license would go to its highest-valued use, but the government could make billions of dollars for something that it had previously provided free to the most qualified applicant, a determination that was both subjective and political.

Returning to Figure 13.1, it might appear that if we go region-by-region through the country, the company with the highest value for each region should win it, regardless of the allocation process used. If this happens, we have the following allocation of regions to companies:

NorthWest: NECO 40	North: NECO 60	NorthEast: NECO 80
West: SWCO 40		East: NECO 60
SouthWest: SWCO 60	South: SWCO 40	SouthEast: SECO 0

The problem with this allocation is that SECO in the SouthEast will receive 0, not the 55 shown in the SouthEast square, because it failed to acquire a neighboring region. The overall profit that the companies receive is 380, which is clearly inefficient because either NECO or SWCO could operate the SouthEast region profitably because they have neighboring holdings.

Before proceeding further with this hypothetical example, it is important to note that although we will focus on corporate profits to determine the relative efficiency of an auction's outcome, most of the benefit gained from these licenses ultimately accrues to the consumers who use the services that employ them. Because the winner of an auction still has to compete with several other frequencies and services in his region, profits more closely reflect the satisfaction of consumers than they do any pricing power granted to their owner. Therefore, in the absence of any evidence to the contrary, it is fair to assume corporate profits are roughly proportional to the overall surplus that the use of a license generates.

Be aware that if the winner of a license does not offer its services to consumers on competitive terms, profits can be a poor proxy for total surplus because the benefits of consumers will not be properly conveyed to the auction market. In particular, forcing the winners to provide services unconditionally and predetermining the prices that consumers are charged can sever the link between the benefits that consumers receive and what the winning companies make from providing them. Similarly, if the winners are unregulated and able to exercise significant market power, their ability to extract surplus from consumers, and not the surplus itself, will drive the bidding.

Having noted the possible limitations of using corporate profits as a measure of auction efficiency, we will now consider how different mechanisms would allocate the regions. If we were to hold simultaneous sealed-bid auctions for the eight regions, all four companies would recognize that without an adjacent license they could each pay for licenses that would turn out to be worthless. The weight of this uncertainty could seriously depress their bids, leading not only to reduced revenues for the government, but also to an allocation of licenses governed more by the bidding strategies of the companies than by their value to them and their customers.

Matters are somewhat improved if the sealed-bid auctions are conducted sequentially, with all parties knowing the outcome of each auction before the next one proceeds. It is now easier for companies to avoid ending up with isolated licenses; however, the outcome of the auction will be highly dependent on the order in which the licenses are auctioned off. Once a company obtains a license, its willingness to bid on the neighboring licenses increases because it can be certain of achieving critical mass. Despite this improvement, significant inefficiencies are likely to remain because once the wrong company gets into a region, misallocations in neighboring regions become more likely.

The FCC initially dealt with this problem using a traditional English auction of all licenses, in this case frequencies for Personal Communications Services (PCS) licenses, simultaneously. Of course, those auctions involved many more regions and companies, but the basic idea was the same as this simple example. The rules for the auction were complex, and have grown more so over time. The most important rules concerned the actions that a company had to take to keep its status as an authorized bidder in the auction. These rules were instituted to keep companies from free-riding off the price discovery process; in order to receive a license, a company had to grant the implicit options contained in its bids at each stage in the auction process.

Under this sort of process, it is likely that SECO, noticing it was cornered on the North and West by NECO and SWCO, respectively, would drop out of the bidding rather than risk being stuck with a worthless SouthEast license. If NECO prevails and every other license goes to its highest-value bidder, the allocation of licenses becomes:

NorthWest: NECO 40	North: NECO 60	NorthEast: NECO 80
West: SWCO 40		East: NECO 60
SouthWest: SWCO 60	South: SWCO 40	SouthEast: NECO 40

Adding the profits (surpluses) together gives 420, which is an improvement over the 380 received when SECO won the SouthEast.

Even if we consider any money that the government raises from the auction to be gravy, the question remains as to whether the allocation given above is efficient. In the simple Marshallian world of a single supply curve and a single demand curve, efficiency fell out naturally from a competitive pricing mechanism that drove the price to where supply and demand cross. For this allocation problem, however, we have no curves to aid us. Instead, we need to consider every possible way that regions could be divided up among the four companies, which gives over 65,000 different possible allocations. In this case, many allocations are clearly inefficient and finding the efficient allocation boils down to figuring out what to do with the SouthEast region and its adjacent regions.

In a typical FCC spectrum auction, the number of combinations that make reasonable candidates for efficiency can number in the billions or more. Any mechanism that can sort through such a vast number of possibilities would have to be extraordinarily intelligent, and a simple price mechanism is not up to the task.

Again, looking at Figure 13.1, the efficient allocation of licenses to companies turns out to be the following:

NorthWest: NECO 40   North: NECO 60   NorthEast: NECO 80
West: SWCO 40   East: NECO 60
SouthWest: SWCO 60   South: SECO 35   SouthEast: SECO 55

This allocation generates a total surplus of 430, which is 10 more than the previous allocation in which SWCO got the South and NECO got the SouthEast. While it is possible that this allocation could naturally arise from any of the auction mechanisms described above, in most cases SECO will simply get squeezed out of the market by its neighboring rivals and an inefficient allocation will result. In this example, the loss from SECO's absence in the market is relatively small—only 10 in the best case—but one can easily construct more intricate examples in which the failure to exploit synergies can lead to inefficiencies that consume much of the available surplus.

Combinatorial Auctions: Optimization on the Fly

The presence of synergies leads to an even more profound failure of the Law of a Single Price than the one we uncovered in the previous chapter. Viewed in isolation, the price of each license should be zero; it is only in combination with other licenses that any license has value. Mechanisms that value these licenses individually are treating them as if the Law of a Single Price holds, when it does not. As things are set up, prices are meaningful only when they are attached to baskets of adjacent licenses. Unfortunately, there are many ways to partition the eight licenses into baskets.

The solution to creating baskets on the fly is a smart market mechanism known as a *combinatorial* or *combined-value auction*. Combinatorial auctions are designed so that they can compute the optimal way to fill any set of bids for baskets of licenses. This ability to optimize gives combinatorial auctions their intelligence; indeed, in complex situations they can find combinations of licenses far beyond the capabilities of any human dealmaker.

The basket-building markets examined in the previous chapter can be viewed as a rudimentary type of combinatorial auction designed to supplement an existing continuous trading system. Although we used the frequency spectrum example to kick off this chapter, the FCC was relatively late to the combinatorial auction party. The earliest combinatorial auctions were designed in the laboratory to handle far more advanced allocation problems. In addition, these markets were too illiquid to support continuous trading of any kind, and so their intelligence must be used when the items are first offered.

The first combinatorial auction (and smart market mechanism) to make its way into print was developed in the late 1970s by Stephen Rassenti, a researcher at Bell Laboratories, as part of his doctoral work at the University of Arizona. Rassenti was a student in Arizona's Systems and Industrial Engineering Department and his dissertation was supervised by Professor Robert Bulfin, who is now at Auburn University.

Rassenti and Bulfin first devised an auction to help the Public Broadcasting Service (PBS) determine which shows to broadcast over its network and what to charge its local affiliates for the network programs they carried. While John Ferejohn and Roger Noll, two of the faculty participants in Vernon Smith and Charles Plott's original Caltech seminar, had previously performed experiments that dealt with this problem, Rassenti and Bulfin sought to modify it to take into account the synergy between different programs. It was only natural that they would meet up with Vernon Smith in Arizona's economics department to test how smart markets performed relative to their ordinary counterparts. Together, they explored the introduction of smart markets into a related market, commercial passenger airlines, which became a test case for deregulation in the United States.

The deregulation of airlines in 1978 almost immediately lowered fares and increased traffic. Consequently, some of the busier airports began to run out of both the gates and runway slots required for flights to take off and land. In order for a passenger aircraft to fly, it must have four airport resources: a departure gate, a take-off slot, a landing slot, and an arrival gate. Absent just one of these, the flight must be canceled. Clearly, a market mechanism that sold only one of these at a time would make flight planning difficult.

Using the airport problem as inspiration, Rassenti, Smith, and Bulfin designed a series of experiments using a simplified version of this problem in which subjects received redemption schedules roughly along the lines of the regional telecommunications example given above. Each individual item (gate or slot) was worth nothing by itself, but each subject could purchase combinations for which the experimenter would pay him according to a schedule of redemption values. Subjects could then submit bids for combinations that interested them. The bids were then entered into a computer and an optimization procedure was used to determine which combination of bids would generate the best allocation. The winners of this auction were then allowed to trade freely in an aftermarket to try to improve on the computer's allocation. As in the double oral auction experiments, the same setup was repeated several times to see if the auction would converge.

The findings of this series of experiments were encouraging, with the auctions reaching almost, but not quite, perfect efficiency. By contrast, significant inefficiencies dominated the results of an earlier version of this experiment conducted at Caltech by David Grether, Mark Isaac, and Charles Plott, which limited each auction to a single item and did not employ computerized optimization, relying solely on trade in the aftermarket to compensate for misallocations made during the initial auctions.

NASA's Awesome Wind Tunnel

Caltech struck back with the next breakthrough in combinatorial auctions: an even smarter market that was both adaptive and interactive. The impetus for this new market was Caltech's connection to the National Aeronautics and Space Administration (NASA), for whom they managed the Jet Propulsion Laboratory (JPL) north of Caltech's campus in Pasadena.

NASA was continually faced with complex resource allocation problems. The demands placed on its manned missions by the scientific community were particularly difficult to juggle. A great many experiments were ideal for the weightless conditions of an orbiting spacecraft; however, the resources required to perform them were in very short supply. Not only would each experiment take up precious space aboard the craft, it might also require electricity to power it and an astronaut's time to monitor it, both of which were scarce.

Until it heard the distant drumbeat of deregulation in the 1980s, NASA was content to allocate resources to scientific experiments like any other government bureaucracy—it assigned a committee to evaluate formal proposals submitted by scientists to determine which experiments would fly and with what level of support. As this game played out over time, scientists would tend to request more resources than they needed because NASA would rarely grant more than a fraction of the resources specified in any proposal. NASA charged non-NASA scientists cost-based fees for their experiments, but these fees were sufficiently low that they likely served only to deter frivolous proposals. Over time, the real requirements of science got lost in the bureaucratic shuffle.

The allocation of scientific resources on Space Shuttle missions had become increasingly confounding. The 1986 Challenger disaster drastically reduced the number and frequency of missions, and so new allocation mechanisms were considered. Scheduling was expected to get even trickier once the proposed space station was in orbit because it could host long-term experiments.

The Jet Propulsion Laboratory studied this scheduling problem extensively and ultimately decided to conduct a series of market experiments that were run by a JPL research scientist, David Porter, in collaboration with Caltech faculty members including John Ledyard and Charles Plott. From JPL's point of view, the experiments provided a *testbed* environment for alternative mechanisms, just as its wind tunnels were an aerodynamic testbed for its spacecraft.

Although uncertainty is present in all economic activities, it plays an overarching role in space exploration. Both the timing of missions and the availability of resources on them are subject to tremendous uncertainty. Missions virtually never take off according to their original schedules, and unexpected events can suddenly require resources previously assigned to experiments. A mechanism for allocating these resources must take uncertainty into account directly. In this setting, contingencies are no longer restricted to prices, as they are in basket trading, but to when a mission is launched. Hence, scheduling an experiment on a space mission involves not only assigning resources, but also creating a contingency plan for their use.

To deal with the added complexity of the space station problem, John Ledyard and David Porter along with Jeffrey Banks at the University of Rochester invented a new auction mechanism that they called the Adaptive User Selection Mechanism (AUSM, pronounced "awesome"). The idea behind the mechanism was that rather than have subjects submit bids that the market uses to compute a single final allocation of goods based on its optimization, the computer continually displays a tentative optimal allocation based on the existing bids and will freely accept new bids from buyers hoping to get in on the action. As such, AUSM is an elaborate form of English auction in which many items under many contingencies are up for sale at the same time.

Buyers competed not only for resources on the space station, but on the priority that they would receive if circumstances dictated that experiments be bumped off a mission. Based on the bids in the system at any point in time, AUSM determined which set of bids to accept in order to generate the highest revenues. In practice, this optimization could be so time-consuming that the market might only be able to compute an approximation to it; indeed, many times it was as if the computer and the buyers are working collaboratively to optimize surplus, something that neither side is capable of doing on its own.

While use of the electromagnetic spectrum involves enormous synergies, the synergies present in space station experimentation are far more limited. The optimal allocation of resources tends to involve cleverly fitting in as many experiments as possible instead of a few, large experiments. While AUSM performed admirably in solving this large-scale jigsaw puzzle, its efficiency topped out at 80 percent of total surplus. The inability of small buyers to form coalitions on the fly, known to economists as the *threshold problem*, tilted the auction in favor of the larger buyers and reduced its efficiency in the process. Nonetheless, AUSM made many matches that would otherwise have been missed; in particular, the traditional method of allocating resources was estimated to capture only about half of the available surplus.

When we first considered alternative auction mechanisms, we saw that both in theory and in practice efficiency was easily achieved—both English and second-price sealed bids auctions worked well in this regard—and the only problem that sellers faced was how to extract more than the second-highest reservation price of the buyers. No matter how one organizes a combinatorial auction, the information that must be extracted from buyers to ensure efficiency is sufficiently rich that it is difficult to elicit in any form, much less as a truthful revelation. The simple mechanism that led to an efficient outcome for auctioning off a single item appears to be difficult to extend to auctions where there are synergies linking several items. Still, variants of the Vickery or second-price sealed-bid auction can be applied to combinatorial environments, but they tend to not perform as well in the laboratory as open mechanisms such as AUSM.

Learning by Doing at the FCC

All of the experiments discussed in the previous sections were completed years before the FCC conducted its first auction in 1994. Rather than dive into the combinatorial auction game, the FCC started with the relatively simple auctions described earlier, breaking each frequency up into many geographic regions and auctioning them off in simultaneous English auctions in which contingencies of any kind were not allowed.

The major difference between the FCC spectrum auctions and the NASA shuttle scheduling problems came down to a matter of money. While the value of the experiments aboard a shuttle mission might be worth millions of dollars, in a typical spectrum auction the total value of the licenses runs into the billions. Any mistakes could be quite costly to the U.S. government, and so it was incumbent upon the FCC that they proceed with caution.

The FCC's biggest problem came not from the auction mechanism itself, but from a failure to appreciate the nature of the options their auctions created. The earliest spectrum auctions did not require that participants be financially qualified to make the payments for any licenses that they were awarded. It was easy for speculators to form a corporation for the purposes of bidding in a spectrum auction and then bid to their heart's content. These interlopers sought to steal licenses out from under the big players and then sell their entire company (the sale of individual licenses was prohibited) to reap a windfall profit. While this scheme can be successful if only a single company tries it, when several syndicates attempt it, their competition for licenses may bid them up to unreasonable prices that even an industry giant would be unwilling to pay. This outcome was not a total disaster for the winner; it could always declare bankruptcy, leaving the FCC holding the license. Effectively, the FCC had been granting free call options to the winners of its auctions. They could buy the license if it was worth more than the winning bid; otherwise, they could put it (pun intended) to the FCC by going bankrupt. Large telecom companies with deep pockets could not play this game, but small firms that were created exclusively to participate in spectrum auctions could and did.

The options that the FCC inadvertently granted ended up costing it billions of dollars on paper. The real losses, however, were substantially less and this mishap received little negative press because the FCC still generated billions of dollars in revenues where previously it had nothing to show for the licenses. Clearly, had it taken the bankruptcy option into account, the bidding would never have gone so high, so it is even conceivable that the FCC came out ahead.

In markets where synergies are important, an efficient auction process helps to coordinate the actions of buyers. A troubling problem that designers of an auction must confront is that the coordination they are promoting ceases to be socially beneficial when it leads to *collusion*. Although collusion has a precise legal meaning, we will consider it loosely as any arrangement among buyers that allows them to depress the prices they pay at auction.

Just as we saw that money could be an emergent property of the economy, cooperation can also emerge without any direct communications or advanced planning among the parties to the collusion. The standard example that game theorists use to illustrate the difficulty of cooperation is known as the Prisoner's Dilemma, which was made popular by political scientist Robert Axelrod's pathbreaking study of evolution and emergent behavior in games, *The Evolution of Cooperation*. The Prisoner's Dilemma game is based on a hypothetical situation where the police capture two suspected parties to a crime and interrogate them individually. Each prisoner faces two alternatives: He can help the police by confessing and implicating the other prisoner or he can deny everything. If the two prisoners are able to cooperate by both denying the charges, they will both serve minimal prison time on a lesser charge for which the police have enough evidence for a conviction in court. Each prisoner is told that if he confesses, he will be set free, but only if his testimony is necessary to convict the other prisoner, who will receive a long prison sentence. Finally, if both prisoners confess, they both get moderate prison sentences.

The dilemma that faces each prisoner is that he has a strong incentive to turn the other in, but collectively they are better off denying every-thing. Viewed as isolated choice, which is just the Nash equilibrium con-cept, confessing is always the better strategy. If the other prisoner confesses, a long prison sentence is avoided and if the other prisoners denies, no time is served. When both prisoners think this way, however, they both get moderate sentences instead of the minimal ones they would have gotten had they both stayed quiet.

The prisoner's dilemma neatly captures the issues facing firms who must decide whether to place artificially low bids in an effort to pay less than the competitive price for an item. In a standard sealed-bid auction, any effort that does not involve explicit collusion among all the parties to the auction is virtually doomed to failure; without any means of commu-nication, submitting an artificially low bid accomplishes nothing other than to allow another buyer to get the item. If the situation is repeated, however, cooperation can emerge spontaneously.

The strategic mechanism for enforcing cooperation is punishment. The simplest punishment strategy is known as *tit-for-tat*. In this strategy, whenever the other party undercuts, he or she is turned in on the next round. This kind of signal is simple enough that it is easy to decode.

The simultaneous nature of the FCC's spectrum auctions made them fertile ground for emergence of cooperation. The FCC conducted a wire-less spectrum auction from August 26, 1996 to January 14, 1997 for three wireless licenses in each of 493 regions (1,479 licenses altogether) that lasted 276 rounds and raised over $2.5 billion. The remarkable thing about this auction is that a few of the bidders discovered a way to cooperate us-ing a practice now known as *code bidding*. Bids for licenses were submitted in whole-dollar amounts, and so some bidders began using the last three digits of their bids to send a message to other bidders. Conveniently, a three-digit number identified each region.

Suppose that a bidder wanted to signal to a competitor not to bid on a license in Rochester, Minnesota, which is region 378. This bidder would go to a region where the competitor currently had the highest bid, say $287,000, and place a noticeable higher "punishing bid" such as $313,378, where the final three digits "378" signal interest in that region. If the recip-ient of the signal continues to bid in the targeted region, additional pun-ishment would be meted out with another signal attached to it.

Statistical studies have found that code bidding was quite effective at keeping bids down and the FCC considered the practice to be in direct violation of the rules governing the auctions. The FCC responded by levying fines on auction participants who employed code bidding and by changing the rules for all future auctions to restrict bids to multiples of $1,000.

It is not surprising that when European countries began conducting their own spectrum auctions that the most successful of the early auctions would be created by an expert in *evolutionary game theory*, which is the study of how strategic behavior, such as code bidding, develops over time. Game theorist Ken Binmore's design for Britain's 3G (third generation) wireless spectrum auction was so successful, raising 22.48 billion pounds ($35.4 billion), that he was named the European Information Technology personality for the year 2000 by the IDG News Service. In reaction to this early success (which appears to be a resounding failure for the telecommunications firms cursed by winning the auction), political pressure forced the British government to stop auctioning off the electromagnetic spectrum. Could it be that something was overlooked?

14

Good Intentions

It would be nice to conclude our story by observing that experimental economics is well along the way to finding the perfect mechanism for traditional markets and has raised the intelligence of markets to the point where they can now be used in areas in which markets were long believed to be unsuitable. Such an optimistic assessment, while debatably true, obscures a deeper truth.

Economists initially ignored experimental findings based on their belief that experiments were insufficiently realistic; they intuitively felt that something important was being omitted. While experimental markets may only incorporate those features that experimenters believe are salient to naturally occurring markets, there is no objective evidence that experimental results are fundamentally misleading. (The failure of the author to include any articles that systematically refute the methods of experimental economics in the bibliography reflects his inability to find any.) Indeed, the imperfect reality of experiments is usually overshadowed by the ability of the experimenter to have knowledge of things that are otherwise inaccessible to outside observers, as demonstrated in the bubble experiments.

Experimental economics hit its stride by examining the inner workings of the market mechanism, something that economists had been content to assume away or leave to an invisible hand, to see how they affected the performance of the market. Under the best of circumstances, the Hayekian ideal could be approached; under the worst of circumstances, markets could produce the bubbles and crashes that have long haunted them.

The challenge that experimental economics faces is not getting experimental markets to look "real"; it is moving their market creations from the laboratory to the world outside and protecting their integrity in the transition. The invisible hand moves not only in economic circles, but in political ones as well. Even though it appears that markets can be engineered to compensate for human psychological frailties, for now politics can stop them dead in their tracks.

Many citizens of the developed world, and the United States in particular, live under the illusion that they participate in a free market system. The central message of this book has been that by understanding options, you can understand the invisible hand. As important as the options internal to the market might be, they are overshadowed by an even greater option—the option of the constitutional governments, within specified limits, to overturn any allocation of goods made by the market. Capitalism, for all the strides it has made, operates without explicit constitutional protection.

The government's option is easily forgotten because in the financial markets it is rarely exercised directly. Only under extreme circumstances, such as we explored in some of our cautionary tales (LTCM, Black Monday, etc.), does the possibility of meaningful government intervention arise and so most of the time this option has little value and minimal influence over markets. Where the government's control really matters is when we try to change the rules of the game, either to help unfetter the invisible hand in an existing market or to substitute the market for the authority of regulators.

The previous chapter described several instances where experimenters had created smart markets that could allocate resources more efficiently than existing regulatory regimes. The sad fact is that none of those markets has been implemented. Bureaucrats realize that by turning their regulatory authority over to markets they may greatly reduce their political power. Members of airport authorities and scientific committees found themselves unwilling to relinquish their control to a more efficient computer-based allocation process regardless of how well it performed in the laboratory.

A glimmer of hope that appears against this background of bureaucratic stonewalling is the Federal Communications Commission. Because the FCC's span of control was not limited to a small bailiwick, but rather extended across the entire electromagnetic spectrum, it needed all the help that it could get to allocate that spectrum. Using an auction system to allocate new frequencies not only made good economic sense, it enhanced the FCC's power by making the Commission the source of billions of dollars in government revenue.

The FCC, however, was reluctant to take the giant step from traditional auctions to the smart auctions required to eliminate obvious inefficiencies in the way the spectrum was allocated. In the end, it took one simple word to get the ball rolling: *combinatorial.*

FCC versus SEC

There are millions of words in the federal statutes of the United States and one of those words is "combinatorial." For those of little faith, feel free to consult Title 47, Section 309 of the United States Code where (at least until it is repealed or amended) you will find the following:

> The [Federal Communications] Commission shall, directly or by contract, provide for the design and conduct (for purposes of testing) of competitive bidding using a contingent combinatorial bidding system that permits prospective bidders to bid on combinations or groups of licenses in a single bid and to enter multiple alternative bids within a single bidding round.

This language applies to the 700Mhz band of electromagnetic spectrum and literally required an Act of Congress—the 1997 Balanced Budget Act—to become law. Of course, the only way to test the markets without really allocating the spectrum was to run experiments. After the FCC examined the findings of these experiments at a special conference in May 2000, it promulgated a regulation requiring the use of combinatorial auctions for allocating the 700Mhz band. The first combinatorial auction of the frequency spectrum was originally scheduled for September 2000, but has been subject to repeated postponements.

Fortunately, the development of smart markets has not been held hostage by the federal government of the United States. The rapid growth in experimental economics research has spawned several start-up companies that specialize in market mechanism design, especially markets that can handle combinatorial orders. Such markets have already been deployed for specialized items ranging from pollution emission permits to cargo containers. Smart markets are even finding their way to the fringes of Wall Street; however, that road remains under the watchful eye of federal regulators.

Congress may have driven the telecommunications world into the arms of experimental economists looking to deploy the first national smart market mechanism, but it has kept financial markets safely out of their embrace. As much as the laws governing the actions of the FCC may be painfully specific, those governing the SEC are woefully vague. As part of the deregulation of the financial markets in the Securities Act Amendments of 1975, Congress mandated the establishment of a National Market System for securities and amended the United States Code (Title 15, Chap. 2B, Sec. 78k-1) as follows:

(A) The securities markets are an important national asset which must be preserved and strengthened.

(B) New data processing and communications techniques create the opportunity for more efficient and effective market operations.

(C) It is in the public interest and appropriate for the protection of investors and the maintenance of fair and orderly markets to assure—

(i) economically efficient execution of securities transactions;

(ii) fair competition among brokers and dealers, among exchange markets, and between exchange markets and markets other than exchange markets;

(iii) the availability to brokers, dealers, and investors of information with respect to quotations for and transactions in securities;

(iv) the practicability of brokers executing investors' orders in the best market; and

(v) an opportunity, consistent with the provisions of clauses (i) and (iv) of this subparagraph, for investors' orders to be executed without the participation of a dealer.

(D) The linking of all markets for qualified securities through communication and data processing facilities will foster efficiency, enhance competition, increase the information available to brokers, dealers, and investors, facilitate the offsetting of investors' orders, and contribute to best execution of such orders.

The double auction mechanism along with extensions that facilitate the linkage of markets for different securities would appear to fit nicely within the parameters of the above law; however, securities markets have not moved in that direction. Soon after deregulation became law, there were calls for a consolidated or *central limit order book* (CLOB). Just as Smith's experiments with a centralized market proved more efficient than Chamberlin's distributed bargaining design, many economists believed for several reasons that having all trade for a given stock ultimately flow through a single order book will better satisfy the goals of the National Market System than a hodgepodge of markets and market makers that are loosely linked at best. In fact, in over 25 years of financial deregulation markets have tended to go in the opposite direction, and became increasingly fragmented. Although several *electronic crossing (or communications) networks* (ECNs)—such as Instinet, Island, and Archipelago—operate limit order books for individual securities that closely correspond to the ideal double auction market that works so well in the laboratory, each network maintains its own distinct set of order books.

Although the SEC has passed many regulations that attempt to place individual investors on a more equal footing with their professional counterparts, it has done less to affect the structure of securities markets. While the FCC web site contains enough material on experimental economics and combinatorial auctions for a graduate university course, on the SEC site experimental economics barely appears.

Even without the benefit of experimentation, the SEC shows every indication of moving toward a National Market System based on some form of central limit order book. Wall Street is also coming around—Henry Paulson, chief executive officer of Goldman, Sachs, made his support of such a system public in 1999. Nonetheless, a realistic assessment of how a market system crafted by the SEC might operate should give one considerable pause. While the FCC has made some blunders on the road to the free market, we must shift our attention to California to see just how much damage a poorly designed market system can do.

Powerless

Some regulators merely tolerate inefficiency; others actively encourage it when they only half-heartedly embrace the market mechanism. The deregulation of California's electric utilities in 1996 used the virtues of free markets as a subtext for political deal making. (It is very tempting to enclose the word *deregulation* as it is used in this context in quotes.) In the complex deal that emerged from deregulation, the electric utilities were provided with a bevy of benefits in exchange for moving to a seemingly competitive market for power generation. While the details of this deal are well beyond the scope of this book, its key elements are quite instructive.

As a condition of deregulation, California utilities were forced to divest themselves of their power plants, compromising their ability to coordinate the production and distribution of electricity. The market system provided for them to purchase power was not only dumb it was horribly incomplete. In particular, long-term contracts for the delivery of power were prohibited and replaced with an ineffectual and underutilized market for future delivery. The market was designed to encourage trade on the spot electricity market while discouraging trade in futures. Furthermore, California consumers, who had influential advocates protecting their interests, were granted a long-term freeze on their electric rates that could be lifted only when the utilities had satisfied certain financial requirements.

The California economy rapidly expanded between 1996 and 2000, led by growth in computer- (and electricity-) intensive high-technology industries. Throughout the 1990s, strict state environment regulations served to block the construction of any large-scale power-generating facilities. By 1999 the wholesale price that power generators received for their electricity began a steep ascent, but supply was unable to respond to this signal. At the same time, customers of the utilities continued to see retail prices fixed by regulation, reducing their incentive to conserve. Industrial customers who paid lower electricity rates in exchange for volunteering to shut down their facilities during peak demand times built some demand responsiveness into the system. Unfortunately, the maximum number of hours that any customer could have its service interrupted was set too low to deal with an extended power shortage, so eventually the California power system would be subject to demand unbridled by market forces.

On January 17, 2001, a full-blown electricity crisis finally struck California after several narrow escapes, with unprecedented statewide rolling blackouts that topped the national news and provided punch lines for late-night talk show hosts. Poor planning and bad luck greatly reduced

California's capacity to supply power to its customers. With supply fixed and demand outpacing it, utilities were still legally required to purchase electricity for their customers and so they drove up the wholesale price of electricity. These higher prices, often a tenfold increase at peak times, were not a bubble; instead, they were the market's natural response to the situation. Like the out-of-control cobweb, electricity prices were reaching out to infinity.

The forces unleashed by deregulation did not stop at California's borders. The shielding of California's electricity users from the real cost of power had strong general equilibrium effects, raising the cost of electricity in neighboring states to inefficiently high levels so that they would conserve electricity on behalf of their California neighbors. The spread of California's misery was halted by the Rocky Mountains, which serve as an imposing physical barrier to the transmission of electric power. Just over the mountains is Texas, home to many of the companies that owned power-generating facilities on the Western power grid. In the press, accusations of price gouging and collusion by power generators flew freely, but early government investigations uncovered little or no wrongdoing.

California's utilities—trapped between paying escalating prices for electricity from their suppliers and receiving fixed prices from their customers—were quickly driven into financial distress by the billions of dollars they owed their suppliers and lenders. California continues to work on solutions to its electricity problems, but the market mechanism appears to have been abandoned in the process. The State of California appears to see its salvation in an extreme form of regulation: government ownership.

The absence of an even minimally intelligent market system did not help matters any in California, but it is doubtful that it could have prevented a crisis given how the market was rigged. For this market to become smart enough to work properly, the real place that intelligence was needed was at the source of consumption: the computers, refrigerators, and other power-hungry appliances. Indeed, economists have long recognized the importance of smart appliances as part of a deregulated electricity market. The costs of generating power are disproportionately concentrated on maintaining the capacity necessary for meeting peak loads. Viewed in this way, the supply of electricity at any point in time fits well with Marshall's upward-sloping supply curve—smaller quantities have low unit costs that increase sharply as highly inefficient methods for generating power are brought online to meet peak loads. The big savings in electricity markets comes from reducing peak loads, which requires consumers and their appliances to respond to prices. Auction wizard William Vickery and other economists have written extensively on how to price electricity efficiently by raising prices at peak times.

Appliances that "know" when electricity is expensive based on a signal that is broadcast to them over power lines or the Internet can then go into a low-power mode until either the price drops or it becomes essential to operate at full power. The basic technology to do this has been around for decades in the form of X-10 and other home automation systems, yet only a few primitive remote-control devices, such as one that enables lights and small appliances to respond to a handclap, are widely used. A market mechanism that can manage peak loads does not need to have anything like the intelligence of the market discussed earlier; it just needs to notify the appliances of current market conditions. The potential benefit is vastly greater than California's failed scheme to switch off industrial customers.

The Rules of Engagement

Even if California's electricity market had been properly designed and tested, there is still a significant chance that its government and regulators would have found a way to undermine it. The perfection of the market mechanism can proceed only so far until it bumps into the imperfection of the political system that governs it. We may not be able to get the rules of exchange that constitute the market mechanism right unless the rules of the society in which the market is embedded are sufficiently hospitable.

Kenneth Arrow's development of social choice theory marked the beginning of a flood of research into how the rules of society interact with its economic choices. While economists and philosophers who had fought against the neoclassical ideal of free markets rallied around the notion that the market system was doomed to failure because it rested on any number of fundamental contradictions, social choice theory demonstrates that all social interactions, and not just those involving markets, must coexist with unresolved paradoxes.

Some of the more obvious difficulties with markets can be resolved in large part simply by getting the rules straight from the beginning. Nobel laureate Ronald Coase demonstrated how the delineation of property rights could influence market outcomes. He found that many problems that economists had associated with the market mechanism, known as *externalities*, could be eliminated merely by explicitly assigning rights to individuals. The FCC's spectrum auctions and the growing market for pollution permits are deeply rooted in Coase's work.

Another Nobel laureate, James Buchanan, extended economic analysis from the actions of consumers and firms to those of the government. He recognized that the government was not merely a black box that took its orders from economists, but consisted of individuals with their own agendas. Buchanan, working with a number of collaborators, found that the legislative deal making that can produce ill-conceived laws was a natural consequence of the rational actions of individual legislators behaving in their own best political interests. Several other distinguished economists, including Oliver Williamson and Nobel laureate Douglass North, have studied the legal and political aspects of economic institutions, creating a new discipline within economics known as the *new institutional economics*.

Smart markets can help to resolve some of capitalism's contradictions, but not without raising some new issues. As we saw in Chapter 12, a market mechanism that is smart enough to exploit arbitrage opportunities automatically is likely to be more efficient and stable than the present arrangement of having outside parties perform the functions necessary to bring markets into equilibrium. While outsiders are faced with capitalism's basic contradiction that if they do their job well enough to make markets perfectly efficient they will put themselves out of business, a self-arbitraging market mechanism can sidestep this contradiction. The problem is that such smart markets cannot simply appear; they must be adopted through a process that is likely more political than economic.

Despite politicians' demonstrated talent for manufacturing chaos when they design economic mechanisms—if you doubt this, consider the U.S. tax code—their individual rationality may be the one thing that keeps them within reach of the invisible hand. Politicians and governments that enact and tolerate inefficient economic institutions can unleash strong economic forces against themselves and their self-interests.

The invisible hand that Adam Smith imagined operated within the confines of free markets may loom as a much larger presence in the world. Over time, the invisible hand may not only lead societies toward market-based processes and away from the alternatives, it may also help better market mechanisms to triumph over inferior ones. Indeed, the spontaneous order that F. A. Hayek sensed would arise from the market's operation could also determine which of the many possible market mechanisms would emerge.

The inevitable progress of the invisible hand does not place society in a passive position. While economic and political mistakes may eventually be corrected by nature, the cost in human suffering of blindly (and repeatedly) making the wrong economic and political choices appears to be the great lesson of the twentieth century. We cannot simply have faith that an invisible hand will ultimately guide the markets along the path to perfection; based on the early results that have come out of the laboratory, we have an obligation to participate fully in the economy's evolution.

Notes

Basic facts, including significant dates and names, were verified using online and offline reference materials from *Britannica* and *Microsoft Encarta*. Smith (1991), Davis and Holt (1993), and Kagel and Roth (1995) provided general background for Part I and are all recommended as comprehensive introductions to experimental economics for the more technical reader. Holt (web site) provides a complete bibliography for experimental economics. Basic financial data (stock price ranges, etc.) are from Yahoo!'s financial gateway, finance.yahoo.com. Experimental economics is developing rapidly and so new reference works continue to be introduced. These notes are arranged by topic within each chapter. Internet searches on a topic name provide the fastest and easiest way to get up-to-date information on the field. Titles of major works are given explicitly to save the reader from having to refer to the bibliography. Material on web sites is subject to change or restrictions on access by its owner.

Preface

The invisible hand and physics: The invisible hand and Newtonian gravitation would appear to be a perfect match. Newton provides no mechanism to guide gravitational attraction; it just happens. This "action at a distance," as it was later called, would seem a lot like an invisible hand. Some economic historians (Foley, 1976 and Mirowski, 1989) believe that Adam Smith's invisible hand was inspired by the older, long-discredited physics of

Descartes in which gravitation was caused by invisible vortices. This belief is largely based on an obscure early astronomical writing of Smith that refers to the invisible hand in reference to the planet Jupiter. Smith makes no explicit reference to the physics of either Descartes or Newton, but Smith (1776, p. 238n) does refer to Newton's accounting of silver shipments. Einstein's curved space–time in his 1915 Theory of General Relativity showed how gravity could work without the need for action at a distance. Redman (1997) discusses the links between Adam Smith and Sir Isaac Newton. See also *The Wealth of Nations* in Chapter 3.

John von Neumann: Lee (1994) provides an extended biographical sketch of John von Neumann and describes his work on the EDVAC stored-program computer.

F. A. Hayek: The Nobel Prize was awarded to Hayek jointly with Gunnar Myrdal, a noted Swedish socialist. (All references to the Nobel Prize refer to the Bank of Sweden Prize in Economic Sciences in Memory of Alfred Nobel, which was first awarded in 1969 and is not one of the original prizes established by Alfred Nobel's will.) Experimental economists recognize Hayek's (1945) "The Use of Knowledge in Society" as his masterwork; however, his earlier (1937) "Economics and Knowledge" spells out his basic equilibrium concept. Ebenstein (2001) gives a comprehensive account of Hayek's life and ideas. Ransom (web site) is a source for all things Hayekian. See also *Hayek hypothesis* in Chapter 3 and *Emergence of money* in Chapter 10.

Edward Chamberlin: See Notes to Chapter 2.

Chapter 1

Blue Monday: Details of the minicrash and recovery are taken from Securities and Exchange Commission (1998) and Ross and Sofianos (1998). The SEC Chairman during the event, Arthur Levitt (1998), provides a thoughtful discussion of circuit breakers in his testimony before a Senate subcommittee on securities.

Tacoma Narrows Bridge collapse: The author, who repeatedly viewed film strips of this event while studying applied mathematics in the 1970s, is unaware of any other reference to it in the economics literature. Koughan (1996) provides an excellent online illustrated discussion of the alternative theories for its collapse. The Washington State Department of Transportation (web site) includes a video of the collapse and a continuously updating camera shot of the present-day bridge built in 1950 to replace Galloping Gertie.

Wind tunnels: Koughan (1996) discusses wind-tunnel testing for bridges and Moran (1999) describes the testing of the Deer Isle Bridge in Maine, a smaller version of the Tacoma Narrows Bridge that still stands. Holloway (1999) describes the tests on the Tacoma Narrow Bridges made before its collapse.

Tulip mania: Garber (1990) is one in a series of controversial works in which he argues that the great speculative bubbles of history were not bubbles at all. The issue of the *Journal of Economic Perspectives* in which this article appears has several pro-bubble articles written in the aftermath of Black Monday.

Road map: Notes for topics described in the road map will appear in their respective chapters.

Chapter 2

Nasdaq/Internet bubble: Specifics of the bubble and priceline.com compiled as events unfolded from Yahoo! Finance (finance.yahoo.com), *Wall Street Journal* (wsj.com), *New York Times* (nytimes.com), Bloomberg (bloomberg.com), and other news and financial web sites.

Individual rationality: Rational Choice (Hogarth and Reder, 1987) is an excellent collection of accessible papers that provides a cross-section of viewpoints about the rationality of individuals from many top researchers in economics and psychology. See also *Utility, preferences, and price indexes* in Chapter 9.

Biology and preferences: Robson (2001) surveys the biological basis of individual economic behavior.

Induced valuation: Smith (1982b) provides the theoretical foundations for the induced valuation approach to experimental economics.

Game theory: Dixit and Nalebuff (1991) provide an accessible introduction to game theory and its business application, while *Fun and Games* (Binmore, 1992) gives a broader and more detailed treatment of game theory with less focus on its application and more on its connection with mathematics and philosophy. Stanford Encyclopedia of Philosophy (web site) provides an online introduction to game theory with several useful links. *A Beautiful Mind* (Nasar, 1998) gives the fascinating story of the life of John Nash and is the basis for the film of the same title.

Bargaining: Schelling's influential *The Strategy of Conflict* (1960) covers some of the more subtle behavioral aspects of bargaining. *The Art and Science of Negotiation* (Raiffa, 1982) is the classic bargaining and negotiation textbook. The observation that prices negotiated by students tend to average a bit less than an even split is noted in that text and has been verified by the author in a series of classroom exercises. Davis and Holt (1993) and Kagel and Roth (1995) both provide detailed coverage of bargaining experiments. Nash (1950) provides his original solution to the bargaining problem.

Edward Chamberlin: Blaug (1997) discusses Chamberlin's contributions to economics and draws a parallel between his work and that of Keynes. Chamberlin (1948) reports the results of his experiments. On the other hand, New School University (web site 1) dismisses him as the economic equivalent of a one-hit wonder. Smith (1981) describes what it was like to participate in one of these experiments and notes that graduate students at Harvard generally regarded them as "silly." In an April 3, 2001 conversation Roger Noll, who attended Chamberlin's class after Smith, confirmed his general impressions while noting that the experiment in which he participated converged to the competitive equilibrium, contrary to the results in Chamberlin (1948). See also *Monopolistic competition* in Chapter 9.

Conducting your own experiments: Charles Holt and his colleagues have prepared a series of papers that make it easy to informally run experiments like the major ones described in this book. See Holt (1996), Ball and Holt (1998), Laury and Holt (1999), and Holt and Sherman (1999). Friedman and Sunder (1994) provide a guide to conducting experiments for professional economists. Most of the experimental articles cited in this paper include sample instructions that were distributed to subjects to make it easy to replicate the experiments.

Chapter 3

John Law: Law (1705) presents the diamond/water paradox that is referenced by Adam Smith (1776, p. 32n). A stately full-body portrait of John Law (www.econlib.org/library/Mackay/JohnLaw.jpg) appears in Charles Mackay's (1841) classic work on bubbles of which the first chapter is devoted to Law's Mississippi scheme.

François Quesnay: New School University (web site 2) provides a centralized source of material on Quesnay including links to several versions of his *Tableau Économique*.

The Wealth of Nations: Adam Smith's (1776) classic work in which the invisible hand is mentioned only once. (The version available on the Library of Economics and Liberty web site makes it easy to search the text.) The invisible hand also makes a single appearance in Smith's other masterwork, *The Theory of Moral Sentiments* (1759). Vernon Smith (1998) uses experimental results to reconcile apparent inconsistencies that scholars have found when contrasting Adam Smith's free-market philosophy in *The Wealth of Nations* with his advocacy of social cooperation in *The Theory of Moral Sentiments.*

Classical and neoclassical economic theory: This book's treatment of this important period in the development of economics is designed to provide the reader with the minimal background necessary to appreciate contemporary economics. Blaug (1997) does an excellent job of filling in all the details.

Supply and demand: John Stuart Mill's (1848) *Principles of Political Economy* is where the notion that the natural price for a good depends on the interplay between supply and demand begins. The famous Marshall (1920) scissors quote is from Book V, Chapter III, Paragraph 27. While supply and demand typically form a simple cross with supply rising and demand falling, many other configurations are possible, including multiple crossings of the two curves.

NYSE opening: See *Call markets* in Chapter 8.

Vernon Smith: Smith (1981) provides a detailed account of how he came to run the double oral auction experiment. Smith describes meeting the late Sidney Siegel at Stanford shortly before his death and notes Siegel's influence on him. Siegel and Fouraker's (1960) study of bargaining behavior, although more limited in scope than Smith's, represents a major advance in experimental economics methodology as well as a significant early collaboration between an economist and a psychologist.

Double auction experiment: Smith (1962) is the classic paper and Holt (1996) gives an updated version of the experiment using playing cards. Smith and Williams' (1992) *Scientific American* article gives an overview of market experimentation. The double auction experiment that appears in Figures 3.5 and 3.6 is one of many designs tested by Vernon Smith. Increasing the size of the steps in the supply and demand curves as one moves away from equilibrium, as Smith did in this experiment, reduces the number of subjects required to conduct the experiment without significantly changing the outcome.

Hayek hypothesis: Smith (1982a) discusses experimental market results in the context of the Hayek hypothesis. Beckmann and Werding (1994) present a more elaborate version of the hypothesis while presenting a comprehensive survey of market experiments, including the speculation, asset market, and bubble experiments described in Chapter 4.

Chapter 4

Business cycles: The Jevons sunspot story appears many places in somewhat different forms. The version given here uses details from Heilbroner (1995, p. 263).

Information mirages: Camerer and Weigelt (1991) define information mirages and perform the first laboratory tests to create them.

Schumpeter: Schumpeter's (1950) *Capitalism, Socialism, and Democracy* introduces the concept of creative destruction. This influential and original work begins with a multidimensional analysis of Karl Marx. While Schumpeter recognizes the importance of entrepreneurs in the economy, he also predicts the extinction of capitalism. Heilbroner (1995, pp. 288–310) gives an insightful profile of this influential economist.

Keynesian macroeconomics: Keynes's (1936) *The General Theory* is the seminal work in this area. It seems that Keynes had figured out that if your work was sufficiently ambiguous, an entire industry would develop that was devoted solely to figuring out what you really meant or to twisting your words to suit their purposes. Heilbroner (1995, pp. 248–287) gives the Keynesian view of Keynes.

Cobweb model: This treatment of the cobweb model is based on Henderson and Quandt (1971, pp. 142–145) and similar presentations of this model appear throughout the economics literature.

Rational expectations: See Notes to Chapter 10.

Two-period models: Samuelson (1966) provides the definitive treatment of the two-period model by adapting the seminal contribution of John Williams (1936).

Speculation experiments: Miller, Plott, and Smith (1977) give a complete account of the first speculation experiment. Arlington Williams (1979) replicated the results, adding a control experiment to ensure that the seasonal markets converged to different prices in the absence of carryover. Laury and Holt (1999) provide instructions for conducting a simple speculation experiment. Chamberlin (1957, p. 249 and 1962, p. 29) supports the view that speculation is destabilizing and both contain the quote attributed to him in the text. Plott and Smith (1978) introduce surplus as a way to compare the efficiency of experimental markets conducted using different trading rules.

Asset market experiments: Sunder (1995) presents an excellent survey. Forsythe, Palfrey, and Plott (1982) and Plott and Sunder (1988) are two important early papers.

Bubble experiments: Smith, Suchanek, and Williams (1988) present the first bubble experiments. Porter and Smith (1995) showed that bubbles still form when dividend payments are known in advance. Caginalp, Porter, and Smith (1998 and 2000) show the importance of liquidity and momentum in the formation of bubbles, respectively. Ball and Holt (1998) give instructions for a simple version of the bubble experiment. Lei, Noussair, and Plott (2001) provide experimental evidence that the desire of subjects to trade even in the absence of any economic gain can contribute to bubble formation.

Computerized experimental markets: Williams (1980) describes some of the first experiments run on the PLATO system.

Circuit breaker experiments: King, Smith, Williams, and van Boening (1993) show that circuit breakers only make bubbles worse. Ackert, Church, and Jayaraman (1999) show that circuit breakers are ineffectual under a different set of parameters than those typically used in bubble experiments. This paper also provides a survey of the theoretical literature on circuit breakers.

Chapter 5

Keynesian beauty contest: The General Theory (Keynes, 1936, p. 156) is the source of the beauty contest metaphor. The boom in behavioral finance has brought this metaphor renewed attention.

Cash flow discounting: Taggart (1996) is an excellent introduction to asset valuation using cash flow discounting. Most introductory corporate finance and investments textbooks also cover this topic.

The reality of experimental markets: Plott (1982) makes the case that experimental markets are real markets.

Random walks and efficient markets: Malkiel's (2000) *A Random Walk Down Wall Street* is the classic work in this area. Bernstein (1992) provides a history of the topic and Cootner (1964) is a collection of the classic papers in the field. Thaler (1992 and 1993) and Lo and MacKinlay (1999) provide a variety of evidence intended to refute the efficient-market theory. Stovall (1994) documents the predictive value of the Super Bowl in the U.S. stock market.

Noise: Black's (1986) "Noise" is the source of great financial wisdom on noise traders, whom in later articles he called *nice traders* because their expected losses redounded to the favor of others.

Behavioral economics and finance: Daviss (1998) gives a popular account of recent work in behavioral economics. Hirshleifer (2001) presents a comprehensive survey of the technical literature on the role of psychology in asset pricing. Tversky and Kahneman (1987) provide a survey of their work and the related work of others that shows inconsistencies in individual choice. Camerer (1995) surveys the findings of individual choice experiments. Grether and Plott (1979) give the results of their pioneering preference reversal experiments. Shiller (2000) is an influential account of asset mispricing at the end of the twentieth century.

Blackjack and card counting: The invention of card counting is universally attributed to Thorp's (1966) *Beat the Dealer*, which is an excellent study of logical problem solving. The Internet is teeming with resources on blackjack and card counting. Consult your favorite search engine and beware.

Hedge-fund closures: The information provided is based on news stories from Yahoo! Finance and other financial publications.

Rational bubbles: Marx's (1867, Chapter 10) *Capital* is the source of the rational bubble quote.

Robot traders: See Notes to Chapter 8.

Complete markets: Arrow and Debreu (1954) prove the existence of equilibrium in complete competitive markets. Arrow (1964) is the English version of his classic 1953 article that proves that efficiency is possible with a complete set of securities contingent on every possible state of nature. Flood (1991) is a thorough introduction to complete markets and their importance to financial markets. Plott and Sunder (1988) devise a clever series of experiments with three possible states of the world. In a typical experiment, half of the subjects are privately given information that one state of the world is impossible and the other half is privately told of another state that is impossible. Among all traders, there is sufficient information to determine that the prevailing state of the world must be the one that was not mentioned to any of the traders. Market prices alone do not appear able to convey this information without specific contracts based on the three states of nature. Bossaerts, Fine, and Ledyard (2000) discuss the problems that arise when laboratory markets provide for trade in too many assets and show how combinatorial auctions (see Chapter 13) can help these markets operate more efficiently. Athanasoulis, Shiller, and van Wincoop (1999) discuss how markets based on macroeconomic variables (Gross Domestic Product, etc.) can help make markets more stable and efficient.

Shad-Johnson Accord: Faille (2000) provides an excellent summary of the Shad-Johnson Accord and single-stock futures contracts. Jenkins (2000) supports single-stock futures as a way of preventing bubbles.

Chapter 6

1929 Crash: Galbraith's (1961) *The Great Crash 1929* is the classic narrative account of the Crash. To further distinguish between this Crash and the one on Black Monday, a capital C is always used to designate it.

Black Monday and Terrible Tuesday: University of Western Ontario (1987) provides selected links to additional information and a comprehensive bibliography that includes the various government reports written after the fact.

Firm handshake theory: The author learned of this expression from Professor Herman Leonard, who teaches finance at Harvard University's Kennedy School of Government.

The RAND Corporation: RAND Corporation (web site) gives an overview of RAND's history and links to historical resources. Nasar (1998) describes what life at RAND was like for John Nash. RAND's research in game theory and economics was primarily driven by its potential for military applications.

Portfolio optimization and CAPM: Markowitz's (1959) *Portfolio Selection* is where this line of research began and much of it is quite readable and still relevant. Bodie, Kane, and Marcus's (1998) *Investments* textbook provides a comprehensive technical introduction to all aspects of portfolio analysis. Roll (1977) and Fama and French (1992) are among the more fruitful efforts that use statistical methods to poke holes in the CAPM. Bernstein's (1992) *Capital Ideas* provides the history and biography behind this work.

Option valuation: See Notes to Chapter 7.

Incentives: Spence and Zeckhauser (1971) and Ross (1973) are two notable pioneering works in the theory of incentives.

Portfolio insurance: Bernstein (1992) tells the story of portfolio insurance in Chapter 14, entitled "The Ultimate Invention." The form of the put-call parity relationship given here assumes that the stock pays no dividends; adjustments for dividends are easily incorporated into it. Bodie, Kane, and Marcus (1992, pp. 627–629) give the logic behind this relationship as do advanced options textbooks including Hull (2000).

Chapter 7

Statistical approaches to option valuation: Thorp and Kassouf (1967) is the most notably statistical approach. Bouchard (1998) looks at option valuation from the perspective of econophysics.

Black-Scholes formula and option calculations: Black and Scholes (1973) and Merton (1973) are the classic option valuation articles. Black (1989) provides a first-hand account of how his article with Myron Scholes made it into print. Bernstein (1992 and 1996) provides additional historical background about the formula and option pricing. Miller (1993) provides a variety of option valuation formulas and numerical option valuation methods written in Mathematica. Many free option value calculators are available online and are easily found using popular search engines.

Advanced option models: Hull (2000) is the standard reference to the wide variety of option valuation models available, including the full version of the trinomial model used in the example and an introduction to the various swaps mentioned at the beginning of this chapter. Kurz and Motolese (2000) provide a rational beliefs model with endogenous volatility. Derivatives Strategy (web site) is a leading web site with information on options and derivatives.

Real options: Real Options (web site) provides a wealth of resources and articles from business publications on real options.

Securitization and embedded options: Fabozzi (2000) provides a broad overview of fixed-income securities, the options embedded with them, and the process of securitization. Frank Fabozzi has numerous books that go into more depth for specific kinds of securities.

Default options: Merton (1974) and Geske (1977) explored how to estimate the probability that a bond would default. Miller (1998) demonstrates the superior predictive power of the KMV's default prediction model.

Decimalization: Opdyke and Zuckerman (2001) report some negative reactions by traders to the conversion to decimals on the NYSE.

Chapter 8

Cost of trading: Perold (1988) provides a comprehensive treatment of all the costs of trading and develops his own measure of these costs that he calls the *implementation shortfall.*

Market manipulations: Niederhoffer (1997) provides a wealth of details about how Wall Street can manipulate markets from the point of view of a finance professor who moved on to a career as a speculator.

Free-rider problem and public goods: Clarke (1980) provides a comprehensive treatment of the issues involved in getting individuals to reveal their demand for public goods.

Robot traders: Rust, Miller, and Palmer (1992) describe the Santa Fe Institute double auction tournament and its results. Gode and Sunder (1993) show how robot traders programmed to behave randomly will converge to the competitive equilibrium under double auction rules.

Call markets: Bacidore and Lipson (2001) describe the mechanics of the call markets used to open and close the NYSE. Attribution of the phrase "truth without consequences" to Charles Polk comes from private correspondence with Evan Schulman and Charles Polk.

One-sided auctions: John Miller (1997) discusses William Vickery's life and includes the roller-skating story. Vickery (1961) is the seminal work in auction theory. Cox, Smith, and Walker (1983) describe the first experimental tests of Vickery's theory. Smith (1989) gives an excellent summary of auction theory and the experimental evidence.

Chapter 9

Monopolistic competition: Chamberlin (1962) is the updated book version of Edward Chamberlin's doctoral dissertation on monopolistic competition. Spence (1976a and b) kicked off a revival of interest in such models using rigorous analytical methods.

Lemons and "Groucho" Marx: Akerlof (1970) is the source of the lemons model and is discussed a great many places in the economics literature, most notably in Schelling (1978), which includes a discussion of why the front rows in auditoriums tend to fill up last. The Groucho quote has worked its way into the English language through Woody Allen and many other writers.

Signaling and related models: Spence's (1973) article and the book version of his doctoral dissertation (1974) provide the original exposition of the signaling model. The equilibrium concept that Spence uses has been refined and many variants of the model have been studied.

Asymmetric information experiments: The signaling experiments described here come from Miller and Plott (1985). Lynch, Miller, Plott, and Porter (1986 and 1991) describe the FTC-sponsored lemons experiments. Holt and Sherman (1999) describe a classroom version of the lemons experiment.

Financial signaling: Some notable financial elaborations of the signaling model are Rothschild and Stiglitz (1976) and Stiglitz and Weiss (1981). That signaling behavior might influence a firm's financial decisions runs counter to the traditional Modigliani–Miller theories of corporate finance in which these decisions are irrelevant because investors can rearrange their portfolio to counterbalance them. Ross (1977) is a seminal work that shows how signaling affects corporate financial decisions.

Thorstein Veblen: Veblen's (1899) conspicuous consumption foreshadows Spence's signaling model, with consumption serving as a signal of social status. Heilbroner's (1995, pp. 213–247) biographical sketch of Veblen highlights his eccentricities.

Price invertibility: Grossman and Stiglitz (1980) explore the inconsistencies that arise when traders attempt to infer the state of the world from market prices rather than incur the cost of gathering the information needed to anchor prices. Forsythe, Nelson, Neumann, and Wright (1991) describe the Iowa Presidential Stock Market. Iowa Electronic Markets (web site) is where the political and other markets being conducted by the University of Iowa are located.

Stock indexes: Malkiel (2000) was instrumental in making the case to the public for index funds. Bernstein (1992) describes the early days of indexing at Wells Fargo.

Utility, preferences, and price indexes: A discussion of utility functions and individual preferences is a standard part of all microeconomics textbooks. Samuelson (1947) provides the rigorous foundations of modern utility. The use of the jolly as a unit of utility comes from Roger Noll's intermediate microeconomics course at Caltech in the early 1970s. Neither the author nor Professor Noll is aware of any other use of that term. In the United

States, a group of distinguished economists known as the Boskin Commission worked to change the way that price indexes are computed to eliminate several biases. Advisory Committee to Study the Consumer Price Index (1996) gives their findings and includes a comprehensive overview of the major issues in price index theory. Tversky and Kahneman (1987) discuss behavioral alternatives to utility theory.

Utilitarianism: Blaug (1997) discusses the role of Bentham and his fellow utilitarians in the development of economic thought.

Optimal taxation: The optimal income taxation is structurally similar to the signaling problem, which it predates, if we view income (observable) as a signal of ability (unobservable). Mirrlees (1971) is the pioneering paper in the area and was part of an enormous boom in the study of optimal taxation in the early 1970s that included work by Anthony Atkinson, Peter Diamond, Ray Fair, Eytan Sheshiniski, and other economists.

Voting and social choice: Sen (1970) provides an excellent overview of the major issues of social choice theory. Arrow (1963) builds the foundations of the theory with a detailed analysis of the possibility of consistent social choice. Levine and Plott (1977) is the first agenda manipulation experiment. Sen (1995) presents an overview of a special issue of the *Journal of Economic Perspectives* on the economics of voting.

Chapter 10

Gold and fiat money: Bernstein (2000) gives a historical account of hard currency and the economic rationale for fiat money.

Monetarism: Blaug (1997) provides a historical perspective on the quantity theory of money and the many writings of Milton Friedman give the contemporary perspective from the master.

Rational expectations: Lucas (1972) shows how changes in the money supply will not affect output in a rational expectations equilibrium.

Money illusion: Modigliani and Cohn (1979) looked at money illusion for a declining stock market and Miller and Schulman (1999) revisited it in a rising stock market. Fehr and Tyran (2000) provide early experimental evidence supporting the existence of money illusion.

Emergence of money: Duffy and Ochs (1999) describe the experiment from which money emerges. Duffy (1998) surveys the experiments conducted in monetary economics.

Future money: The Internet is awash with discussions of the future of money in an electronic age. Jerry Jordan (1996) of the Federal Reserve Bank provides a brief and readable introduction to the issues. Business Wire (1998) gives the postmortem press release from the failed Manhattan electronic money trial.

Chapter 11

Traffic gridlock: Budiansky (2000) discusses how gridlock has become a hot topic in contemporary physics.

Salomon Brothers: Lewis (1989) provides entertaining background material on John Meriwether and his early days at Salomon Brothers. Dunbar (2000, pp. 110–112) and Lowenstein (2000, pp. 20–22) give independent accounts of the circumstances under which LTCM's principals left Salomon Brothers.

Long-Term Capital Management: Dunbar (2000) and Lowenstein (2000) provide complementary book-length descriptions of the LTCM affair. Dowd (1999) provides a critical examination of whether LTCM was really too big to fail. The Bank for International Settlements (1999) and the President's Working Group on Financial Markets (1999) are the official reports generated by the formal investigations of the affair. Perold (1999) is the Harvard Business School case study of the affair. Although none of the accounts of the affair view it as a form of gridlock, Perold (1999) and Dunbar (2000) provide the best insights into the difficulties that LTCM faced and how they could be squeezed by conflicting valuations.

Limits of arbitrage: Shleifer and Vishny (1997) is the most celebrated model of how arbitrage may not be able to rid the market of inefficiencies. De Long, Bradford, Shleifer, Summers, and Waldmann (1990) is a notably early effort along the same lines. Lowenstein (2000) provides evidence that Robert Merton was aware of the Shleifer-Vishny model and dismissed it as irrelevant to their situation. Perold (1999) explains the lengths to which LTCM went to insure that it was funding over the long-term, thereby allowing them to avoid the liquidity problems of the Shleifer-Vishny model only to fall victim to the related problem of a valuation squeeze. Abelson (2001) is the source for the Keynes remark, which he in turn got from Barton Biggs at Morgan Stanley.

Artificial intelligence: The Internet, which has developed alongside the field of artificial intelligence, has vast resources available on the topic accessible by your favorite search engine, which undoubtedly incorporates what at one time would have been considered artificial intelligence technology. Barger (web site) gives an entertaining introduction to the field.

Stock baskets: American Stock Exchange (web site) has links to information on the stock baskets that trade on the exchange. FOLIOfn (web site) provides further information on how its folios work.

Chapter 12

Basket trading and all-or-none contingencies: The examples given here are simplified versions of the examples that appear in Miller (1990) and Miller (1996) and were offshoots of a theory of the market mechanism developed in Miller (1986). All the algorithms described in this chapter are in the public domain and Miller (1990) is referenced by two basic priceline.com (see Chapter 2) patents: U.S. 6,085,169 and U.S. 6,134,534. Norris (2001) discusses a regulatory action involving all-or-none orders on Nasdaq.

Market friction: Black (1995) describes friction and assorted other ideas about automated market systems.

Recombinant securities markets: Bureau of the Public Debt (web site) answers basic questions on the U.S. Treasury's STRIPS program. Keynes (1936, p.158) is the source of the casino quote.

Chapter 13

Monopoly game: ADENA (web site) presents a collection of alternative views of the history of the Monopoly game.

Combinatorial auction experiments: Ferejohn and Noll (1976) give their pioneering public goods experiment on the choice of PBS programming. Grether, Isaac, and Plott (1981) is the original airplane slot experiment, and Rassenti, Smith, and Bulfin (1982) is the combinatorial auction version. Banks, Ledyard, and Porter (1989) provide the background for the AUSM experiments. McCabe, Rassenti, and Smith (1989 and 1991) describe experiments for a pipeline network and survey the early smart market experiments, respectively.

Spectrum auctions: Kwerel and Rosston (2000) provide the inside view of the FCC spectrum auctions from both political and economic perspectives. Cramton and Schwarz (1999) is a comprehensive study of the code bidding that occurred in earlier auctions and is the source of the example used in this chapter. Federal Communications Commission (web site 1) contains both current and historical information about the wireless spectrum auctions. Axelrod's (1984) *The Evolution of Cooperation* describes a computerized prisoner's dilemma tournament that was the inspiration for the Santa Fe double auction tournament. Rohde (2000) describes the European spectrum auction experience in the context of Ken Binmore's selection as European Information Technology personality of the year 2000.

Chapter 14

FCC and combinatorial auctions: Federal Communications Commission (web site 2) gives comprehensive references from the May 5–7, 2000 conference on combinatorial auctions.

SEC and the National Market System: Securities and Exchange Commission (web site) includes numerous documents on the National Market System. Reuters (1999) reports Henry Paulson's support of a single electronic market system.

California electric crisis: This discussion is based largely on information gathered from Yahoo! and the Los Angeles Times (web site).

Ronald Coase: Coase (1959 and 1960) contain his contributions on the FCC and the importance of delineating property rights, which is the basis for the theorem that bears his name.

James Buchanan: Buchanan (web site) has many of his major works. Congleton (1999) describes the "Virginia School" that Buchanan founded. The experimental economics contributions of Charles Plott were influenced by the fact that he was one of Buchanan's students.

Bibliography

Original publication dates are used for all citations with historic significance. Publication dates that are more recent may be used for modern sources that have undergone significant revisions since their original publication. Web addresses are subject to change and content at web sites is subject to change or discontinuance. Every effort was made to choose sites that were the most likely to persist over time. A search engine may be able to relocate moved sites or find related information.

Abelson, Alan, 2001. "False Bottom." *Barron's* (March 26), pp. A5–A6.

Ackert, Lucy F., Bryan K. Church, and Narayanan Jayaraman, 1999. "An Experimental Study of Circuit Breakers: The Effects of Mandated Market Closures and Temporary Halts on Market Behavior." Federal Reserve Bank of Atlanta, Working Paper 99-1 (March). Available at *www.frbatlanta.org/publica/work_papers/wp99/wp9901.pdf*.

ADENA, web site. "Who Invented Monopoly?" Available online at *www.adena.com/adena/mo*.

Advisory Committee to Study the Consumer Price Index, 1996. "A More Accurate Measure of the Cost of Living." (December 4.) Available online at *www.ssa.gov/history/reports/boskinrpt.html*.

Akerlof, George A., 1970. "The Market for 'Lemons': Qualitative Uncertainty and the Market Mechanism." *Quarterly Journal of Economics*, Vol. 84, No. 3 (August), pp. 488–500.

American Stock Exchange, web site. "Exchange Traded Funds (ETFs)—Overview." Available online at *www.amex.com/indexshares/index_shares_over.stm*.

Arrow, Kenneth J., 1963. *Social Choice and Individual Values*, 2nd ed. New Haven and London: Yale University Press. First published 1951.

Arrow, Kenneth J., 1964. "The Role of Securities in the Optimal Allocation of Risk Bearing." *Review of Economic Studies*, Vol. 31, No. 1 (April), pp. 91–96. First published (in French) 1953.

Arrow, Kenneth J., and Gerard Debreu, 1954. "Existence of Equilibrium for a Competitive Economy." *Econometrica*, Vol. 22, No. 3 (July), pp. 265–290.

Athanasoulis, Stefano, Robert Shiller, and Eric van Wincoop, 1999. "Macro Markets and Financial Security." *Economic Policy Review (Federal Reserve Bank of New York)*, Vol. 5, No. 1 (April). Available at *www.ny.frb.org/rmaghome/econ_pol/499van.pdf*.

Axelrod, Robert, 1984. *The Evolution of Cooperation*. New York: Basic Books.

Bacidore, Jeffrey Michael, and Marc L. Lipson, 2001. "The Effects of Opening and Closing Procedures on the NYSE and Nasdaq." Presented at the *2001 Meetings of the American Finance Association (January)*. Available online at *http://papers.ssrn.com/sol3/papers.cfm?abstract_id=257049*.

Ball, Cheryl B., and Charles A. Holt, 1998. "Classroom Games: Bubbles in an Asset Market." *Journal of Economic Perspectives*, Vol. 12, No. 1 (Winter), pp. 207–218. Available at *www.people.virginia.edu/~cah2k/bubbletr.pdf*.

Bank for International Settlements, 1999. "A Review of Financial Market Events in Autumn 1998." Committee on the Global Financial System Publication No. 12 (October), Basil, Switzerland. Available at *www.bis.org/publ/cgfs12.pdf*.

Banks, Jeffrey S., John O. Ledyard, and David P. Porter, 1989. "Allocating Uncertain and Unresponsive Resources." The *RAND Journal of Economics*, Vol. 20, No. 1 (Spring), pp. 1–25.

Barger, Jorn, web site. "The Outsider's Guide to Artificial Intelligence." Available online at *www.robotwisdom.com/ai/index.html*.

Beckmann, Klaus, and Martin Werding, 1994. "Markets and the Use of Knowledge Testing the 'Hayek Hypothesis' in Experimental Stock Markets." Unpublished working paper (May 3). Available at *http://netec.wustl.edu/WoPEc/data/Papers/wpawuwpex9405001.html*.

Bernstein, Peter L., 1992. *Capital Ideas: The Improbable Origins of Modern Wall Street.* New York: Free Press.

Bernstein, Peter L., 1996. *Against the Gods: The Remarkable Story of Risk.* New York: Wiley.

Bernstein, Peter L., 2000. *The Power of Gold.* New York: Wiley.

Binmore, Ken, 1992. *Fun and Games: A Text on Game Theory.* Lexington, MA: D. C. Heath.

Black, Fischer, 1986. "Noise." *Journal of Finance,* Vol. 41, No. 3 (July), pp. 529–543. Reprinted in Thaler, 1993.

Black, Fischer, 1989. "How We Came Up with the Option Formula." *Journal of Portfolio Management,* Vol. 15, No. 2 (Winter), pp. 4–8.

Black, Fischer, 1995. "Equilibrium Exchanges." *Financial Analysts Journal,* Vol. 51, No. 3 (May–June), pp. 23–29.

Black, Fischer, and Myron Scholes, 1973. "The Pricing of Options and Corporate Liabilities." *Journal of Political Economy,* Vol. 81, No. 3 (May–June), pp. 637–654.

Blaug, Mark, 1997. *Economic Theory in Retrospect,* 5th ed. Cambridge, UK: Cambridge University Press.

Bodie, Zvi, Alex Kane, and Alan Marcus, 1998. *Investments,* 4th ed. New York: McGraw-Hill.

Bossaerts, Peter, Leslie Fine, and John Ledyard, 2000. "Inducing Liquidity in Thin Financial Markets Through Combined-Value Trading Mechanisms." Caltech Social Science Working Paper 1095R (August). Available at *http://xxx.hss.caltech.edu/SSPapers/wp1095R.pdf.*

Bouchard, J.-Ph., 1998. "Elements for a Theory of Financial Risks." Available online at *www.soton.ac.uk/abs/cond-mat/9806101.*

Buchanan, James M., web site. "Collected Works of James M. Buchanan." Available online at *www.econlib.org/library/Buchanan/buchCContents.html.*

Budiansky, Stephen, 2000. "Engineering: The Physics of Gridlock." *Atlantic Monthly,* Vol 286, No. 6 (December). Available online at *www.theatlantic.com/issues/2000/12/budiansky.htm.*

Bureau of the Public Debt, web site. "Treasury STRIPS." Available online at *www.publicdebt.treas.gov./of/ofstrips.htm.*

Business Wire, 1998. "Chase, Citibank, MasterCard and Visa to Conclude New York Smart Card Program; Program Provides Valuable Learnings." New York (November 3).

Caginalp, Gunduz, David Porter, and Vernon Smith, 1998. "Initial Cash/Asset Ratio and Asset Prices: An Experimental Study." *Proceedings of the National Academy of Sciences of the United States of America*, Vol. 95 (January), pp. 756–761.

Caginalp, Gunduz, David Porter, and Vernon L. Smith, 2000. "Momentum and Overreaction in Experimental Asset Markets." *International Journal of Industrial Organization,* Vol. 18, No. 1 (January), pp. 187–204.

Camerer, Colin, 1995. "Individual Decision Making." In Kagel and Roth, 1995, pp. 587–703.

Camerer, Colin, and Keith Weigelt, 1991. "Information Mirages in Experimental Asset Markets." *Journal of Business,* Vol. 64, No. 4 (October), pp. 463–493.

Chamberlin, Edward H., 1948. "An Experimental Imperfect Market." *Journal of Political Economy,* Vol. 56, No. 2 (April), pp. 95–108. An annotated version appears in Chamberlin, 1957.

Chamberlin, Edward H., 1957. *Towards a More General Theory of Value.* New York: Oxford University Press.

Chamberlin, Edward H., 1962. *The Theory of Monopolistic Competition,* 8th ed. First published 1933. Cambridge, MA: Harvard University Press.

Clarke, Edward H., 1980. *Demand Revelation and the Provision of Public Goods.* Cambridge, MA: Ballinger.

Coase, Ronald H., 1959. "The Federal Communications Commission." *Journal of Law and Economics,* Vol. 2, No. 1 (October), pp. 1–40.

Coase, Ronald H., 1960. "The Problem of Social Cost." *Journal of Law and Economics,* Vol. 3, No. 1 (October), pp. 1–44.

Congleton, Roger D., 1999. "Buchanan and the Virginia School." Unpublished working paper. Available at *www.gmu.edu/jbc/fest/files/congleton.htm.*

Cootner, Paul, ed., 1964. *The Random Character of Stock Market Prices.* Cambridge, MA: MIT Press.

Cox, James C., Vernon L. Smith, and James M. Walker, 1983. "A Test That Discriminates Between Two Models of the Dutch-First Auction Non-Isomorphism." *Journal of Economic Behavior and Organization,* Vol. 4, No. 3 (June–September), pp. 205–219.

Cramton, Peter, and Jesse A. Schwartz, 1999. "Collusive Bidding in the FCC Spectrum Auctions." *Econometric Society World Congress 2000 Contributed Papers,* Paper #1210. Available at *www.bc.edu/RePEc/es2000/1210.pdf.*

Davis, Douglas, D., and Charles A. Holt, 1993. *Experimental Economics.* Princeton, NJ: Princeton University Press.

Daviss, Bennett, 1998. "Let's Get Emotional." *New Scientist,* Vol. 159, No. 2151 (September 19).

De Long, J. Bradford, Andrei Shleifer, Lawrence H. Summers, and Robert J. Waldman, 1990. "Noise Trader Risk in Financial Markets." *Journal of Political Economy,* Vol. 98, No. 4 (August), pp. 703–738. Reprinted in Thaler, 1993.

Derivatives Strategy, web site. Available online at *www.derivativesstrategy.com.*

Dixit, Avinash K., and Barry J. Nalebuff, 1991. *Thinking Strategically: The Competitive Edge in Business, Politics, and Everyday Life.* New York: W. W. Norton.

Dowd, Kevin, 1999. "Too Big to Fail? Long-Term Capital Management and the Federal Reserve." Cato Institute Briefing Paper No. 52 (September 23). Available at *www.cato.org/pubs/briefs/bp52.pdf.*

Duffy, John, 1998. "Monetary Theory in the Laboratory." Federal Reserve Bank of St. Louis, *Review,* Vol. 80, No. 5 (September–October), pp. 9–26. Available at *www.stls.frb.org/docs/publications/review/98/09/9809jd.pdf.*

Duffy, John, and Jack Ochs, 1999. "Emergence of Money as a Medium of Exchange: An Experimental Study." *American Economic Review,* Vol. 89, No. 4 (September), pp. 847–877.

Dunbar, Nicholas, 2000. *Inventing Money: The Story of Long-Term Capital Management and the Legends Behind It.* Chichester, UK: Wiley.

Eatwell, John, Murray Milgate, and Peter Newman, eds., 1989. *The New Palgrave: Allocation Information and Markets.* New York and London: W. W. Norton.

Ebenstein, Alan, 2001. *Friedrich Hayek: A Biography.* New York: Palgrave.

Fabozzi, Frank J., 2000. *The Handbook of Fixed Income Securities,* 6th ed. New York: McGraw-Hill.

Faille, Christopher, 2000. "Congress Relieved: Regulators Agree on Shad-Johnson Reform." *HedgeWorld Daily News* (September 18). Available online at *www.hedgeworld.com/news/read_excite.cgi?storyfile=/sections/legl/legl70.html.*

Fama, Eugene E., and Kenneth R. French, 1992. "The Cross-Section of Expected Stock Returns." *Journal of Finance,* Vol. 47, No. 2 (June), pp. 427–465.

Federal Communications Commission, web site 1. "Combinatorial (Package) Bidding." *www.fcc.gov/wtb/auctions/combin/combin.html.*

Federal Communications Commission, web site 2. "Wireless Telecommunications Bureau Auction Topics." Available online at *www.fcc.gov/wtb/auctions/.*

Fehr, Ernest, and Jean-Robert Tyran, 2000. "Does Money Illusion Matter? An Experimental Approach." IZA Discussion Paper No. 174 (July). Available at *http://papers.ssrn.com/sol3/papers.cfm?abstract_id=250116.*

Ferejohn, John A., and Roger G. Noll, 1976. "An Experimental Market for Public Goods: The PBS Station Program Cooperative." *American Economic Review Papers and Proceedings*, Vol. 66, No. 2 (May), pp. 267–273.

Flood, Mark D., 1991. "An Introduction to Complete Markets." Federal Reserve Bank of St. Louis, *Review,* Vol. 73, No. 2 (March–April), pp. 32–57.

Foley, Vernard, 1976. *The Social Physics of Adam Smith.* West Lafayette, IN: Purdue University Press.

FOLIOfn, web site. "FOLIOfn—Online Folio Investing." Available online at *foliofn.com.*

Forsythe, Robert, Robert Nelson, George Neumann, and Jack Wright, 1991. "The Iowa Presidential Stock Market: A Field Experiment." In *Research in Experimental Economics,* Vol. 4, edited by R. M. Isaac. Greenwich, CT: JAI Press, pp. 1–43.

Forsythe, Robert, Thomas R. Palfrey, and Charles R. Plott, 1982. "Asset Valuation in an Experimental Market." *Econometrica*, Vol. 50, No. 3 (May), pp. 537–568.

Friedman, Daniel, and Shyam Sunder, 1994. *Experimental Methods: A Primer for Economists.* New York: Cambridge University Press.

Galbraith, John Kenneth, 1961. The *Great Crash 1929.* Sentry edition. Boston: Houghton, Mifflin. First published 1954.

Garber, Peter M., 1990. "Famous First Bubbles." *Journal of Economic Perspectives,* Vol. 4, No. 2 (Spring), pp. 35–54.

Geske, Robert, 1977. "The Valuation of Corporate Liabilities as Compound Options." *Journal of Financial and Quantitative Analysis,* Vol. 12, pp. 541–552.

Gode, Dhananjay K., and Shyam Sunder, 1993. "Allocative Efficiency of Markets with Zero-Intelligence Traders: Market as a Partial Substitute for Individual Rationality." *Journal of Political Economy,* Vol. 101, No. 1 (February), pp. 119–137.

Grether, David M., R. Mark Isaac, and Charles R. Plott, 1981. "The Allocation of Landing Rights by Unanimity Among Competitors." *American Economic Review Papers and Proceedings*, Vol. 71, No. 2 (May), pp. 166–171.

Grether, David M., and Charles R. Plott, 1979. "Economic Theory of Choice and the Preference Reversal Phenomenon." *American Economic Review*, Vol. 69, No. 4 (September), pp. 623–638.

Grossman, Sanford J., and Joseph E. Stiglitz, 1980. "On the Impossibility of Informationally Efficient Markets." *American Economic Review*, Vol. 70, No. 3 (June), pp. 393–408.

Hayek, F. A., 1937. "Economics and Knowledge." *Economica*, N.S. Vol. 4, No. 1 (February), pp. 33–54. Reprinted in Hayek, 1948, pp. 33–56. Available at *www.virtualschool.edu/mon/Economics/HayekEconomicsAndKnowledge.html*.

Hayek, F. A., 1945. "The Use of Knowledge in Society." *American Economic Review*, Vol. 35, No. 4 (September), pp. 519–530. Reprinted in Hayek, 1948, pp. 77–91. Available at *www.virtualschool.edu/mon/Economics/HayekUseOfKnowledge.html*.

Hayek, F. A., 1948. *Individualism and Economic Order*. Chicago and London: University of Chicago Press.

Heilbroner, Robert L., 1995. *The Worldly Philosophers: The Lives, Times, and Ideas of the Great Economic Thinkers*, 7th ed. New York: Touchstone.

Henderson, James H., and Richard E. Quandt, 1971. *Microeconomic Theory: A Mathematical Approach*, 2nd ed. New York: McGraw-Hill.

Hirshleifer, David, 2001. "Investor Psychology and Asset Pricing." *Journal of Finance*, Vol. 56, No. 4 (August), pp. 1533–1597. Available at *http://papers.ssrn.com/sol3/papers.cfm?abstract_id=265132*.

Hogarth, Robin M., and Melvin W. Reder, 1987. *Rational Choice: The Contrast Between Economics and Psychology*. Chicago and London: University of Chicago Press. First appeared as a supplement to the *Journal of Business*, Vol. 59, No. 4, 2 (October 1986).

Holloway, C. Michael, 1999. "From Bridges and Rockets, Lessons for Software Systems." *Proceedings of the 17th International System Safety Conference*, pp. 598–607. Available at *http://shemesh.larc.nasa.gov/people/cmh/ISSC99/cmh-issc-lessons.html*.

Holt, Charles A., 1996. "Classroom Games: Trading in a Pit Market." *Journal of Economic Perspectives*, Vol. 10, No. 1 (Winter), pp. 193–203. Available at *www.people.virginia.edu/~cah2k/pitmkttr.pdf*.

Holt, Charles A., web site. "Bibliography of Experimental Economics." Available online at *www.people.virginia.edu/~cah2k*.

Holt, Charles A., and Roger Sherman, 1999. "Classroom Games: A Market for Lemons." *Journal of Economic Perspectives*, Vol. 13, No. 1 (Winter), pp. 205–214. Available at *www.people.virginia.edu/~cah2k/lemontr.pdf*.

Hull, John, 2000. *Options, Futures, and Other Derivative Securities*, 4th ed. Englewood Cliffs, NJ: Prentice-Hall.

Iowa Electronic Markets, web site. Available online at *www.biz.uiowa.edu/iem/*.

Jenkins, Holman W., Jr., 2000. "Business World: Future Shock for the Next Bubble Stock?" *Wall Street Journal* (May 31), p. A27.

Jordan, Jerry L., 1996. "Governments and Money." *Cato Journal*, Vol. 15, Nos. 2–3 (Fall–Winter). Available at *www.cato.org/pubs/journal/cj15n2-3-2.html*.

Kagel, John H., and Alvin E. Roth, eds., 1995. *The Handbook of Experimental Economics*. Princeton, NJ: Princeton University Press.

Keynes, John Maynard, 1936. *The General Theory of Employment, Interest, and Money*. New York: Harcourt, Brace.

King, Ronald R., Vernon L. Smith, Arlington W. Williams, and Mark van Boening, 1993. "The Robustness of Bubbles and Crashes in Experimental Stock Markets." In *Nonlinear Dynamics and Evolutionary Economics*, edited by Richard H. Day, and Ping Chen. New York and Oxford: Oxford University Press, pp. 183–200.

Koughan, James, 1996. "The Collapse of the Tacoma Narrows Bridge, Evaluation of Competing Theories of Its Demise, and the Effects of the Disaster of Succeeding Bridge Designs." Department of Mechanical Engineering, University of Texas at Austin (August 1). Available online at *www.me.utexas.edu/~uer/papers/paper_jk.html*.

Kurz, Mordecai, and Maurizio Motolese, 2000. "Endogenous Uncertainty and Market Volatility." Unpublished working paper. Available at http://*www-econ.stanford.edu/faculty/workp/swp99005.html*.

Kwerel, Evan R., and Gregory L. Rosston, 2000. "An Insiders' View of FCC Spectrum Auctions." *Journal of Regulatory Economics*, Vol. 17, No. 3, pp. 253–289.

Laury, Susan K., and Charles A. Holt, 1999. "Multi-Market Equilibrium and the Law of One Price." *Southern Economic Journal*, Vol. 65, No. 3 (January), pp. 611–621. Available at *www.people.virginia.edu/~cah2k/onepritr.pdf*.

Law, John, 1705. *Money and Trade Considered*. Edinburgh: Heirs and Successors of Andrew Anderson. Available as prepared by Rod Hay at *www.yale.edu/lawweb/avalon/econ/mon.htm*.

Lee, J. A. N., 1994. "John Louis von Neumann." Available online at *http://ei.cs.vt.edu/~history/VonNeumann.html*.

Lei, Vivian, Charles N. Noussair, and Charles R. Plott, 2001. "Nonspeculative Bubbles in Experimental Asset Markets: Lack of Common Knowledge of Rationality vs. Actual Irrationality." *Econometrica*, Vol. 69, No. 4 (July), pp. 831–859.

Levine, Michael E., and Charles R. Plott, 1977. "Agenda Influence and Its Implications." *Virginia Law Review*, Vol. 63, No. 4 (May), pp. 561–604.

Levitt, Arthur, 1998. "Concerning Circuit Breakers." Testimony Before the Subcommittee on Securities of the Senate Committee on Banking, Housing and Urban Affairs (January 29). Available at *www.sec.gov/news/testimony/testarchive/1998/tsty0198.txt*.

Lewis, Michael, 1989. *Liar's Poker: Rising Through the Wreckage on Wall Street*. New York: W. W. Norton.

Lo, Andrew W., and Archie C. MacKinlay, 1999. *A Non-Random Walk Down Wall Street*. Princeton, NJ: Princeton University Press.

Los Angeles Times (web site). Available online at *www.latimes.com*.

Lowenstein, Roger, 2000. *When Genius Failed: The Rise and Fall of Long-Term Capital Management*. New York: Random House.

Lucas, Robert E., Jr., 1972. "Expectations and the Neutrality of Money." *Journal of Economic Theory*, Vol. 4, No. 2 (April), pp. 103–124.

Lynch, Michael, Ross M. Miller, Charles R. Plott, and Russell Porter, 1986. "Product Quality, Consumer Information and 'Lemons' in Experimental Markets." In *Empirical Approaches to Consumer Protection Economics*, edited by P. M. Ippolito and D. T. Scheffman. Washington, DC: Federal Trade Commission, Bureau of Economics, pp. 251–306.

Lynch, Michael, Ross M. Miller, Charles R. Plott, and Russell Porter, 1991. "Product Quality, Informational Efficiency, and Regulations in Experimental Markets." In *Research in Experimental Economics*, Vol. 4, edited by R. M. Isaac. Greenwich, CT: JAI Press, pp. 269–308.

McCabe, Kevin A., Steven J. Rassenti, and Vernon L. Smith, 1989. "Designing 'Smart' Computer-Assisted Markets: An Experimental Auction for Gas Networks." *European Journal of Political Economy*, Vol. 5, pp. 259–283.

McCabe, Kevin A., Steven J. Rassenti, and Vernon L. Smith, 1991. "Experimental Testing of Smart Computer-Assisted Markets." *Science*, Vol. 254 (October 25), pp. 534–538.

Mackay, Charles, 1841. *Extraordinary Popular Delusions and the Madness of Crowds*, 1989 reprint with a foreword by Bernard M. Baruch. New York: Barnes & Noble. Available at *www.econlib.org/library/classics.html*.

Malkiel, Burton, G., 2000. *A Random Walk Down Wall Street*. New York: W. W. Norton. First published 1973.

Markowitz, Harry, 1959. *Portfolio Selection*. New Haven, CT and London, UK: Yale University Press.

Marshall, Alfred, 1920. *Principles of Economics*, 8th ed. London: Macmillan. First published 1890. Available at *www.econlib.org/library/classics.html*.

Marx, Karl, 1867. *Capital*. Volume I. Available online at *www.socsci.mcmaster.ca/~econ/ugcm/3ll3/marx*.

Merton, Robert C., 1973. "Theory of Rational Option Pricing." *Bell Journal of Economics and Management Science*, Vol. 4 (Spring), pp. 141–183.

Merton, Robert C., 1974. "On the Pricing of Corporate Debt: The Risk Structure of Interest Rates." *Journal of Finance*, Vol. 29, No. 2 (May), pp. 449–470.

Miller, John, 1997. "A Maverick Wins the Nobel Prize in Economics." *Dollars and Sense* (January–February).

Miller, Ross M., 1986. "Markets as Logic Programs." In *Artificial Intelligence in Economics and Management*, edited by L. F. Pau. Amsterdam: North-Holland, pp. 129–136.

Miller, Ross M., 1990. "The Design of Decentralized Auction Mechanisms that Coordinate Continuous Trade in Synthetic Securities." *Journal of Economic Dynamics and Control*, Vol. 14, No. 2 (May), pp. 237–253.

Miller, Ross M., 1993. "Option Valuation." In *Economic and Financial Modeling with Mathematica*, edited by Hal R. Varian. Santa Clara, CA: TELOS/Springer-Verlag, pp. 266–285. Source code from this paper is available online at *www.mathsource.com/Content/Applications/Economics Finance/0209-270*.

Miller, Ross M., 1996. "Smart Market Mechanisms: From Practice to Theory." *Journal of Economic Dynamics and Control*, Vol. 20, No. 6 (June), pp. 967–978.

Miller, Ross M., 1998. "Refining Ratings." *Risk*, Vol. 11, No. 8 (August), pp. 87–91.

Miller, Ross M., and Charles R. Plott, 1985. "Product Quality Signaling in Experimental Markets." *Econometrica,* Vol. 53, No. 4 (July), pp. 837–872.

Miller, Ross M., Charles R. Plott, and Vernon L. Smith, 1977. "Intertemporal Competitive Equilibrium: An Empirical Study of Speculation." *Quarterly Journal of Economics,* Vol. 91, No. 4 (November), pp. 599–624. Reprinted in Smith, 1991.

Miller, Ross M., and Evan Schulman, 1999. "Money Illusion Revisited." *Journal of Portfolio Management,* Vol. 25, No. 3 (Spring), pp. 45–54.

Mill, John Stuart, 1848. *Principles of Political Economy.* Available online at *www.econlib.org/library/classics.html.*

Mirowski, Philip. 1989. *More Heat Than Light: Economics as Social Physics; Physics as Nature's Economics.* Cambridge, UK: Cambridge University Press.

Mirrlees, James, 1971. "An Exploration in the Theory of Optimal Income Taxation." *Review of Economic Studies,* Vol. 38, No. 1 (April), pp. 175–208.

Modigliani, Franco, and Richard A. Cohn, 1979. "Inflation, Rational Valuation and the Market." *Financial Analysts Journal,* Vol. 35, No. 2 (March/April), pp. 24–44.

Moran, Barbara, 1999. "A Bridge that Didn't Collapse." *Invention & Technology* (Fall). Available online at *www.americanheritage.com/scripts/redir1.asp?/i&t/1502/bridgec.htm.*

Nasar, Sylvia, 1998, *A Beautiful Mind.* New York: Simon and Schuster.

Nash, John, 1950. "The Bargaining Problem." *Econometrica,* Vol. 18, No. 2 (April), pp. 155–162.

New School University, web site 1. "Edward Chamberlin." Available online at *http://cepa.newschool.edu/het/profiles/chamberlin.htm.*

New School University, web site 2. "François Quesnay." Available online at *http://cepa.newschool.edu/het/profiles/quesnay.htm.*

Niederhoffer, Victor, 1997. *The Education of a Speculator.* New York: Wiley.

Norris, Floyd, 2001. "Trader Pays $25,000 to Settle Stock Case." *New York Times* (May 4).

Opdyke, Jeff D., and Gregory Zuckerman, 2001. "Decimal Move Brings Points of Contention from Traders." *Wall Street Journal* (February 12).

Perold, André, 1988. "The Implementation Shortfall: Paper versus Reality." *Journal of Portfolio Management,* Vol. 14, No. 3 (Spring), pp. 4–9.

Perold, André, 1999. "Long-Term Capital Management, L.P. (A-D)." Harvard Business School Case Studies. Order from *www.hbsp.harvard.edu.*

Plott, Charles R., 1982. "Industrial Organization Theory and Experimental Economics." *Journal of Economic Literature*, Vol. 20, No. 4 (December), pp. 1485–1527.

Plott, Charles R., and Shyam Sunder, 1988. "Rational Expectations and the Aggregation of Diverse Information in Laboratory Securities Markets." *Econometrica*, Vol. 56, No. 5 (September), 1085–1118.

Plott, Charles R., and Vernon L. Smith, 1978. "An Experimental Examination of Two Exchange Institutions." *Review of Economic Studies*, Vol. 45, No. 1 (February), pp. 133–153.

Porter, David P., and Vernon L. Smith, 1995. "Futures Contracting and Dividend Uncertainty in Experimental Asset Markets." *Journal of Business*, Vol. 68, No. 4 (October), pp. 509–541.

President's Working Group on Financial Markets, 1999. "Hedge Funds, Leverage, and the Lessons of Long-Term Capital Management." Washington, D.C. (April). Available at *www.ustreas.gov/press/releases/docs/hedgfund.pdf*.

Raiffa, Howard, 1982. *The Art and Science of Negotiation*. Cambridge, MA and London: The Belknap Press of Harvard University Press.

RAND Corporation, web site. "RAND's History." Available online at *www.rand.org/history*.

Ransom, Greg, web site. "The Friedrich Hayek Scholars' Page." Available online at *www.hayekcenter.org/friedrichhayek/hayek.html*.

Rassenti, S. J., V. L. Smith, and R. L. Bulfin, 1982. "A Combinatorial Auction Mechanism for Airport Time Slot Allocation." *Bell Journal of Economics*, Vol. 13, No. 2 (Spring), pp. 402–417.

Real Options, web site. Available online at *www.real-options.com*.

Redman, Deborah, 1997. *The Rise of Political Economy as a Science: Methodology and the Classical Economists*. Cambridge, MA: MIT Press.

Reuters, 1999. "Goldman Sachs CEO Urges One E-Stock Mkt." (November 4).

Robson, Arthur J., 2001. "The Biological Basis of Economic Behavior." *Journal of Economic Literature*, Vol. 39, No. 1 (March), pp. 11–33.

Rohde, Laura, 2000. "Euro IT Person of the Year: Ken Binmore." IDG News Service (December 14). Available at *www.security-informer.com/english/crd_3g_315970.html*.

Roll, Richard, 1977. "A Critique of the Asset Pricing Theory's Tests." *Journal of Financial Economics*, Vol. 4 (March), pp. 129–176.

Ross, Katharine, and George Sofianos, 1998. "An Analysis of Price Volatility October 27 and 28, 1997." NYSE Working Paper 98-04 (November). Available at *www.nyse.com/pdfs/wp98-04a.pdf.*

Ross, Stephen A., 1973. "The Economic Theory of Agency: The Principal's Problem." *American Economic Review Papers and Proceedings*, Vol. 63, No. 2 (May), pp. 134–139.

Ross, Stephen A., 1977. "The Determination of Financial Structure: The Incentive-Signaling Approach." *Bell Journal of Economics*, Vol 8, No. 1 (Spring), pp. 23–40.

Rothschild, Michael, and Joseph Stiglitz, 1976. "Equilibrium in Competitive Insurance Markets: An Essay on the Economics of Imperfect Information." *Quarterly Journal of Economics,* Vol. 90, No. 3 (August), pp. 629–650.

Rust, John, John Miller, and Richard Palmer, 1992. "Behavior of Trading Automata in a Computerized Double Auction Market." In *The Double Auction Market: Institutions, Theories, and Evidence*, edited by Daniel Friedman, and John Rust. Reading, MA: Addison-Wesley, pp. 155–198.

Samuelson, Paul A., 1947. *Foundations of Economic Analysis*, 1983 enlarged edition. Cambridge, MA: Harvard University Press.

Samuelson, Paul A., 1966. "Intertemporal Price Equilibrium: A Prologue to the Theory of Speculation." In *The Collected Papers of Paul A. Samuelson*, Vol. II, edited by J. E. Stiglitz. Cambridge, MA: MIT Press. First published 1957.

Schelling, Thomas C., 1960. *The Strategy of Conflict*. Cambridge, MA: Harvard University Press.

Schelling, Thomas C., 1978. *Micromotives and Macrobehavior*. New York: W. W. Norton.

Schumpeter, Joseph A., 1950. *Capitalism, Socialism and Democracy*, 3rd ed. New York: HarperPerennial. First published 1942.

Securities and Exchange Commission, 1998. "Trading Analysis of October 27 and 28, 1997." A Report by the Division of Market Regulation (September). Text available at *www.sec.gov/news/studies/tradrep.htm.*

Securities and Exchange Commission, web site. Available online at *www.sec.gov.*

Sen, Amartya, 1970. *Collective Choice and Social Welfare*. San Francisco: Holden Day.

Sen, Amartya, 1995. "How to Judge Voting Schemes." *Journal of Economic Perspectives*, Vol. 9, No. 1 (Winter), pp. 91–98.

Shiller, Robert J., 2000. *Irrational Exuberance*. Princeton, NJ: Princeton University Press.

Shleifer, Andrei, and Robert W. Vishny, 1997. "The Limits of Arbitrage." *Journal of Finance*, Vol. 52, No. 1 (March), pp. 35–55.

Siegel Sidney, and Lawrence E. Fouraker, 1960. *Bargaining and Group Decision Making: Experiments in Bilateral Monopoly*. New York: McGraw-Hill.

Smith, Adam, 1759. *The Theory of Moral Sentiments*. Available online at *www.econlib.org/library/classics.html*.

Smith, Adam, 1776. *An Inquiry into the Nature and Causes of the Wealth of Nations*, 1994 edition by Edwin Canaan. New York: Modern Library. Available at *www.econlib.org/library/classics.html*.

Smith, Vernon L., 1962. "An Experimental Study of Competitive Market Behavior." *Journal of Political Economy*, Vol. 70, No. 3 (June), pp. 111–137. Reprinted in Smith, 1991.

Smith, Vernon L., 1981. "Experimental Economics at Purdue." In Smith, 1991.

Smith, Vernon L., 1982a. "Markets as Economizers of Information: Experimental Examination of the 'Hayek Hypothesis.'" In Smith, 1991.

Smith, Vernon L., 1982b. "Microeconomic Systems as an Experimental Science." *American Economic Review*, Vol. 72, No. 5 (December), pp. 923–955.

Smith, Vernon L., 1989. "Auctions." In Eatwell, Milgate, and Newman, 1989.

Smith, Vernon L., ed., 1991. *Papers in Experimental Economics*. Cambridge, UK: Cambridge University Press.

Smith, Vernon L., 1998. "The Two Faces of Adam Smith." *Southern Economic Journal*, Vol. 65, No. 1 (July), pp. 1–19.

Smith, Vernon L., Gerry L. Suchanek, and Arlington W. Williams, 1988. "Bubbles, Crashes, and Endogenous Expectations in Experimental Spot Asset Markets." *Econometrica*, Vol. 56, No. 5 (September), pp. 1119–1151.

Smith, Vernon L., and Arlington W. Williams, 1992. "Experimental Market Economics." *Scientific American*, Vol. 276, December, pp. 116–121.

Spence, A. Michael, 1974. *Market Signaling: Informational Transfer in Hiring and Related Processes*. Cambridge, MA: Harvard University Press.

Spence, A. Michael, 1976a. "Product Differentiation and Welfare." *American Economic Review Papers and Proceedings,* Vol. 66, No. 2 (May), pp. 407–414.

Spence, A. Michael, 1976b. "Product Selection, Fixed Costs, and Monopolistic Competition." *Review of Economic Studies,* Vol. 43, No. 2 (June), pp. 217–235.

Spence, Michael, 1973. "Job Market Signaling." *Quarterly Journal of Economics,* Vol. 87, No. 3 (August), pp. 355–374.

Spence, Michael, and Richard Zeckhauser, 1971. "Insurance, Information, and Individual Action." *American Economic Review Papers and Proceedings,* Vol. 90, No. 2 (May), 380–387.

Stanford Encyclopedia of Philosophy, web site. "Game Theory." Available online at *http://plato.stanford.edu/entries/game-theory*.

Stiglitz, Joseph E., and Andrew Weiss, 1981. "Credit Rationing in Markets with Imperfect Information." *American Economic Review,* Vol. 71, No. 3 (June), pp. 393–410.

Stovall, Robert H., 1994. "Still on a Winning Streak: The Super Bowl Stock Market Predictor." *AAII Journal,* Vol. 16, No. 8 (September), pp. 6–7.

Sunder, Shyam, 1995. "Experimental Asset Markets: A Survey." In Kagel and Roth, 1995, pp. 445–500.

Taggart, Robert A., Jr., 1996. *Quantitative Analysis for Investment Management.* Upper Saddle River, NJ: Prentice-Hall.

Thaler, Richard, 1992. *The Winner's Curse: Paradoxes and Anomalies of Economic Life.* Princeton, NJ: Princeton University Press.

Thaler, Richard, ed., 1993. *Advances in Behavioral Finance.* New York: Russell Sage Foundation.

Thorp, Edward O., 1966. *Beat the Dealer.* New York: Random House. First published 1962.

Thorp, Edward O., and Sheen T. Kassouf, 1967. *Beat the Market.* New York: Random House.

Tversky, Amos, and Daniel Kahneman, 1987. "Rational Choice and the Framing of Decisions." In Hogarth and Reder, 1987, pp. 67–94.

University of Western Ontario, web site. "The Crash of 1987—Ten Years Later." Available online at *www.lib.uwo.ca/business/crash87.html*.

Veblen, Thorstein, 1899. *The Theory of the Leisure Class,* 1994 edition. New York: Penguin. Available at *www.socsci.mcmaster.ca/~econ/ugcm/3ll3/veblen/leisure/index.html*.

Vickery, William, 1961. "Counterspeculation, Auctions, and Competitive Sealed Tenders." *Journal of Finance*, Vol. 16, No. 1, pp. 8–37.

Washington State Department of Transportation, web site. "MPEG Video of Tacoma Narrows Bridge Collapse." Available online at *ftp://www.wsdot.wa.gov/wsdot/other/tacnb.mpg*. Real-time photo of present-day bridge at *http://images.wsdot.wa.gov/ORFlow/016cc0047.jpg*. Homepage is http://*wsdot.wa.gov*.

Williams, Arlington W., 1979. "Intertemporal Competitive Equilibrium: On Further Experimental Results." In *Research in Experimental Economics*, Vol. 1, edited by V. L. Smith. Greenwich, CT: JAI Press, pp. 255–278.

Williams, Arlington W., 1980. "Computerized Double-Auction Markets: Some Initial Experimental Results." *Journal of Business*, Vol. 53, (July), pp. 235–258.

Williams, John, 1936. "Speculation and the Carryover." *Quarterly Journal of Economics*, Vol. 50, No. 3 (May), pp. 436–455.

Index